The New York Times
60-Minute Gourmet

The New York Times
60-Minute Gourmet

Pierre Franey

WITH AN INTRODUCTION BY

Craig Claiborne

Fawcett Columbine • New York

THE NEW YORK TIMES 60-MINUTE GOURMET

Published by Fawcett Columbine Books, CBS Educational and
Professional Publishing, a division of CBS Inc., by arrangement with
Times Books, a division of Quadrangle/The New York Times Book
Co., Inc.

ISBN: 0-449-90045-2

Printed in the United States of America

First Fawcett Columbine Printing: April 1981

12   11   10   9   8   7   6   5   4   3

This book
is dedicated to
Barbara Gelb

Contents

Introduction

I first met Pierre Franey as part of a reportorial fluke.

Suffice it to say that, although I was restaurant critic of *The New York Times* for more than a decade, I was not ushered from the cradle into the luxury restaurants in this world with an inbred knowledge of the world's great cuisines. Far from it. I was raised in a small town in Mississippi, and my knowledge of the world's gastronomy was limited to that of traditional Southern culture.

I had, in a sense, found myself and my identity when I was thirty-three years old. At that advanced age my credits included a degree in journalism from the University of Missouri, an avid if amateur interest in cooking, and a job in Chicago where I eked out (but barely) a living in public relations for a broadcasting company. I was bored to death. And desperate.

Through some miracle too intricate to outline here, I applied for and was accepted by the Hotel School of the Professional Hotel Keepers' Association in Lausanne, Switzerland. It was then, and to my mind still is, the pre-eminent school for hotel management in the world. It was there, within a thirteen-month period, I discovered that horizons in food were unlimited. I discovered white wine sauces and the thousands of things one can do with mayonnaise and hollandaise and puff pastries; I learned about omelets, soufflés and fish dishes based on something called meunière. I also learned the fine points of table service and menu planning and banquets. Prior to that training I knew painfully little about wines, but at that school I learned the intimate details about how to pour it.

When I came back to America, I arrived in New York and unpacked my bags. And by scrimping here and there I saved enough money to visit some of the best restaurants in the city. And what I found was appalling. Sauces with the consistency of mucilage, the most unimaginative, stereotyped menus, incompetent waiters with soiled uniforms and soiled fingernails.

Not many months after my arrival I joined *The New York Times* as food editor and, in that capacity, I could afford to dine, and often, in the best restaurants the city had to offer. I found the same dreadful sameness from the Brooklyn Bridge to the Battery. I must say that the restaurant scene today bears little resemblance to what it did then. There are now dozens of fine, elegant, and imaginative French restaurants in town. They have style or class or name it what you will. Not then.

There was in those days only one restaurant whose kitchen and table service seemed to approximate in quality what I had been taught at that hotel school. That was the then flourishing Le Pavillon, in its heyday at the time. It was considered by most connoisseurs to be—and there was no doubt in my mind that it was—the finest French restaurant in America. The late Ludwig Bemelmans, a man of unswerving taste, once stated that it was to his mind the best French restaurant in the world. Under the direction of Henri Soulé, uncompromising in his standards, it made the rest of the city's watering places—even the best known—look like bistros.

Thus that kid (no longer a kid) from the sticks decided to take on all the French restaurants in town. I decided to write an article, for which I subsequently won a publisher's award, about the terrible state of French restaurants in Gotham. It appeared on a Sunday with the headline, "The Decline of Elegance in New York's Restaurants."

In the article I stated quite flatly that Le Pavillon was the only restaurant in town with the style and quality of a first-rate establishment. And that included the now defunct but well-known Colony and the Chambord, which had fallen into incompetent hands.

To accompany the article an illustration was necessary, and I telephoned Soulé to ask if I might photograph his chef in the Pavillon kitchen. I was scared to death of him, but he responded with kindness and I was invited into those hallowed premises beneath the dining room.

When I arrived with my photographer I was introduced to the chef. A man of modest height and somewhat athletic build, wearing a toque blanche and an immaculately starched white uniform with apron, his name was Pierre Franey.

He was photographed standing before a silver platter containing a whole baked striped bass with a champagne sauce. It was simply but spectacularly garnished with puff pastry crescents and sculptured, turban-shaped mushrooms.

After the photography session we sat down to dine and we founded a friendly rapport which has continued for nearly twenty years. During the course of those years we have cooked and worked together, discussing and preparing thousands of dishes, in the beginning mostly on weekends and his days off.

A few years ago *The New York Times* decided to greatly expand its food coverage and introduced a section called "Living." As part of this expansion, (Le Pavillon had been closed for several years) Pierre Franey was engaged as a member of the food staff. Somewhat hesitatingly, a member of the upper hierarchy of the editorial staff proposed that he write a column on fine dishes that could be prepared in an hour or less. A column for those who might be pressed for time—after work, spur-of-the-moment occasions, sudden guests, and so on. It had been felt that with his background, he might find it a mission impossible or demeaning.

Pierre found the idea interesting, and justly so. On reflection he realized that a good many of the dishes he has cooked since his childhood require less than an hour, start to finish, to prepare. Some dishes, as he points out here, must be cooked as hastily as possible to be perfect. In that category one could number a hundred fish dishes, dishes made with eggs, and so on.

This book contains the complete range of cooking times. There are omelets that can be made in seconds as well as lamb chops rouennaise, which demand the outer limit of sixty minutes. There are broiled fish dishes that require about fifteen minutes, sautéed chicken dishes that demand about half an hour, and so on.

It should be added that this book is not only for those who would cook in haste. It is a serious book that is based on Pierre's solid background in French cooking. Many of the recipes could be reproduced in books on the classic French tradition dating back to Escoffier and before.

Craig Claiborne
East Hampton, New York
May 1979

The New York Times
60–Minute
Gourmet

The Gourmet
in the Kitchen

There are seemingly numerous fantasies in the public mind about the daily grind in the kitchens of what are called the grand luxe restaurants of the world. Paramount among these is the notion that all great chefs, particularly the French, are men of violence and emotion, more temperamental than opera stars. Most of the first-rate chefs I've known in my career are gentle and oftentimes meek. They like to ski and dance and make love, and one or two that I know may even enjoy, when they spend a quiet evening at home, a martini or two before dinner.

There is a second prevailing notion that, with the exception of dishes like salade niçoise and céleri rémoulade, all the dishes that go from stove burner to table top are intricately involved, endlessly complicated dishes, any of which requires the better part of a day and night to bring to the proper state of perfection.

It simply isn't true. There are many dishes, to be sure, that require numberless hours of simmering and skimming and stirring and putting through sieves to yield an ultimate result. These involve bases like fonds bruns or brown sauces for fish and poultry; things like glazes and half glazes to enrich and ennoble sauces for fish, meat, and whatever; Quenelles of fish and veal and so on.

But there are, to balance this, countless thousands of dishes that can be—indeed, must be—made in seconds to bring them to their state of absolute perfection. This would embrace a volume of recipes that includes fish and seafood—fillets of sole, clams, mussels and so on—and egg dishes such as omelets or such a simple masterpiece as scrambled eggs with tarragon. Reckoning in minuted rather than seconds, there are the grilled and broiled foods, among the most popular on luxury menus. And the sautéed dishes. To choose but one example of the latter, there is the excellent sauté of chicken beausejour with its thyme, garlic, and bay leaf, a dish that requires less than forty-five minutes to prepare, start to finish. The ingredients are to be found in any supermarket and any conscientious home cook can prepare it with ease and expertise. You don't have to be a budding Escoffier to master it. This book, then, is dedicated to the proposition that the home cook can prepare dishes of elegance and excellence, with the exigencies of time considered.

[3]

If you wish to cook in a hurry and without frustration, there are certain factors to be considered. Certain hints and admonitions to ease the burden—if you think of it like that—and increase the pleasure of cooking when time is telescoped.

If I had to name the two most important considerations for cooking in haste and in pleasure, they would be these. First off, outfit your kitchen with the best equipment, the cost of which will fit your purse or pocketbook and budget. That is not to say that you need indulge in a costly professional range, although if your bank account can accommodate it, I would certainly recommend it; a good range is forever. It is also not to say that you must outfit your pot racks with the grandest, most costly tin-lined copper pots and saucepans from Europe. Not at all.

What I do recommend is that you buy the finest cookware that you can afford, adding to your collection as the budget allows. In saucepans and skillets you should look for those with heavy bottoms and, to the greatest degree possible, easy to clean. A heavy black iron skillet is dandy, but it does rust unless you take scrupulous care of it. If you can't afford heavy copper, heavy aluminum skillets and heavy enamel-coated cast iron skillets are generally excellent and so are the utensils in heavy metal called Calphalon. The word "heavy" is accented here because if the metal used, particularly in skillets, is thin, foods are very apt to burn unless they are watched constantly.

You needn't have a "battery" of equipment to cook well. You should have one large and one small appropriate skillet; a large saucepan or small kettle for boiling things in quantity and for cooking pasta such as spaghetti; a medium-size saucepan and a small saucepan.

Among your most important utensils, you should count at least one large and one small first-class knife. The large knife should have a heavy stainless blade and in this you should not stint. The knives should be of first-quality stainless. Stainless is stressed here because certain "acid" vegetables such as onions and shallots will be discolored if chopped with a non-stainless steel blade. The knives will also rust if allowed to sit in the sink. By all means buy a food processor, even if it is one of the least expensive models. And a coffee maker. And a cork screw.

You will also need a flat, sturdy chopping board or surface, which brings up another point. Most amateurs in the kitchen believe that if they have a counter made of wood such as maple block, then that is to chop on. That's not the way professionals do it. You need a portable chopping board or surface—one that lies flat and stays in place as you work. I frankly prefer the relatively new, white polyethylene chopping surfaces. They are portable, they are easily cleaned, and they can be placed in the dishwasher for thorough cleaning. One of these "boards" that measures about ten by seventeen inches is suitable for most purposes, although I prefer a larger size, one that measures sixteen by twenty inches. That is a personal idiosyncracy, however, and for ordinary home use I recommend the smaller size. It is easier to store and to clean. Wood surfaces, in time, become nicked and breed bacteria.

At the end of this chapter there is a lengthier discussion of utensils and gadgets that would be of value in a very well equipped kitchen.

To name the second most important asset for hasty cooking with comfort and ease, I would state without qualification that it is organization. This "organization" should commence before you buy a single ingredient or take a saucepan down from the rack. You should take into thorough consideration, making a list as necessary, of the ingredients and utensils you will need to prepare the dishes you have in mind. Don't take anything for granted, be it a pound of butter you "thought" you had in the refrigerator or the carton of cream you were "sure" was sitting next to the milk.

Once you are ready to attack a dish, I strongly recommend that you assemble all the ingredients necessary for the preparation of the dish in one area. To choose one simple and obvious dish, consider the preparation of fish chowder. Bring to your work surface the following: onions, celery, potatoes, the fish, milk, butter, and whatever else the recipe requires. Gather these into a neat grouping. Get out the proper saucepan or small kettle and put it on the stove.

You will save yourself a good deal of time and bother if you lay out a length of waxed paper on the work surface and start peeling and trimming the onions, celery ends, and so on. When the peeling and trimming are done, simply gather the sheet of paper together and discard it.

Now proceed to the cubing of the potatoes (which must be dropped into cold water to prevent discoloring), the chopping of the onions and celery, adding them to glass measuring cups as they are prepared. Keep the ingredients neatly grouped and always keep your working surface wiped and clean between the cubing, chopping, and so on. Always keep in mind that clutter is distracting, a hindrance, and an enemy of time.

And incidentally, have a place for everything—the salt container, the pepper, the milk, and so on. Don't shift things about from day to day. Have a spot for the butter, the milk, and the cream in the refrigerator so that your hand projects automatically to the right place. It's a great time saver.

You can save yourself time and money if you will exercise forethought a day or an evening ahead. For example, if a dish you have planned for tomorrow's dinner calls for cooked shrimp, lobster, or chicken you will greatly simplify matters if you cook the shrimp, lobster, or whatever the night before. Remember that pre-cooked seafood, to choose one example, costs more than the raw product.

And there are many vegetables and seasonings that can be chopped or minced or otherwise prepared the evening before. Garlic can be finely minced and stored compactly in a small container and covered with plastic wrap so that air does not circulate around it. (It can also be covered with a little oil to keep air out.) Onions can be chopped, added to a bowl, and covered with plastic wrap and kept for many hours without damage to taste. So can shallots and fresh parsley.

Lettuce leaves can be rinsed clean in cold water and patted or spun dry before storing in plastic wrap or bags for use the next day. Potatoes can be peeled and cubed and kept in a basin of cold water in the refrigerator for a day or so. You can scrape carrots the day before, core green peppers or cabbage, and so on.

Think twice before throwing things out, half an onion, say. If you only use one-half for a meal, cover the other half closely in plastic wrap and refrigerate. It will be in good condition for at least one more day.

If circumstances permit (and there are rare exceptions in my mind when they would not) you might consider extending your night-before programming to the dinner table. If you know you will be pressed for time when you come home to prepare a meal, it would seem the most logical thing in the world if your preparations included setting the table as completely as possible to receive guests. Place mats or tablecloths could be installed on the table, the places set with silver, napery, wine glasses, and the like. If you're going to be all-out fancy with flowers, an arrangement of blossoms will also keep very neatly in the refrigerator.

If you are a really conscientious host or hostess and are pressed for time, as this book presumes you to be, you will probably want to serve coffee at the end of the meal. Therefore, as long as you are organizing to the last degree, you might make all preparations the night before for coffee brewing and serving. Make ready the coffee cups and spoons, have the cream in a pitcher in the refrigerator (if the cream is fresh it won't spoil) and the sugar spooned into a proper server. If you plan to serve cordials or after-dinner liqueurs, bring those glasses out, too.

You will probably serve a beverage of some sort, probably wine or beer (if there is sauerkraut). You can deposit a bottle of white wine in the refrigerator the night before. As a matter of fact, you can uncork it the night before if you recork it immediately and refrigerate it. The red wine can be placed in a cool place, but don't refrigerate it the night before. I hasten to add that, to my taste, some red wines benefit from a little chilling, a Beaujolais or an Italian wine, say, half an hour before they are served. The red wines can and should be opened about an hour before you are ready to serve them. You might open the red wines before you start the meal.

If you have a fine hand at cooking, if you cook at all properly, you will need access to a decent number of herbs and spices. In season I use fresh herbs to the greatest extent possible. My herb garden is fairly modest, but throughout the summer I have a constant supply of such herbs as tarragon, rosemary, thyme, parsley, sorrel, and basil. I have a fresh bay bush for bay leaves, but that is a rarity. I buy other herbs in season at a greengrocer—fresh coriander, dill, and so on.

In winter, however, like everyone else I am largely dependent on dried herbs and spices. These, with the exception of bay leaf and thyme, are kept in a cool, dark place in the pantry to preserve their color and flavor. I have my bay leaf and thyme in a cool place next to the stove, and the reason for this is that I use both in considerable quantity while testing recipes. Otherwise I would leave these, too, in a cool, dark place. Remember that a bright color, even for dried herbs and spices, is an indication of freshness in flavor.

There follows an alphabetical list of dried herbs and spices that I would consider essential for a spice rack. The most important of these are italicized, with bay leaf and thyme the most important of them all.

Allspice, whole or ground
Basil
Bay leaves
Caraway seeds
Cayenne pepper or hot ground red pepper
Chili powder
Cinnamon, ground and/or in stick form
Cloves, whole and/or ground
Coriander, seeds or ground
Cumin, seeds or ground
Curry powder
Marjoram
Mustard powder
Nutmeg, whole and/or ground
Oregano
Paprika
Black peppercorns and ground black pepper
White peppercorns and ground white pepper
Hot red pepper flakes and/or whole dried hot red pepper pods
Rosemary
Saffron, in stem form or powdered
Tarragon
Thyme
Vanilla extract

For a ''complete'' spice shelf, you might consider the following:
Anise seeds
Cinnamon seeds and/or ground
Celery seeds and/or salt
Fennel seeds
Ginger, ground
Juniper berries
Mace, ground
Mint leaves
Pickling spices
Poppy seeds
Savory, summer
Sesame seeds

Turmeric
Vanilla beans

And the following non-spices:
Monosodium glutamate
Saltpeter
Cream of tartar

I am one of those people—as many of my friends are—who believe that some foods are equally if not more delicious when used as leftovers rather than when freshly cooked. Like many another, I prefer cold turkey sandwiches with fresh mayonnaise to the original roast bird. Cold leftover poached fish makes one of the best cold salads. Cold leftover duck is delicious although it must not be kept too long. And turkey soup made with the carcass and other bits of leftovers is superb.

If you dine and/or entertain often at home, and time is a factor (which is almost assuredly the case if you are reading this), there are many delectables—standbys, if you will—that you might consider always keeping in stock either in the refrigerator or on the pantry shelf, such as the case may be. Some of the finest meals I can recall were those that required no more effort than slicing and arranging foods in an appetizing fashion on platters. You might keep on hand well-flavored salamis and smoked meats, head cheese and pâtés (the keeping time of these goods varies, of course, and some must be eaten within a reasonably short time after purchase). Have on hand for a platter of such charcuterie (or cold meats or cold cuts, as it is listed in America) a jar or two of fine imported mustards (kept in the refrigerator) and imported cornichons (small, sour French pickles) to use as garnish. Plus a crusty French or Italian loaf. Stocks of such breads, tightly wrapped, keep well in the freezer and can be reheated before serving.

I also almost always have in my home refrigerator a wheel or two of Brie or Camembert or other cheeses that could be served on the spur of the moment. When tightly wrapped in plastic wrap or foil and refrigerated, the shelf life of most cheese is far greater than most people suspect. And, for cooking purposes, I always have—closely wrapped—a supply of Swiss or Gruyère cheese for "gratinéed" dishes, plus Parmesan (whole chunks; Parmesan is always best if freshly grated the moment before it is used) for gratinéed dishes or to sprinkle on pasta.

In addition to this, on my pantry shelves I keep a constantly replenished supply of canned fish products—sardines, tuna, and salmon mostly—for hasty meals. For such meals—whether of sliced meats or sardines—I would generally serve a cold salad and there will almost always be in my refrigerator fresh cucumber, tomatoes, and eggs for hard-cooking and/or turning into fresh mayonnaise.

Which reminds me that many new cooks over the years have asked about how best to maintain salad oils such as olive oil if they are to be maintained over a long period of time. Refrigeration is the answer, although I must confess that in my own home, oils, whether olive or corn oil, are used in such quantitites that rancidity through nonuse is almost out of the question.

A few words might be added here about expediting the cooking of certain foods. If you have a dish that is to be baked—let us say a chicken that is to be cut into serving pieces and baked with a liquid poured around it—it will hasten the cooking time a great deal if you use a metal baking dish, one that can be heated on top of the stove. Place the dish on the stove and get the liquid to the boil before placing the dish in the oven.

I am also often asked if I make everything from scratch, especially such stapel and often called for ingredients as chicken stock or beef broth, and the answer is no. It is certainly true that I prefer to use fresh chicken or beef broth, but like everyone else, I am frequently caught in the web of needing either chicken or beef broth on the spur of the moment. Thus I keep in my larder for such emergencies an ample supply of canned broths. Plus bottles of clam broth, which can—in an emergency—be substituted for fish stock. I also almost always have a case or so of canned tomatoes on my shelves, and tomato paste. I would no more use a can of tomato sauce (the flavor is terrible) than dehydrated onion or garlic, or instant rice (an abomination and insult to a cook's intelligence) because a sauce made with canned tomatoes is infinitely preferable and easy to make. And when fresh tomatoes are out of season, canned tomatoes are far superior for other uses as well.

I would also point out that the freezer is a great boon for home cooks. The use of a TV dinner is, to my mind, unthinkable. But there are many foods that can be frozen to advantage—including tomato sauces, meat casseroles, and so on.

A word of caution about reheating foods that have been frozen. Freezing tends to dilute the strength of various spices in any dish. Therefore, it is best to always taste the defrosted product and add more seasonings according to taste. And speaking of seasonings, always use salt sparingly when cooking. Remember that it can always be added at the end of cooking time. It can't be taken away, no matter what people say about adding raw potatoes to the dish to extract the salt.

At times there have been two "quarrels" with the column known as "60-Minute Gourmet" and by way of expiation I would like to point out the following:

It has been said that there might seem to be an excessive number of recipes for rice, noodles, and potatoes. The answer is that these foods have been considered, in the finest kitchens in the world, the basic and ideal accompaniments for main courses. Certain stews and ragouts, for example, simply go with noodles in one form or another. Rice is the best and most logical accompaniment for many dishes, be they meat, poultry, or fish. The same is true of potatoes. For subtle, psychological reasons, these "starches" are not always interchangeable where taste is concerned. I have done my utmost in the menu planning here to choose the ideal accompaniment (noodles, rice, or potatoes) and to vary the preparation to the greatest degree possible.

It has further been said that there is no emphasis on dessert. To my mind, desserts that might be labeled "gourmet" are for the most part too intricate to be included in the planning of a meal to be executed in less than an hour. The preparation time for a first-rate dessert is simply too elaborate In the long run, fruit with cheese is probably the greatest of all ways to end a meal. And the home cook has at his or her disposal a number of foods that may be purchased at the grocery and supermarket. Ice cream (with a variety of liqueur toppings added at home) is excellent and takes seconds to prepare and serve. To tell you the truth, the one dessert most often served in my home when I am pressed for time is the following, the fruits and berries of which change with the season:

Macédoine de Fruits
(A mixed fruit dessert)

1½ cups seedless grapes	1½ cups fresh berries such as
1½ cups seedless or seeded orange	strawberries or blueberries or a
sections	mixture of berries
3 cups fresh fruit such as peaches	5 tablespoons confectioners' sugar
and plums, seeded and cut into	3 tablespoons cognac
wedges	3 tablespoons Kirsch
	3 tablespoons Grand Marnier.

1. Combine all the fruits in a mixing bowl and sprinkle with sugar. Blend well. Chill until ready to serve.

2. When ready to serve, add the cognac, Kirsch and Grand Marnier. Stir to blend and serve immediately.

Yield: About six servings.

Earlier on, at the beginning of this chapter, I stated that a more elaborate discussion of kitchen equipment would be appended. In addition to the appliances and gadgets mentioned earlier, you can make your cooking more comfortable and pleasurable if you have the following:

A wire whisk of respectable weight and size; a large, plain metal spoon; a large, slotted or perforated metal spoon; a kitchen timer; a large two-pronged fork; a pancake turner; a swivel-bladed vegetable scraper; a colander or sieve of suitable size; a set of graduated glass measuring cups (from one to four cups); a standard set of metal measuring spoons; a nest of mixing bowls; a can opener; a beer can opener; a flour sifter; a grater with assorted grating surfaces; a heavy pair of kitchen scissors; a salad basket (preferably a spin-dry utensil); rubber or plastic spatulas.

Other utensils or gadgets that would be valuable if not essential include a pair of kitchen tongs; a large spatula; a lemon squeezer; a large wooden spoon for stirring; a rolling pin; a pastry blender; a dish-draining rack; a spice rack; an ice pick; a dispenser for paper towels, plastic wrap, waxed paper, and aluminum foil; an electric juice extractor; and a pastry brush. You may wish to add an electric toaster, although I prefer toast made in the oven.

Poultry

WHEN I HAVE BEEN ASKED OVER THE YEARS THE most basic thing an aspiring cook could be taught, the answer is almost invariable. If you learn a few basic techniques of cookery, the rest of it is only applied logic. There are astonishingly few ground rules for the various forms of cookery. If you can make a basic mayonnaise, for example, you can make a sauce rémoulade or a sauce tartare with the simple additions of a few ingredients such as chopped anchovy, capers, pickles, and so on.

Similarly, if you can make a basic hollandaise, the technique of making variations on it—béarnaise, sauce Choron, and so forth—are easy to come by. A basic white sauce becomes a mornay with the addition of cheese, and a brown sauce becomes a sauce madère with the addition of Madeira wine.

One of the most basic foods, if hasty cooking is your goal, to be learned is a basic method of sautéeing chicken. If you know the few easily learned steps involved, your range in flavors is almost limitless. You simply start with the base and add flavors according to your taste and imagination. Your inventiveness can run riot.

To illustrate what I mean, a basic sauté is outlined here. It is as simple as this: You brown cut-up pieces of chicken in butter. When cooked on both sides, the pieces are removed for a brief period. You pour off the fat (most of it) from the skillet and add chopped shallots, then wine. The wine is reduced briefly and chicken broth is added. You swirl in a touch of butter and return the chicken pieces to the sauce. That's all there is to it.

The second recipe is a basic variation. This is the addition of a single herb, rosemary. It could be tarragon. Or you might use any of a dozen other herbs or spices. For the wine, you might substitute red for white. Or use tomatoes in lieu of the chicken broth. And you might add heavy cream to mention but one more of a hundred—perhaps a thousand—possibilities.

Serve the dish, if you will, with buttered noodles.

Poulet Sauté
(A basic sauté of chicken)

1 2½-pound chicken, cut into serving pieces	3 tablespoons butter
Salt and freshly ground pepper to taste	1 tablespoon finely chopped shallots
	2 tablespoons dry white wine
	½ cup chicken broth.

1. Sprinkle the chicken pieces with salt and pepper.

2. Heat 2 tablespoons of butter in a heavy skillet and when it is melted add the chicken pieces, skin side down. Cook about 10 to 15 minutes or until golden brown on one side.

3. Turn the pieces and cook 10 to 15 minutes longer, turning the pieces occasionally. Cook 10 to 15 minutes longer.

4. Remove the chicken pieces and arrange them neatly on a serving dish, piling them up as necessary. Keep warm.

5. Pour off the fat from the skillet and add one tablespoon finely chopped shallots. Cook, stirring briefly, and add the wine. Cook until reduced by half.

6. Add the chicken broth and simmer, stirring, about one minute, or until sauce is reduced to about half a cup. Add salt and pepper to taste. Swirl in the remaining tablespoon of butter. Pour the sauce over the chicken and serve.

Yield: Four servings.

Poulet Sauté au Romarin
(Chicken sauté with rosemary)

1 **2½-pound chicken, cut into serving pieces**	1 **teaspoon finely chopped fresh rosemary leaves**
Salt and freshly ground pepper to taste	1 **tablespoon finely chopped shallots**
3 **tablespoons butter**	2 **tablespoons dry white wine**
	½ **cup chicken broth.**

1. Sprinkle the chicken pieces with salt and pepper.

2. Heat 2 tablespoons of the butter in one or two heavy skillets and, when it is melted, add the chicken pieces, skin side down. Cook 15 minutes or until golden brown on one side.

3. Turn the pieces and add the chopped rosemary. Cook 10 to 15 minutes longer, turning the pieces occasionally.

4. Remove the chicken pieces and arrange them neatly on a serving dish, piling them up as necessary. Keep warm.

5. Pour off the fat from the skillet and add the shallots. Cook, stirring briefly, and add the wine. Cook until reduced by half.

6. Add the chicken broth and simmer, stirring to blend well, about 1 minute. Continue to cook and when the sauce is reduced to about one-half cup, swirl in the remaining tablespoon of butter. Pour the sauce over the chicken and serve immediately.

Yield: Six to eight servings.

DURING THE COURSE OF PRODUCING THIS BOOK, I have tried to keep in mind—quite diligently—that those who may read it with the thought of producing worthwhile meals in the course of an hour will not all be equipped with the same dexterity in wielding a knife or stirring vigorously with a wire whisk.

Within the past months I have made an effort to get down to the most elementary techniques in cooking while keeping the end product at a "gourmet" level.

The book now contains basic broiled fish dishes, broiled meats, and the simplest method for preparing a chicken sauté plus variations on that method.

I have also decided to include a basic recipe for a broiled chicken, if for no other reason than that I consider a simply broiled chicken one of the natural good things on earth.

The recipe is listed in detail but it consists of nothing more than arranging the chicken halves, brushed with oil and sprinkled with salt and pepper, in a shallow pan. The pan is placed under the broiler, a judicious distance from the source of heat. The cooking of the dish is then completed by keeping the pan with the chicken in the oven with the thermostat set to about 400 degrees. The chicken is served with the pan juices, if desired, and preferably accompanied by fluffy rice.

Or, if you prefer, and you have a neat skill in the kitchen, you may wish to prepare and serve the chicken with what is known as a beurre bercy (a butter sauce made with shallots and a dry white wine). Actually, this is a delicious and somewhat sophisticated sauce for broiled foods. It is easy to make, but you must exercise caution on one point. The butter beaten into the sauce must not be overheated in the saucepan with the shallots and reduced wine. If the sauce is subjected to too-high heat, it will more likely than not "separate" or curdle.

In case you wondered about the name, Bercy is a quarter of Paris, long known as a center for wine commerce.

Poulet Grillé
(Broiled chicken)

1 2½-pound chicken split for broiling Salt and freshly ground pepper to taste	1 tablespoon peanut, vegetable, or corn oil.

1. Preheat the broiler to high. If the broiler and oven units have separate thermostats, preheat the oven, simultaneously, to 400 degrees.

2. To facilitate broiling, have the backbone removed from the chicken when it is split. Turn the chicken skin side down on a flat surface. Using a sharp knife, carefully split the joint half way down where the leg and thigh bone

meet. Do not split all the way through. This split will insure more even cooking at this joint.

3. Rub the chicken halves, the neck, gizzard, and chicken liver with the oil. Place the chicken skin side down on a shallow baking dish. Arrange the neck, liver, and so on around and between the chicken halves.

4. Place the chicken in the broiler about five or six inches from the source of heat. Broil about 5 to 10 minutes and remove from the oven.

5. Using a fork, turn over all the pieces of chicken including the neck, gizzard, and so on. Put back in the oven and continue broiling about 10 minutes. It may be necessary to lower the baking dish if the chicken starts to burn. It should be nicely browned, however.

6. If the oven and broiler work on the same thermostat, lower the temperature to 400 degrees. Return the chicken to the oven and bake 10 minutes. The total cooking time should be about 25 to 30 minutes.

7. Remove the chicken from the oven and baste lightly with the pan juices.

Yield: Four servings.

Beurre Bercy
(Butter sauce with shallots and white wine)

2	tablespoons finely chopped shallots	¼	pound butter at room temperature
2	tablespoons dry white wine		Salt to taste, optional.
¼	teaspoon freshly ground black pepper		

1. Blend the shallots and wine in a small heavy saucepan and bring to the boil. Cook, shaking the saucepan until the liquid evaporates. Take care not to burn the shallots.

2. Remove from the heat and let cool about 3 minutes. Stir the shallots occasionally as they stand.

3. Do not return the saucepan to the heat. Start beating the shallots with a wire whisk and gradually beat in the butter, shaking the pan constantly. The important thing in making this butter sauce is that the saucepan be cooled briefly but it must still remain hot enough so that the butter will thicken like a béarnaise. If the butter becomes too hot it will curdle. Serve with broiled fish, broiled meats, and so on.

Yield: About half a cup.

IN THE SCHEME OF THINGS, IT DOESN'T SEEM IN the least surprising that of the various categories in this book—veal, beef, fish, and so on—there are more than twice as many chicken recipes as in any other category.

To my mind as a chef (and part-time home cook) chicken is probably the most versatile of all foods. It also is, as has been pointed out elsewhere, historically the least expensive of basic foods. Long before Henry the Fourth declared that every peasant should have a chicken in every pot (and long before they named the poule au pot after him), chicken was known as the food of both the poor and nobility alike. Chickens are simply one of the easiest of all edible creatures to feed and propagate. With the possible exception of fish, however, but the coast-lines and waters of this world are too far apart for a universal catch.

One of my favorite chicken preparations is completed with a basic assembly of ingredients that are known in their blend as a persillade (there is also a beef salad with a good deal of chopped parsley that is known simply as a persillade). These traditional ingredients are fresh bread crumbs, garlic and/or shallots, and a handful of chopped parsley. The name, incidentally, derives from the French word for parsley, persil.

Once the ingredients for the persillade are blended, the other preparation and cooking of the dish is a child's game. Pieces of seasoned, cut-up chicken are turned in butter and broiled. The pieces are turned once and broiled again. The chicken is sprinkled with the parsley and bread crumb mixture and baked without much further ado until done. As a final step, you may run the dish under the broiler for a split second to give a browner and more desirable texture.

A buttered vegetable such as broccoli or cauliflower are complementary with this dish. The vegetable should be cooked until crisp-tender and a lemon butter poured over. The recipe given here is for broccoli with lemon butter.

Poulet en Persillade
(Chicken with parsley sauce)

1	2½-pound chicken, cut into serving pieces	2	tablespoons finely chopped shallots
	Salt and freshly ground pepper to taste	1	small clove garlic, finely minced
4	tablespoons butter	2	tablespoons finely chopped parsley.
¼	cup bread crumbs		

1. Preheat the broiler.
2. Sprinkle the chicken pieces with salt and pepper.
3. Heat the butter in a heat-proof baking dish large enough to hold the chicken pieces in one layer. Turn the pieces in butter. Arrange the pieces skin

side down in the baking dish and place under the broiler about six inches from the source of heat.

4. When the chicken has broiled about 5 minutes, remove from the oven and turn the pieces skin side up. Return to the oven and continue broiling about 5 minutes longer.

5. Blend the bread crumbs, shallots, garlic, and parsley. Blend well. Sprinkle this over the chicken and baste to coat well with the butter.

6. Set the oven heat at 400 degrees and add the chicken. Bake 10 minutes.

7. Just before serving, reheat the broiler. Run the chicken briefly under the broiler to brown quickly.

Yield: Four servings.

Brocoli au Citron
(*Broccoli with lemon butter*)

1 small bunch broccoli	**Juice of half a lemon**
Salt to taste	**Freshly ground pepper to taste.**
2 tablespoons butter	

1. Cut and trim the broccoli into flowerettes. The pieces should be bite-size but not too small.

2. Bring enough water to the boil to cover the broccoli when added. Add salt to taste and add the broccoli pieces. Cook briefly, about 3 to 4 minutes or until crisp-tender. Drain well.

3. Heat the butter in a saucepan and add the lemon juice. Pour this over the broccoli. Sprinkle with salt and pepper and serve.

Yield: Four servings.

THERE IS A HASTILY MADE CHICKEN DISH REPRE-
sented here that has an interesting legend behind it. In its
original form it was called chicken Marengo and was served
to Napoleon on the day he defeated the Austrians on the battlefield near the
village of Marengo in the northwest of Italy in mid-June 1800. Culinary history
states that Napoleon's chef was a man named Dunand.

With victory at hand, the chef sent scouts into the countryside to find provi-
sions for a meal. They returned with crayfish from a nearby stream or river,
chicken, eggs, tomatoes, garlic and oil from a nearby farm, and a skillet.

Dunand cooked the chicken in oil, then added tomatoes, a little water, and
garlic. The dish was served with the crayfish steamed over the chicken and
fried eggs as a garnish. Napoleon is said to have told his chef that it was one of
the finest meals he'd ever eaten. The legend continues that on his return to
France, the General asked the chef to repeat the dish. He did. But he omitted
the crayfish, which he considered out of place with chicken. He used wine in
lieu of water and added fresh mushrooms—champignons de Paris—to the ingredients. The commander complained vehemently and the crayfish garnish
was restored; crayfish are now always used with a true Marengo.

What Dunand, back in France, had created was a chicken à la provençale,
which is the dish outlined here. It is a true regional specialty, incorporating in
its ingredients chopped anchovies and green onions in the style of Provence. It
is, indeed, simply made. Chicken parts are seasoned and cooked in oil. The
pieces are then cooked in a mixture of wine and tomato with mushrooms, plus
the inevitable provençale seasonings—garlic, bay leaf, and thyme. The total
cooking time for the dish is approximately half an hour. And while it simmers
there is plenty of time to prepare the rice dish which, for reasons unknown to
me, is called riz egyptienne or Egyptian rice. This is a simply made fluffy rice
dish containing among its elements one chicken liver (taken from the chicken
cooked à la provençale) and small cubes of cooked ham. The chicken dish goes
well with a dry white wine, a rosé from Provence, or a somewhat robust dry
red wine.

Poulet Sauté Provençale
(*Sautéed chicken with tomatoes*)

1   2½- to 3-pound chicken, cut into
    serving pieces
    Salt and freshly ground pepper
    to taste
3   tablespoons olive oil
½   pound mushrooms, left whole if
    small; otherwise halved or
    quartered, depending on size
1   bay leaf
¼   teaspoon dried thyme

¾   cup finely chopped onion
1½ teaspoons finely chopped garlic
2   tablespoons flour
½   cup dry white wine
1   cup crushed tomatoes
¾   cup fresh or canned chicken
    broth
6   flat fillets of anchovies, chopped
24 bottled, small, pitted, green
    olives, drained.

1. Sprinkle the chicken pieces with salt and pepper. If desired, set the chicken liver aside to prepare rice with liver as a side dish for the chicken.

2. Heat the oil in a skillet and add the chicken pieces, skin side down. Cook over moderately high heat 3 to 5 minutes or until golden brown. Turn the pieces and continue cooking about 3 minutes or until golden brown on the second side.

3. Add the mushrooms and continue cooking. Add the bay leaf, thyme, onion, and garlic. Cook, shaking the skillet and stirring the chicken pieces so that the other ingredients are evenly distributed around and between the pieces.

4. When the chicken has cooked about 10 or 12 minutes (total cooking time, start to finish), remove the pieces to a serving dish.

5. Sprinkle the ingredients with flour, stirring to blend evenly.

6. Add the wine and tomatoes and broth. Stir and bring to the boil.

7. Return the chicken pieces to the skillet. Add the juice that may have accumulated around them. Add anchovies, salt and pepper to taste. Cover closely and simmer 5 minutes.

8. Add the olives and continue to cook 5 minutes.

Yield: Four servings.

Riz Egyptienne
(*Rice with chicken livers*)

---

1 **chicken liver**	1 **cup rice**
1 **tablespoon plus two teaspoons butter**	1½ **cups fresh or canned chicken broth**
¼ **cup finely chopped onion**	⅔ **cup cooked ham, cut into quarter-inch dice.**
⅔ **cup fresh mushrooms, cut into half-inch dice**	

1. Cut the liver in quarter-inch pieces. Set aside.

2. Heat one tablespoon of the butter and add the onion and mushrooms. Cook, stirring occasionally, until wilted. Add the rice and cook, stirring, until rice is coated. Add the broth and bring to the boil. Cover closely and cook 17 minutes.

3. Meanwhile, heat the remaining butter in a skillet and add the livers and ham. Cook, shaking the skillet and stirring until liver is cooked and ham is heated through.

4. Add the liver and ham to the rice and toss gently with a two-pronged fork to blend the ingredients.

Yield: Four servings.

MONG THE FOODS BEST SUITED TO A HASTY MEAL
(with the exception of the egg, of course, which can make a
super supper scrambled or turned into an omelet) are those
that are skinless and boneless and tender besides.

Few foods fit that category better than skinless, boneless chicken breasts,
which are readily available in supermarkets and, what's more, are generally
sold at what could be called a relative bargain.

Chicken breasts take well to an endless variety of flavors, and there is almost
no seasoning that won't complement them, from a pungent bit of garlic to
something as delicately flavored as basil or tarragon.

I recently prepared a quickly cooked platter of chicken véronique, a dish
adapted from my Burgundy childhood. Véronique is actually of Parisian origin
and means a dish in which grapes—generally white and seedless—figure in the
food's preparation. No one knows precisely when the name véronique was first
applied to such dishes, and I doubt, as some propose, that it has biblical conno-
tations after St. Veronica.

Most dishes labeled véronique are quite bland by nature, and the quickly
cooked chicken dish I have in mind is highly complemented by a dish of
curried rice.

Generally, the cooking time for rice is only seventeen minutes. The cooking
time for the chicken is less than ten. Therefore, I would recommend first
preparing all the ingredients for both these dishes; once the rice is put on to
cook there will be ample time for cooking the chicken. The rice, incidentally,
may be kept warm several minutes after cooking without damage to flavor or
texture.

Suprêmes de Volaille Véronique
(Chicken breast with grapes)

1¾ pounds skinless, boneless chicken breasts	1½ tablespoons finely chopped shallots
½ cup fresh or canned seedless grapes	½ cup dry white wine
3 tablespoons butter	1½ cups heavy cream
Salt and freshly ground pepper to taste	curried rice (see recipe).

1. Trim off all traces of fat, white membranes and so on from the chicken
breasts. Place the pieces on a flat surface, and using a flat mallet, pound them
lightly. Using a sharp knife, cut the breasts into half-inch strips. There should
be about 3 cups.

2. If canned grapes are used, drain them and set aside. If fresh grapes are
used, remove the stems. Rinse and drain well. Set aside.

3. Heat the butter in a large, heavy skillet, and when very hot but not brown

add the chicken breasts. Sprinkle with salt and pepper. Cook over high heat, stirring constantly so that the pieces cook evenly. Cook just until pieces lose their raw look and are barely cooked through, about 3 to 5 minutes.

4. Using a slotted spoon, transfer the pieces to another skillet.

5. Add the shallots to the skillet. Cook briefly, stirring, and add the wine. Cook over high heat, shaking the skillet and stirring. As juices accumulate around the chicken pieces in the second skillet, drain them into the cooking liquid. When the wine has cooked down by half, add the cream. Cook over high heat.

6. If fresh grapes are available, add them to the sauce. Cook over high heat about 4 or 5 minutes or until the cream mixture takes on a saucelike consistency. Add salt and pepper to taste. If canned grapes are used, add them at the last minute of cooking, just to heat through.

7. Spoon the chicken into the sauce and heat through. If desired, pack the rice into a buttered round mold just large enough to hold it. Unmold onto a round platter. Spoon the chicken and grapes around and serve.

Yield: Four servings.

Riz à l'Indienne.
(*Curried rice*)

1	cup rice	1	tablespoon curry powder
1	small apple, peeled and cored	½	bay leaf
3	tablespoons butter	1½	cups fresh or canned chicken
½	cup finely chopped onion		broth.
1	clove garlic, finely minced		

1. Measure the rice and set aside.

2. Cut the apple into slices about one-quarter inch thick. Stack the slices and cut them into strips about half an inch thick. Cut the strips into quarter-inch cubes. There should be 1 cup. Do not use more. Set aside.

3. Heat 2 tablespoons of the butter in a saucepan and add the onion and garlic. Cook until onion wilts.

4. Add the apple and curry powder and stir. Add the rice, bay leaf, and chicken broth. Cover closely and cook exactly 17 minutes.

5. Add the remaining tablespoon butter and fluff it into the rice, using a two-pronged fork.

Yield: Four servings.

I N FRENCH KITCHENS, CHEFS AND COOKS OFTEN communicate in the form of a code that has been used for generations. You say, "Add a bouquet garni," instead of, "Make a bundle of herbs and spices including parsley sprigs, thyme, and bay leaf." You say, "Give me a duxelles," instead of, "Make a hash of chopped mushrooms cooked in butter with a touch of shallots." And you say, "Use a soubise," instead of, "Make a purée of onions simmered down until thickened."

Similarly, in menu writing a catalogue of names serves as a code. Dishes made with carrots are called crécy, a place name; dishes made with cauliflower are listed for some mysterious reason as du barry, and dishes relating to asparagus are called argenteuil, another place name. Perhaps the best known of these menu names in America is florentine, which appears on thousands of menus all over this country and abroad. It indicates the presence of spinach in any given dish; historians are imprecise as to the exact relation between spinach and the city on the banks of the River Arno.

Chicken breasts florentine are an excellent entrée, and I must say that one of the choicest items in many supermarkets in America is boneless chicken breasts. If they are not in your supermarket, your local butcher (if he is accommodating enough) will quickly bone chicken breasts for you.

To make the dish, you could use breasts that are not only boneless but skinless, but if you have a choice it is best to leave the skin on. The breasts, when cooked, retain their shape better.

To prepare chicken breasts florentine, the breasts must be cooked in a blend of wine and broth. The cooking liquid is used to prepare a sauce. As the chicken poaches, there is ample time to cook the spinach, press it and reheat it in butter. The sauce requires a very few minutes to make, and that's the sum of it. Chicken breasts florentine, a salad, and perhaps cheese could make an excellent meal any season of the year.

Suprêmes de Volaille à la Florentine
(Chicken breasts with spinach)

4 whole, unsplit, boneless chicken breasts with or without the skin, about 2½ pounds Salt and freshly ground pepper to taste	2 sprigs parsley 2 10-ounce packages fresh spinach cooked as for épinards en branche (see recipe)
2 tablespoons plus 2 teaspoons butter	2 tablespoons flour
1 tablespoon finely chopped shallots	1 cup heavy cream
½ cup dry white wine	1 egg yolk, lightly beaten
½ cup chicken broth	1 or 2 tablespoons grated Gruyère or Parmesan cheese.

1. Place the chicken breasts open up on a flat surface, skin side down. Sprinkle with salt and pepper. Fold the chicken breasts, reshaping them skin-side out. Smooth the skin over.

2. Butter the bottom of a skillet with 2 teaspoons butter and sprinkle with shallots. Add the reshaped breasts, seam side down, and add the wine, chicken broth, and salt and pepper to taste. Add the parsley and bring to the boil. Cover and simmer about 15 to 20 minutes, until breasts are just cooked through. Remove from the heat.

3. As the chicken cooks, prepare the spinach according to the recipe.

4. Drain and reserve all the liquid from the chicken breasts. There should be about 1½ cups. Keep the chicken breasts covered.

5. Heat the remaining 2 tablespoons butter in a saucepan and add the flour, stirring with a wire whisk until blended. Add the reserved cooking liquid to the butter-flour mixture, stirring with the whisk. When thickened and smooth, simmer about 5 minutes. Add the heavy cream and cook about 2 minutes.

6. Remove from the heat and add the yolk, stirring briskly.

7. Preheat the broiler.

8. Spoon the spinach into the center of a heatproof serving dish. Arrange the chicken breasts seam side down over the spinach. Spoon the sauce over the chicken and spinach. Sprinkle the cheese on top of the breasts and run under the broiler until bubbling on top.

Yield: Four servings.

Épinards en Branche
(Spinach with butter)

---

2 **10-ounce packages fresh spinach**
2 **cups water**
   Salt and freshly ground pepper to taste

⅛ **teaspoon freshly grated nutmeg**
1 **tablespoon butter.**

1. Pull away and discard any tough stems and blemished leaves from the spinach. Rinse and drain the spinach.

2. Pour the water in a kettle and bring to the boil. Add salt to taste and the spinach. Stir down to wilt.

3. Bring to the boil, stirring occasionally, and cook about 5 minutes. Empty the spinach into a colander and drain. Press with the back of a wooden spoon to extract most of the liquid. Squeeze between the hands to extract additional moisture.

4. Put the spinach on a flat surface and chop coarsely.

5. Add salt, pepper and nutmeg.

6. To a skillet add the butter, and when it starts to brown add the spinach. Cook, tossing and stirring, just to heat through.

Yield: Four servings.

OVER A PERIOD OF TIME I HAVE HEARD NUMEROUS readers lament: "But some of your recipes are so l-o-n-g." The fact is that, with certain exceptions, the length of a recipe isn't necessarily related to the cooking time. The recipe for the following dish is a case in point. It consists of nine "steps." If you read carefully, however, you will note that the first four steps are nothing more than telling you to trim and cut carrots and asparagus in a certain way and to cook them quickly in boiling water. Nothing complicated there.

The reason for the steps is primarily to improve the presentation of the dish once it is finished and ready to be served. The dish itself is an easily made, very simple sauté of chicken breasts, using the most basic "classic" technique. In that the breasts are skinless and boneless, the cooking time is shortened considerably. And the technique is this:

The breasts are seasoned and coated lightly with flour. The flour will aid in the quick-browning process. The breasts are cooked on two sides in butter, about ten minutes in all, and then removed from the skillet.

Shallots, an almost indispensable ingredient in fine French cookery, are added, then a dry white wine. The wine (it will dissolve the skillet's brown particles, which add flavor) is cooked down and a bit of tomato paste is added. The tomato paste will give a smattering of flavor, but it is primarily for color. A little chicken broth will "extend" the sauce, and heavy cream—only two tablespoons—will enrich and smooth it.

The accompaniment? Buttered noodles simply cooked and served with chopped fresh tomatoes quickly sautéed in butter.

Suprêmes de Volaille Printanier
(Chicken breasts with asparagus and carrots)

4 cups water	1 to 2 tablespoons flour
Salt to taste	3 tablespoons butter
8 fresh large asparagus spears	1 tablespoon finely chopped shallots
1 carrot	½ cup dry white wine
2 skinless, boneless chicken breasts split in half, about 1½ pounds, ready-to-cook weight	1 tablespoon tomato paste
	¼ cup fresh or canned chicken broth
	2 tablespoons heavy cream.
Freshly ground pepper to taste	

1. Bring 4 cups of water to the boil with salt to taste.

2. Scrape the sides of the asparagus spears, leaving the tips (about two inches from the top) unscraped. Cut off and discard the tough base of the spears. Set aside.

3. Scrape the carrot and trim off the end. Cut the carrot crosswise into two-inch lengths. Cut each length into quarter-inch slices. Stack the slices and cut them into quarter-inch strips (like small french fries). Set aside.

4. Drop the vegetables into the boiling water and cook about 4 minutes or until crisp tender. Do not overcook. Drain well and set aside.

5. Sprinkle the four chicken pieces with salt and pepper to taste. Dredge lightly in flour and shake off excess.

6. Heat 2 tablespoons of the butter in a skillet. When quite hot but not brown, add the chicken pieces. Cook on one side over moderately high heat about 4 minutes. Turn and cook on the other side until golden brown, about 2 to 4 minutes. Cover and cook about 4 to 5 minutes until tender.

7. Transfer the pieces to a warm platter, arranging them neatly. To the skillet add the shallots. Stir and cook briefly. Add the wine and cook until reduced by half. Add the tomato paste, stir and add the chicken broth. Stir in the cream.

8. Heat the remaining tablespoon of butter in a skillet. Add the asparagus and carrots, salt and pepper to taste. Cook just to heat through and coat with butter.

9. Arrange equal portions of asparagus and carrots between the chicken breast pieces. Spoon the sauce over the chicken and serve.

Yield: Four servings.

Nouilles à la Tomate
(*Noodles with fresh tomato*)

½ **pound thin noodles**
Salt to taste
1 **large, red, ripe tomato, about**
¾ pound

2 **tablespoons butter**
Freshly ground pepper to taste.

1. Bring enough water to the boil to cover the noodles when added. Add salt to taste.

2. Core and peel the tomato and cut it into half-inch cubes.

3. Drop the noodles into the boiling water and cook until tender.

4. Meanwhile, heat 1 tablespoon of the butter in a saucepan and add the tomato, salt and pepper to taste. Cook about 1 minute, stirring occasionally.

5. Drain the noodles and return them to the kettle. Add the remaining tablespoon butter, salt and pepper to taste.

6. Serve the noodles with the tomatoes spooned over.

Yield: Four servings.

TO JUDGE FROM THE QUESTIONS PUT TO ME over a period of years, the occasional cook seems little aware that the techniques for cooking are in most cases both staple and repetitive. A good case in point are the various breaded dishes that, if you are properly organized, are a snap to prepare. Particularly, meats such as veal scallopine or breast of chicken require a minimum of cooking time in the skillet.

With rare exceptions, the procedure for breading foods follows a standard outline. The foods, depending on their thickness and basic tender nature, may be pounded lightly with a flat mallet, the side of a heavy knife, or the bottom of a small, heavy, clean skillet. The "flattening" should be gentle but firm. It also helps if the food is placed between pieces of clear plastic wrap, or, as a second choice, wax paper.

Use three flat utensils for the breading process. In one add flour seasoned with a little salt and pepper. In the second add a beaten egg or two (depending on the amount of meat to be coated) blended with a small spoonful or so of water. To the third add a supply of fresh bread crumbs, ample enough to coat the meat. Dip the pieces of meat first in flour, patting to coat and shake off excess. Add the pieces of meat one at a time to the egg, patting with the fingers to coat well. Immediately add the meat pieces one at a time to the crumbs and pat to coat. At this point the meat may be transferred to a pastry rack and allowed to stand until ready to cook. It can be cooked immediately.

That's all there is to it other than cooking the foods either in butter or a combination of butter and oil. If all butter is used, the foods may brown too quickly and burn. With the oil the burning point is considerably lowered and they may cook for a longer period.

Breaded foods in French are called à l'anglaise, which is to say English-style. One of the most easily made of such dishes are chicken breasts, flattened, breaded, and cooked until golden all over. They are served with lemon wedges. An excellent accompaniment for the dish are zucchini and carrots with chopped fresh mint. Recipes for those—to be cooked start to finish in less than an hour—are given here.

Suprêmes de Volaille Panés à l'Anglaise
(Breaded chicken breasts)

2	whole skinless, boneless chicken breasts, about 1 pound total weight	1	egg
		2	tablespoons water
		1	cup or more bread crumbs
¼	cup flour	¼	cup peanut, vegetable, or corn oil
	Salt and freshly ground pepper to taste	1	tablespoon butter
			Seeded lemon slices for garnish.

1. Slice the chicken breasts in half. Trim off thin cartilage and other extraneous matter.

2. Place the breasts, one at a time, between two sheets of plastic wrap and pound lightly with a flat mallet or the bottom of a heavy skillet.

3. Dredge the breasts on all sides in flour seasoned with salt and pepper.

4. Beat the egg with the water in a flat dish. Dip the meat on all sides in egg, patting with the fingers.

5. Dip the breasts in bread crumbs to coat on all sides. Tap the sides lightly with the flat part of a heavy knife to help the crumbs adhere.

6. Heat the oil and butter in one or two skillets and add the pieces. Cook until golden brown on one side, about 3 to 5 minutes. Turn and cook about 3 to 5 minutes on the other side. Remove and serve hot garnished with lemon slices.

Yield: Four servings.

Courgettes et Carottes à la Menthe
(Zucchini and carrots with fresh mint)

---

3 carrots, about ½ pound, trimmed and scraped

2 zucchini, about ¾ pound, ends trimmed

2 tablespoons butter

Salt and freshly ground pepper to taste

2 teaspoons finely chopped mint or parsley.

1. Cut the carrots into quarter-inch rounds and set aside.

2. Cut the zucchini into quarter-inch rounds and set aside.

3. Heat the butter in a heavy skillet and add the carrots and salt and pepper. Cover and cook about 3 to 5 minutes or until half cooked.

4. Add the zucchini and cover. Shake the skillet occasionally. Cook 4 to 5 minutes or until all the vegetables are crisp-tender. Sprinkle with salt, pepper, and mint.

Yield: Four servings.

ALTHOUGH I HAVE SPENT THE MAJORITY OF MY years in one kitchen or another, I find myself rarely bored by cooking. It was an adventure for me when I was an apprentice and it is an adventure now that all the young chefs start to look more and more like children.

Creating dishes, combining unaccustomed ingredients, can be an interesting pastime, and that's the way I feel about the dish here.

Chicken and avocado in a cream sauce is, to the best of my knowledge, an unaccustomed liaison. Like most such creations, it was the result of linking together two things that wound up one morning in my shopping cart.

I must confess that I had never seen an avocado before I came to this country in 1939 for the New York World's Fair. Although avocados—avocats, as they are called in France—are today quite common, they were very much a rarity in my youth. Available, perhaps, in specialty shops such as Fauchon on the Place Madeleine, but I'm not even certain of that.

In any event, they are an interesting fruit because they depend to such a great degree not so much on what they are but on what they are served with, be it French dressing or onion and chilies as in guacamole.

The total cooking time for this creation—it also includes quartered or sliced mushrooms and a light lacing of cognac—is about ten minutes. Here again, I recommend rice as an ideal accompaniment. And because of the somewhat bland nature of this dish, curried rice makes a nice contrast.

The rice preparation will require the usual seventeen minutes of baking in the oven. Thus the chicken and avocado dish may be put together and cooked as the rice bakes.

Poulet et Poire d'Avocat à la Crème
(*Chicken and avocado in cream*)

1½	pounds skinless, boneless chicken breasts	¼	pound mushrooms, quartered or cut into slices
	Salt and freshly ground pepper to taste	2	tablespoons cognac
2	tablespoons butter	1½	cups heavy cream
1	tablespoon finely chopped shallots	1	avocado peeled, seeded, and cut into ½-inch strips.

1. Cut each chicken breast into six or seven strips. Sprinkle with salt and pepper.

2. Heat the butter in a heavy skillet and when it is very hot but not browned, add the chicken. Cook over high heat, stirring and shaking the skillet 3 to 4 minutes or until chicken pieces have lost their raw look.

3. Remove the pieces of chicken with a slotted spoon and set aside.

4. To the skillet, add the shallots and mushrooms and cook briefly, stirring.

Sprinkle with the cognac. Add the cream and cook down over high heat about 5 minutes. Add salt and pepper to taste. Add the avocado and cook gently to heat through. Add the chicken gently and heat in the sauce. Serve with curried rice.

Yield: Four servings.

Riz à l'Indienne
(*Curried rice*)

2½ tablespoons butter	1 tablespoon curry powder
2 tablespoons minced onion	1½ cups chicken broth
¼ teaspoon minced garlic	2 springs parsley
1 cup uncooked rice	½ bay leaf.

1. Preheat the oven to 400 degrees.

2. Melt 1 tablespoon butter in a heavy saucepan and cook the onion and garlic stirring with a wooden spoon, until the onion is translucent. Add the rice and stir briefly over low heat until all the grains are coated with butter. Sprinkle with curry powder and stir to blend.

3. Stir in the broth, making sure there are no lumps in the rice. Add the parsley and bay leaf. Cover with a close-fitting lid and place in the oven.

4. Bake the rice exactly 17 minutes. Remove the cover and discard the parsley and bay leaf. Using a two-pronged fork, stir in the remaining butter. If the rice is not to be served immediately, keep covered in a warm place.

Yield: Four servings.

MANY FACTORS ARE INVOLVED IN THE TIME RE-quired to prepare any dish, be it a simple dinner or an elaborate dish, such as a coulibiac, which may require as many as six different preparations combined in one single presentation. It helps enormously, of course, if you know how to cut and slice and chop efficiently. But the proper tools or equipment are a great aid in any form of hasty cooking. A dull knife can hinder a cook as much as a cluttered work surface, which is the bane of a professional. As you work you should clean and rid your immediate work area of unnecessary ingredients and any other nonessentials. You should also plan ahead, determine the ingredients to be used, and decide the order in which they should logically be cleaned and otherwise made ready for cooking.

There are certain "tricks," too, that will expedite the preparation of food. I am often asked why my recipes call for starting a dish on top of the stove before it is placed in the oven, and the answer is basic: it hastens the baking time. The heat that is rapidly generated on top of the stove may save as much as five or ten minutes baking.

That pertains to the 60-minute dish here, parsleyed chicken with vegetables. There is another "trick" outlined in the recipe. Cooks are instructed to make a slit at the bend where each chicken thigh and leg meet without severing the two pieces. This is frequently a good idea whenever thighs and legs of chickens are cooked together without splitting the pieces apart. That joint requires more cooking time than the rest of the chicken and with a partial cut, the cooking is hastened.

Poulet Persillé aux Légumes
(*Parsleyed chicken with vegetables*)

1	3- to 4-pound chicken, cut into quarters	3	tablespoons finely chopped shallots
	Salt and freshly ground pepper to taste	1	teaspoon finely chopped garlic
3	tablespoons butter	3	tablespoons finely chopped parsley
½	cup bread crumbs		assorted vegetables (see recipe for marmite de légumes).

1. Preheat the oven to 425 degrees.

2. Using a sharp knife such as a boning knife, make a slit at the bend between each leg and thigh without severing the pieces.

3. Sprinkle the chicken pieces, including the liver, gizzard, and neck, if they are used, with salt and pepper.

4. Grease a shallow heatproof baking pan large enough to hold the chicken in one layer with 1 tablespoon of butter. Arrange the quartered chicken pieces over it. Dot the chicken with remaining 2 tablespoons of butter. Add the liver, neck and gizzard between the pieces.

5. Place the baking dish on top of the stove and heat to sizzling. Place the dish in the oven and bake 30 minutes, basting occasionally.

6. Meanwhile, blend the crumbs with the shallots, garlic, and parsley.

7. After the half hour of baking, remove the dish from the oven. Baste the chicken liberally and sprinkle with the crumb mixture. Return the chicken to the oven for 10 minutes or until crumbs are golden brown.

8. Scatter the vegetables over the chicken, if desired, or serve them separately.

Yield: Four servings.

Marmite de Légumes
(*Assorted vegetables*)

8 small baby carrots or 2 large carrots, about ¼ pound	¼ pound green beans, trimmed and cut into 2-inch lengths
1 white turnip, about ¼ pound, peeled	Salt to taste
1 Idaho potato, about ¼ pound, peeled	12 small white onions, peeled
	2 tablespoons butter
	Freshly ground pepper to taste.

1. Scrape the carrots and leave them whole if they are small. Otherwise, cut the larger carrots in half crosswise. Cut each half in two to make eight pieces. Set aside.

2. Peel the turnip and potato. Cut them in half. Cut each half into eight segments.

3. Add the green beans and carrots to a saucepan and add water to cover and salt to taste. Bring to the boil and simmer 8 minutes.

4. Add the potatoes, turnips, and onions and cook about 3 minutes. Drain well.

5. Heat the butter in a skillet and add the vegetables, salt and pepper to taste. Cook about 5 minutes, stirring and shaking the skillet so that the vegetables cook evenly.

Yield: Four servings.

WE WERE REMINISCING—FOR THE THOUSANDTH
time, of course—on the elaborate changes that have been
made in American taste and food habits within recent mem-
ory. My memory stretches back to that World's Fair of 1939 when I first came
here to work in the restaurant of the fair's French pavilion.

Many of the dishes created in the pavilion kitchen were not overly daring,
and yet they were at the time a novelty to the thousands of fairgoers and were
consumed with obvious relish. Chicken in red wine sauce—particularly coq au
vin—and boeuf bourguignon were among the dishes in which the public in-
dulged with uncommon enthusiasm.

Both those dishes have become so familiar by now that they seem almost as
American as they were French. In a way, it seems a shame that both dishes
have lost some of their original éclat, for both dishes have an honest and inherent goodness. And one of them, chicken in red wine sauce, is a snap to
make. The most basic such dish is a simple sauce with mushrooms, chopped
shallots, and red wine, with herbs and spices. The cooking time for browning
the chicken in butter is about twelve minutes. After that you simply add wine
and seasonings, cover and cook until the chicken is done, and the sauce is
ready to be strained.

I have deliberately avoided calling it coq au vin, for that dish in its classic in-
carnation is a bit more complicated and time-consuming, calling as it does for
rendered pieces of salt pork (lardons), glazed small white onions, and, finally,
croutons.

Thus, the recipe here is called au brouilly. The day the dish was recently
made I used a glass of Brouilly, an excellent beaujolais that happened to be
handy. Any good dry red wine, preferably a burgundy, would suffice. The
chicken and a hastily prepared gratin made with noodles and cheese are a fine
combination. That plus a salad would suffice.

Poulet Sauté au Brouilly
(*Chicken in red wine sauce*)

1	2½- to 3-pound chicken, cut into serving pieces and including back, neck, gizzard, and liver Salt and freshly ground pepper to taste	1	teaspoon finely chopped garlic
		2	tablespoons flour
		1½	cups dry red wine, preferably a Brouilly
2	tablespoons butter	½	cup plus 2 tablespoons chicken broth
¼	pound mushrooms, left whole if very small; otherwise halved, quartered, or sliced	1	bay leaf
		1	sprig parsley
¼	cup chopped shallots	2	sprigs fresh thyme or less, or
		¼	teaspoon dried thyme.

1. Sprinkle the chicken pieces with salt and pepper.
2. Heat the butter in a skillet large enough to hold the chicken parts in one layer without crowding. Add the chicken pieces skin side down.
3. Cook the chicken over moderately high heat until golden brown, about 6 or 7 minutes. Turn the pieces and cook about 5 minutes longer.
4. Add the mushrooms, shallots, and garlic and stir to blend. Cook about 1 minute and sprinkle the flour evenly over all.
5. Add the wine and half a cup of broth and bring to the boil.
6. Add the bay leaf, parsley sprig, and thyme. Add salt and pepper to taste and cover. Cook 15 to 20 minutes.
7. Using a slotted spoon, transfer the meaty parts of the chicken to a heat-proof casserole. Add the mushrooms, but leave the back, gizzard, and so on in the skillet.
8. Strain the sauce over the chicken, pressing with the back of a wooden spoon to extract juices from the solids. Add the remaining 2 tablespoons of broth and swirl it around to thin the sauce remaining in the skillet. Strain this over the chicken. Reheat thoroughly.

Yield: Four servings.

Nouilles au Fromage
(*Noodles with cheese*)

¾   **pound medium or fine egg noodles**
    Salt
2   **tablespoons butter**
    Freshly ground pepper to taste
⅛   **teaspoon freshly grated nutmeg**

1   **cup heavy cream**
¼   **pound grated Gruyère or Swiss cheese, about 1¼ cups loosely packed.**

1. Preheat the broiler.
2. Cook the noodles in boiling salted water until tender. Drain. Return the noodles to the kettle and add half the butter, salt, pepper, and nutmeg. Toss to blend.
3. Spoon the noodles into a hot serving dish. Heat the cream and pour it over the noodles.
4. Sprinkle the cheese over the noodles and dot with the remaining butter. Run under the broiler until cheese melts.

Yield: Four servings.

IT IS A FALLACY, OF COURSE, TO SAY THAT THERE'S no accounting for taste. Taste can be accounted for on an elaborate scale, and it is more accurate to use the old bromide that man is what he eats.

The 60-minute suggestion offered here set me to thinking about dishes in French cooking that are called à la diable, deviled or in the devil's style.

The French kitchen uses far fewer hot spices than any other of which I am aware. Recently, Chinese restaurants have become celebrated for the fiery hot dishes of Szechwan and Hunam cooking. Although Indian cooking is not one mass of dishes fired with chilies, there are many dishes whose success depends on mouth-burning ingredients. Similar things could be said about foods of Mexico, Thailand, the American Southwest and of certain Japanese recipes that call for liberal sprinklings of hot ground chilies.

Although in French cooking there are numerous recipes that call for cayenne pepper, only the least trace of it is used in the classic kitchen—a dash or two in lobster bordelaise or américaine, sauce Nantua and a few cheese dishes. Hot chilies, except along the French-Spanish border, are rarely used in regional cooking. Thus, when some chef, who knows how many decades ago, first prepared a recipe that called for an abundance of mustard and une pointe de cayenne, it must have seemed very hot or piquant to his taste. "Une pointe" is generally an eighth of a teaspoon or less.

Chicken is one of the foods most often prepared à la diable, and it is an excellent dish for cooking when time is a consideration. Although the chicken (in this case the legs with thighs are used) must be tended to several times as it cooks under the broiler, the total time for that is less than fifteen minutes. There is an additional baking time of less than thirty minutes and it cooks with a minimum of watching. There is ample time to prepare and cook the asparagus with sesame seeds recommended as a side dish.

Cuisses de Volaille à la Diable
(Deviled chicken legs)

4	chicken legs with thighs attached, about 3 pounds	5	tablespoons dry white wine
	Salt and freshly ground pepper to taste	⅛	teaspoon cayenne pepper
4	tablespoons butter	8	tablespoons fine fresh bread crumbs
2	tablespoons imported mustard such as Dijon or Düsseldorf	3	tablespoons finely chopped parsley.

1. Preheat the broiler to high.

2. Partly cut the chicken thighs and legs at the joint. Cut about halfway through, but do not sever the legs and thighs. This will speed up the cooking process. Sprinkle the chicken with salt and pepper.

[3 6]

3. Melt the butter in a baking dish large enough to hold the legs. Heat the dish and add the chicken pieces, turning once to coat with butter.

4. Arrange the pieces skin side up. Place the dish under the broiler and broil about four inches from the source of heat. Cook about 7 minutes and turn. Cook another 7 minutes.

5. Baste the chicken with butter (at this point it would be skin side down).

6. Blend the mustard, 1 tablespoon wine, and cayenne. Brush the chicken with the mustard mixture and sprinkle each leg and thigh with 1 tablespoon of bread crumbs.

7. Reduce the oven heat to 450 degrees.

8. Place the chicken pieces in the oven and bake 10 minutes.

9. Turn the chicken pieces. Brush with the remaining mustard mixture and sprinkle with remaining crumbs. Return to the oven and bake 15 minutes longer.

10. Transfer the chicken pieces to a warm platter. Add the remaining wine to the baking dish and stir to dissolve the brown particles that cling to the bottom and sides of the pan. Add the parsley and spoon the sauce over the chicken.

Yield: Four servings.

Asperges Sautées aux Graines de Sésame
(Sautéed asparagus with sesame seeds)

24	asparagus spears, 1½ pounds	1	tablespoon soy sauce
2	tablespoons butter	2	tablespoons sesame seeds.
½	teaspoon sugar		

1. Trim off the asparagus about one inch from the bottom. Using a swivel-bladed vegetable parer, scrape the sides of the asparagus to about two inches from the tops. Cut the asparagus on the diagonal into one-inch pieces.

2. Heat the butter in a skillet and cook the asparagus, tossing and shaking the skillet, about 1 minute. Sprinkle with sugar and toss, cooking about 30 seconds. Sprinkle with soy sauce and cook, tossing about 30 seconds. Take care not to overcook.

3. Meanwhile, heat the sesame seeds in a skillet, shaking and stirring so that they cook evenly. When golden brown, remove from the heat.

4. Sprinkle the asparagus with sesame seeds and serve.

Yield: Four servings.

FROM ITALIAN FRIENDS I HAVE LEARNED THAT THE name of the dish, chicken scarpariello, means chicken shoemaker-style. It is an interesting name because the lowest compliment you can pay a French chef is to say, "He cooks like a shoemaker."

In any event, a friend and colleague, Luigi Nanni, chef-patron of two of New York's best Italian restaurants—Nanni's and Il Valleto—was contacted by telephone, and he explained briefly that the dish is a sauté of chicken cooked until golden brown in olive oil and quickly finished with a bit of garlic, white wine, and lemon juice. It is a dish from the south of Italy.

On the day I decided to cook this dish, one of the first shipments of broccoli di râpé appeared in the vegetable section of one of the largest supermarkets in Southampton.

My knowledge of this somewhat bitter but excellent vegetable also came to me through a good friend and excellent cook, Ed Giobbi, the artist and cookbook author of Katonah, N.Y. Broccoli di râpé is easily prepared. It is necessary to simply trim away any tough bottom stalks. All the rest of the vegetable is edible—the leaves, stems, and "buds" or flowers. When these are washed and drained briefly, the vegetable is cooked in olive oil with a bit of garlic and crushed hot red pepper. It cooks quickly.

Some may complain that it is bad planning to link two dishes containing olive oil and garlic in the same menu. To my taste the two dishes complement each other and a bit of flexibility would seem in order where menu-planning is concerned.

The logical way to prepare this menu is to begin with the chicken. As it cooks, the broccoli di râpé can be trimmed and washed and put on to cook shortly before the chicken is ready.

The important thing to keep in mind in preparing this menu is to use your judgment in cooking the chicken. It should be browned over high or moderately high heat. The heat must be reduced somewhat so that the chicken will be cooked throughout at the end of the cooking time. The total cooking time for one three-and-one-half-pound chicken to serve four is from about twenty to twenty-five minutes.

It is recommended that this menu include the usual salad with cheese as a second course and, if desired, a final course of fresh fruit or a purchased or previously made dessert.

Poulet Scarpariello
(Chicken in white wine)

1 3½-pound chicken, cut into serving pieces	2 tablespoons butter
Flour for dredging	2 teaspoons finely minced garlic
Salt and freshly ground pepper to taste	½ cup dry white wine
	Juice of 1 lemon
¼ cup olive oil	3 tablespoons finely chopped parsley.

1. Dredge the chicken all over in flour seasoned with salt and pepper.

2. Heat the oil in a heavy skillet large enough to hold the chicken pieces in one layer. Add the chicken pieces skin side down and cook until golden brown, 8 to 10 minutes. Do not cover.

3. Turn the chicken pieces and cook 10 to 12 minutes longer. Do not cover. At the end of this time the chicken should be cooked through to the bone. Adjust the heat and cooking time accordingly.

4. Carefully pour all the fat from the skillet, leaving the chicken in the skillet. Add the butter to the skillet and when it is hot, add the garlic. Pour the wine around the chicken and bring to the boil. Squeeze the lemon juice over the chicken and sprinkle with parsley. Cover closely and cook 3 minutes longer.

Yield: Four servings.

Brocoli di râpé à la vapeur
(*Steamed broccoli di râpe*)

---

1 pound tender, bright green, unblemished broccoli di râpé (see note)	**1 hot dried red pepper, crushed with seeds or ½ teaspoon hot red pepper flakes**
¼ cup olive oil	**Salt and freshly ground pepper to taste.**
1 tablespoon finely minced garlic	

1. Using a small paring knife, cut off and discard the bottom stalks. The tender leaves and stems plus the buds of the vegetable should be left intact. Rinse the vegetable well and place it in a colander. Drain but allow the water that clings to the leaves to remain.

2. Heat the oil in a heavy skillet or casserole with a tight-fitting lid. Add garlic and red pepper. Immediately add the prepared broccoli di râpé and stir, using a two-pronged fork, turning the vegetable in the oil until the leaves start to wilt. Sprinkle with salt and pepper and cover closely. Let cook about 3 to 5 minutes, turning the vegetable occasionally so that it cooks evenly.

Yield: Four servings.

Note: Broccoli di râpé is available in some supermarkets and stores that specialize in Italian foods.

I HAD NEVER COOKED BEFORE I WAS PACKED OFF ON a train to go to Paris to become apprenticed as a chef shortly after my fourteenth birthday. At that time I lived in the small village of St. Vinnemer in Burgundy, and the total population was said to be exactly 396 people. The town is not listed in most atlases. Legend had it that when anyone moved, someone else arrived; when someone died, another child was born, and so on.

My father served the town proudly in two capacities. He was both mayor and chief fireman. He also took pleasure in the thought that I had chosen cooking as a profession.

The time of my first visit home one year later coincided with St. Barbe's Day and St. Barbe just happened to be the patron saint of firemen.

It was a time of considerable revelry, and my father volunteered that I would cook the meal for all the volunteer firemen in town and their families, a total of about thirty people.

I hadn't the courage to tell him that in the first year of apprenticeship in any kitchen of France back in those days, your time was spent peeling potatoes and onions, sweeping floors and cleaning pots and pans. Serious cookery would come later.

In any event, I couldn't disappoint him, so after brooding over the problem I decided there was one dish I could concoct without fear or trembling. It was one of the most basic dishes of the entire French repertory, a simply boiled chicken with a sauce suprême or cream sauce with chicken broth as its foundation. It was a huge success, and that dish to this day remains a favorite of mine.

The chicken requires thirty minutes to simmer. The broth in which it is cooked may be used in cooking the rice to accompany the dish and the sauce to spoon over it. If on the other hand you have a spare quantity of broth in the refrigerator or freezer, you might use this for the rice and sauce and the total cooking time would be reduced to slightly more than half an hour.

It is recommended that this menu include the usual salad with cheese as a second course and, if desired, a final course of fresh fruit or a purchased or previously made dessert.

Poulet Poché Sauce Suprême
(*Poached chicken in cream sauce*)

1 2½-pound chicken, trussed	1 cup rice
5 cups water or chicken broth	3 cups chicken broth (broth in
1 bay leaf	which chicken is cooked here may
1 small onion stuck with two cloves	be used)
2 allspice	2 tablespoons butter
1 large carrot, cut in half widthwise	2 tablespoons flour
3 large ribs celery, each about 6	1 cup heavy cream
inches long	Juice of half a lemon
Salt to taste	Freshly ground pepper to taste
6 peppercorns	⅛ teaspoon nutmeg
2 sprigs fresh thyme or ½ teaspoon	Pinch of cayenne.
dried thyme	

1. Place the chicken in a small kettle or large saucepan and add the water, bay leaf, onion with cloves, allspice, carrot, celery, salt, peppercorns and thyme. Bring to the boil and partly cover. Simmer 30 minutes.

2. Place the rice in a saucepan and add 2 cups of chicken broth (the rice may be cooked before or after the chicken is finished). Bring to the boil and cook 20 minutes.

3. Meanwhile, melt the butter in a saucepan and add the flour, using a wire whisk. When blended, add remaining 1 cup of chicken broth, stirring rapidly with the whisk. Cook about 5 minutes and add the cream. Simmer about 10 minutes. Add salt to taste and the remaining ingredients.

4. To serve, untruss the chicken. Remove the skin from the chicken (except the wing skin).

5. Arrange the hot rice on a dish. Cut the carrots and celery into two-inch portions. Place the chicken on the rice, along with the carrots and celery. Spoon the sauce over the chicken and serve.

Yield: Four servings.

IT WOULD BE INTERESTING TO KNOW THE NAME OF the cook or chef who first discovered that a splash of spirit would enhance the flavor of a dish. The name of the dish and the circumstances of that landmark decision will never be known, but posterity owes him a debt.

Of course, there's almost no category of food to which a bit of cognac, a dash of rum, or, in some cases, even a jigger of gin can't add a curiously interesting fillip.

The rule applies to the sherry in the turtle soup, the pernod in the bouillabaisse, the orange liqueur in duck á l'orange and the cognac in the sauce for lobster americaine. Kirsch gives character to an endless number of desserts including cakes and cream—pastry creams or ice cream.

Bourbon, perhaps the most thoroughly American of drinks outside of Coca Cola, has fairly widespread usage in French cookery. It goes in several dishes, including lobster au whisky. Two of the best-known ''American'' dishes in the French repertory count on bourbon as a seasoning agent. These are chicken Washington and chicken Maryland, both conceived in France.

Poached chicken is one of the best, least pretentious, and simplest dishes ever concocted in any kitchen, home or professional. It is excellent served in the broth with, perhaps, noodles added. Poached chicken in a cream sauce makes it just a bit more festive and, if a dash of bourbon is added, it takes on an added coloration for the palate. The preparation and cooking of the dish can be accomplished in much less than sixty minutes. Poached chicken in a bourbon-flavored cream sauce is neatly complemented by buttered noodles or rice.

Poulet Poché Sauce au Whisky
(*Poached chicken with bourbon sauce*)

1	3-pound chicken		Salt to taste
1	leek, trimmed and scraped	8	peppercorns, crushed
1	carrot, trimmed and scraped	6	large mushroom caps, about ½
1	onion, peeled		pound
1	bay leaf	1	tablespoon butter
2	sprigs fresh thyme or ½ teaspoon	1	tablespoon flour
	dried thyme	½	cup heavy cream
1	rib celery, broken		Freshly ground pepper to taste
6	cups water	2	tablespoons bourbon whisky.

1. Truss the chicken, if desired, and place it in a kettle. Split the leek in half lengthwise down to but not through the root end. Cut the leek in two, widthwise, and tie the two pieces with string. Add them to the kettle.

2. Add the carrot, onion, bay leaf, thyme, celery, water, salt, and peppercorns. Bring to the boil and simmer 30 minutes.

3. Neatly trim off the stems of the mushrooms and add them to the simmering liquid in the kettle. Cover and simmer 10 minutes.

4. Remove the chicken and mushrooms and set aside. Cook the cooking liquid down to 4 cups.

5. Melt the butter in a saucepan and add the flour, stirring with a wire whisk. Add 1½ cups of reduced chicken broth, stirring rapidly with the whisk. Put the remaining broth to another use. When blended and smooth, add the cream. Add salt and pepper to taste. Add the bourbon. Serve the chicken carved with the mushrooms and bourbon sauce. Serve with buttered noodles (see recipe).

Yield: Four servings.

Nouilles à la Noix de Muscade

| ½ | pound broad noodles | 2 | tablespoons butter |
| | Salt to taste | ¼ | teaspoon freshly ground nutmeg. |

1. Drop the noodles into boiling salted water to cover and stir until water returns to the boil. Cook until noodles are tender, 7 minutes or longer.

2. Drain and return the noodles to the pot. Add the butter and nutmeg and toss well until coated.

Yield: Four servings.

COOKING WELL, LIKE ALMOST ANY PROFESSION OR hobby, is to a great degree psychological. It has to do with "aptitude," which implies a feeling of security in what you are about. Many people are terrified of cooking because they have a mistaken notion that it is an impossible exact science. They're afraid, so to speak, of fitting a round hole with a square peg.

One of the best chicken dishes in the French repertoire is called poulet Vallée d'Auge, chicken in cream sauce, a celebrated dish of Normandy made with cut-up chicken and vegetables and flavored with Calvados, the famed applejack of the region.

Since the chicken and vegetables are first cooked separately and then combined so that they finish cooking together, the first "fear" to come into an amateur cook's mind is probably that either the chicken or the vegetables will be undercooked or overcooked. That they won't "finish the race together."

The thing to remember is that in most cases there is a lot more latitude in cookery than most amateur cooks believe. Of course, you wouldn't want to serve undercooked chicken. Or mushy, overcooked vegetables. But cooking times have a way of compensating for themselves. If the vegetables cook four or five minutes longer than the "ideal" time you would allot them, they are still going to be highly edible. Perhaps a trifle less "toothy" than you would have them, but don't say a word and your guests won't suspect a thing.

In preparing the dish you will note that the chicken is sautéed in butter for the first few minutes of cooking. The vegetables are prepared for cooking and what one calls "blanched" or "parboiled" before the final steps. To go about this, it is preferable to prepare all the ingredients for cooking before you start. Salt and pepper the chicken pieces, then proceed to scraping, peeling, and cutting the vegetables. Then begin.

As the chicken is put on to cook, add the vegetables to a kettle and bring to the boil. Relax. Everything is going to be all right.

Poulet Vallée d'Auge
(Chicken with applejack sauce)

---

1 2½- to 3-pound chicken, cut up for frying Salt and freshly ground pepper to taste	8 small white onions or 4 small- to medium-size onions, about ½ pound, peeled
1 large or 2 medium-size potatoes, about 1 pound peeled	1 zucchini, about ¼ pound
2 carrots, about ⅓ pound	6 tablespoons butter
¼ pound green beans	¼ cup Calvados, cognac, or bourbon
	1 cup heavy cream.

1. Sprinkle the chicken pieces with salt and pepper.
2. If one large potato is used, cut it into eight pieces ("cubes") after

peeling. If two potatoes are used, cut into quarters after peeling. Cover with cold water to prevent discoloration.

3. Trim and scrape the carrots. Cut each carrot in half. Cut each half into thirds.

4. Trim off the ends of the beans. Cut the beans into one-and-a-half-inch lengths.

5. If onions are small, cut them in half. If larger, cut into quarters.

6. Trim the end of the zucchini. Cut in half lengthwise, then cut each half into quarters.

7. Heat 4 tablespoons of butter in a large, heavy skillet and add the chicken, skin side down. Cook about 10 minutes.

8. As the chicken cooks, place the potato, carrots, beans, and onions in a saucepan and add cold water to cover. Add salt to taste and bring to the boil. At the boil cook 1 minute and drain.

9. When the chicken is browned on one side, turn it. Cook 5 minutes.

10. Heat remaining 2 tablespoons of butter in another skillet and add the drained vegetables and zucchini. Sprinkle with salt and pepper and shake the skillet or stir gently occasionally to redistribute the vegetables. Cook about 5 minutes. The vegetables at this point should not be cooked until tender. They will be cooked again with the chicken.

11. Add the Calvados or other spirit to the chicken and cover the chicken. Cook 10 minutes and uncover. Add the cream and vegetables and bring to the boil. Add salt and pepper and cover. Cook 10 minutes and serve.

Yield: Four servings.

IN TRADITIONAL MENU PLANNING, A MAIN COURSE, more often than not, is served with a starch such as rice or potatoes, plus a green vegetable. Quite obviously, when planning a meal to be cooked in limited time, if you can combine all these elements in one casserole—and in less time than it takes to prepare each separately—you are ahead of the game.

The chicken and rice casserole here falls in that category. It contains sautéed chicken, which is further cooked with rice plus mushrooms. Mushrooms are generally and quite justifiably lumped into the green vegetable category.

Those who frown on or shun recipes with long lists of ingredients should also take pleasure in this one. The total number here is less than twelve, including salt and pepper and bay leaf. This dish, incidentally, is prepared with a technique similar to one frequently used for cooking quail rather than chicken breast.

The recommended way to use this recipe is as follows:

Prepare and measure all the necessary ingredients. That is to say, chop the onions, garlic, and mushrooms and have them ready. Measure out the rice, wine, and chicken broth. Then heat the butter in a skillet, add the chicken pieces, which have been sprinkled with salt and pepper, and continue cooking until done.

It is recommended that this menu include the usual salad with cheese as a second course and, if desired, a final course of fresh fruit or a purchased or previously made dessert.

Casserole de Poulet au Riz
(Chicken and rice casserole)

2 whole chicken breasts, split in half, about 2 pounds total weight (4 pieces)

Salt and freshly ground pepper to taste

2 tablespoons butter

½ cup finely chopped onion

1 teaspoon chopped garlic

⅓ pound fresh mushrooms, left whole if very small, otherwise sliced or quartered, depending on size

1 bay leaf

½ cup dry white wine

½ cup raw rice

1 cup chicken broth.

1. Do not skin or bone the chicken breasts. Sprinkle the chicken pieces with salt and pepper.

2. Heat the butter in a skillet and add the chicken pieces, skin side down. Brown about 5 minutes and turn.

3. Scatter the onion and garlic between the chicken pieces and add the mushrooms and bay leaf. Cook about 5 minutes.

4. Add the wine and cook until it is almost all evaporated. Add the rice and broth, taking care that the rice does not rest on top of the chicken pieces. Cover closely and cook about 20 minutes or until rice is tender.

Yield: Four servings.

DURING MY TENURE AS CHEF AT LE PAVILLON RES-
taurant, it almost goes without saying that the clientele that
passed through those doors was both international and celebrated. It also goes without saying that the owner, Henri Soulé, held some of
his customers in higher esteem than others. The gentleman was inclined—a natural inclination—to pamper those of whom he was particularly fond, whether it
was a matter of seating or a complimentary bottle of champagne. His solicitude
and care were never more apparent than when those whom he particularly liked
and/or admired were hospitalized.

He was known by that small segment of his clientele for the Pavillon's poule
au pot, or chicken in the pot. He hated hospital food himself, and whenever he
ascertained that a favored guest, temporarily indisposed, was well enough to
eat, he would dispatch his movable feast to the patient's bedside and not
without ceremony.

The kitchen would be charged with adding a whole, small chicken to an
earthenware crock and over it was ladled a piping hot, rich, and nourishing
broth containing carrots, celery, turnips, leeks, and rice. It was not so much the
healing powers of the dish that spurred him on. Poule au pot also happened
to be one of the dishes on which he personally preferred to dine.

In any event, the chicken and broth in the crock would be covered closely
with the lid and a tablespoon tied on top of it. A personal note would be added,
addressed to such people as John F. Kennedy, Margaret Truman, Cole Porter,
the Duchess of Windsor, and so on. For clients of this caliber he would send
Martin Decre, Soulé's second and right-hand man in the dining room, to see
the small but important details of carving the chicken and serving the broth
while it was still steaming.

At its best, a poule au pot is an excellent dish and certainly one of the easiest
to prepare, simply a matter of cutting up a few vegetables and cooking them as
timing demands. It is, of course, a meal in itself and the success of the dish
depends in large part on how rich, fresh, and strongly flavored the chicken
broth is when it is added to the chicken and vegetables.

This dish, plus fruit and cheese, would be an ample meal for a late spring or
summer evening.

Poule au Pot d'Henri Soulé
(Henri Soulé's chicken in the pot)

1 **3-pound chicken**	1 **cup leeks, quartered lengthwise**
3 **carrots, scraped, quartered**	**and cut into 1½-inch lengths**
lengthwise and cut into 1½-inch	1 **zucchini, trimmed, quartered and**
lengths	**cut into 1½-inch lengths**
3 **ribs celery, trimmed, split**	6 **cups fresh or canned chicken**
lengthwise and cut into 1½-inch	**broth**
lengths	¼ **cup rice**
2 **or 3 turnips, about ½ pound,**	**Salt and freshly ground pepper to**
trimmed and cut into pieces about	**taste.**
the same shape as the celery and	
carrots	

1. Truss the chicken and place it in a kettle. It should fit snugly or else too much water must be added and the subsequent soup will be weak and watery. Cover with water and add the carrots, celery, turnips, leeks and zucchini. Bring to a full boil and drain well.

2. Return the chicken to the kettle and add the chicken broth. Add all the vegetables except the zucchini. Simmer 20 minutes. Add the zucchini and simmer 5 minutes longer.

3. Add the rice and salt and pepper to taste, and cook until it is tender, about 10 minutes.

4. Untruss the chicken. Cut it into serving pieces and serve in four hot soup bowls with equal amounts of vegetables and rice in each bowl.

Yield: Four servings.

PURISTS MAY ARGUE THAT CURRY POWDER IS NOT A proper ingredient for dedicated cooks. I demur. I have dined at several Indian tables both in private homes and in restaurants where the food has been something to marvel at. And yet I see nothing wrong with a first-rate commercially blended curry powder, if it is not used on a static, day-by-day basis.

As a matter of fact, there are numerous brands of curry powder on the market that vary considerably both in strength and flavor, and if you are not out to cook pure Indian, it might be wise to shop around and experiment with several to find a blend that pleases you.

The method I use for preparing curries is as uncomplicated as I believe it to be good and it is one that I have used since my earliest days (a good many years ago) as a qualified chef in Paris. It consists of sautéing meats or poultry or seafood quickly, adding a bit of garlic, cubed apple and banana among other things, the curry powder and chicken broth, and cooking until tender. It may not be what you find in New Delhi but it is delicious nonetheless. The sauce, pushed through a sieve, is smooth and, if desired, enriched with a touch of heavy cream.

At times I have been served curries in Western homes where various side dishes—peanuts, deep-fried coconut shavings, raisins—were served to be sprinkled on the main dish. It is a question of personal taste, but I find this is bothersome and unnecessary.

The curry that I have in mind does go well, however, with a simple and quickly made rice dish that contains among its ingredients both a few raisins and almonds. It is a nice complement for the curry dish.

A salad may or may not go well with this curry: that is up to your individual taste. Cold yogurt would be an excellent accompaniment. And, again Western style, so would bottled chutney.

Poulet au Kari
(*Curried chicken*)

1	3-pound chicken	2	tablespoons curry powder
	Salt to taste	1	bay leaf
	Freshly ground pepper to taste	1	cup apples cut into small cubes
2	tablespoons butter	⅓	cup finely diced banana
¾	cup finely chopped onion	2	teaspoons tomato paste
½	cup finely chopped celery	1½	cups chicken broth
1	teaspoon finely minced garlic	½	cup heavy cream.

1. Sprinkle the chicken pieces with salt and pepper.

2. Heat the butter in a heavy skillet and add the chicken pieces skin side down. Cook until golden on one side, about 5 minutes, and add the onion, celery and garlic. Cook briefly and sprinkle with curry powder. Add the bay leaf,

apples, and bananas. Cook about 5 minutes and add the tomato paste, stirring it around. Add the chicken broth and stir to blend. Cover and cook 15 minutes longer or until chicken is tender.

3. Remove the chicken pieces. Strain the sauce through a fine sieve, pushing to extract as much of the solids as possible. Reheat and add the cream. Return the chicken to sauce, bring to the boil and serve hot with rice.

Yield: Four servings.

Riz Orientale
(Rice with almonds and raisins)

1	tablespoon butter	¼	cup blanched almonds
⅓	cup finely chopped onion	1½	cups chicken broth
1	cup raw rice		Salt to taste
2	teaspoons white or black raisins		Freshly ground pepper to taste.

1. Melt butter in a small saucepan and add the onions. Cook, stirring, until wilted. Add the rice, raisins, and almonds and stir.

2. Add the broth, salt and pepper. Bring to the boil. Cover and simmer 20 minutes or until rice is tender and all the liquid is absorbed.

Yield: Four servings.

THERE SEEMS TO BE A COMMON ASSUMPTION AMONG the restaurant-going public that all the dishes that emerge from a professional kitchen are, of necessity, intricate and complex in their preparation. There are, of course, some dishes that require various stocks and bases which may require a day or more to simmer and reduce to a proper or desired consistency. And there are various creations that do require a highly specialized if not to say arcane knowledge to produce successful results.

I thought of this recently while cooking a quickly made sautéed chicken dish, a dish known as chicken beauséjour. During my years as chef of Le Pavillon in New York, this was a great favorite of the clientele, Europeans and Americans alike. And yet it is as easy to make as any, dish that is sort of elegant in its simplicity. It consists of chicken cut into pieces as for frying, and sautéed in butter with a few herbs, namely bay leaf and thyme. White wine is added and cooked down, and the dish is served traditionally with fine buttered noodles or rice. I prefer noodles.

The cooking time for chicken beauséjour is less than half an hour; preparation time is negligible. The noodles should be cooked, of course, shortly before the chicken is ready to be served.

Serve the dish with a salad and a choice of cheese and a simple purchased dessert.

Poulet Sauté Beauséjour
(*Sautéed chicken with wine and herbs*)

---

1 1¾- to 2-pound chicken, cut into serving pieces Salt and freshly ground pepper to taste	1 large bay leaf 2 sprigs fresh thyme or ½ teaspoon dried thyme
3 tablespoons butter	⅓ cup dry white wine
2 whole cloves garlic, unpeeled	⅓ cup water Buttered thin noodles, optional.

1. Sprinkle the chicken pieces with salt and pepper to taste. To facilitate cooking, make a gash in the underside (opposite the skin side) of each chicken leg.

2. Heat 2 tablespoons butter in a heavy skillet and add all the chicken pieces, skin side down. Do not add the liver. Cook 5 to 7 minutes until golden brown and turn the pieces. Add the garlic, bay leaf and thyme.

3. Add the liver and reduce the heat. Cook over moderate heat, turning the pieces so that they cook evenly. The total cooking time at this point should be from 17 to 20 minutes.

4. Remove the chicken pieces to a hot serving platter and add the wine to the skillet. Cook over high heat, stirring to dissolve the brown particles that

cling to the bottom and sides of the pan. Cook until wine is reduced by half. Add the water and boil briskly about 30 seconds.

5. Swirl in the remaining butter, salt and pepper to taste.

6. Spoon the sauce over the chicken and serve with buttered thin noodles (see recipe).

Yield: Four servings.

Nouilles Fines au Beurre
(*Buttered fine noodles*)

½ **pound thin noodles**	2 **tablespoons butter at room**
Salt	**temperature**
	Freshly ground pepper to taste.

1. Drop the noodles into a large quantity of boiling salted water. Cook about 2 or 3 minutes or until tender. Do not overcook.

2. Drain the noodles and return them to the kettle. Toss them with the butter and add salt and pepper to taste. Serve hot.

Yield: Four servings.

NE OF THE ULTIMATE GOALS OF WHAT MIGHT BE called "fast stove" cookery could be a main course in which the principal components are cooked simultaneously. One of the prime examples of this—and a dish that is, by the way, excellent for special occasions—is what is known in French kitchens as poulet grillé à l'américaine, or grilled chicken American-style.

Just why this dish is called American is not immediately apparent. To the French mind, however, it simply seems like a dish that might have been put together by an American chef. In spirit, at least, it is closely related to the English mixed grill (with mutton chop, kidneys, and so on).

Before you begin this recipe, there is a point to remember: The foods—chicken, bacon, sausages, tomatoes, and mushroom caps—are first broiled and some of the ingredients are later "finished" in a hot oven.

Although grilled chicken American-style requires no great ingenuity in its preparation, it is a dish that requires some concentration because of the varied cooking times of the various foods.

One of the most interesting of the meal's components is the chicken, which is prepared à la diable. That is to say, it is "deviled," or made more tangy, by brushing with mustard thinned with a little dry white wine before breading at the very end.

There is one thing for certain. Although this dish could be said to have class or style, it is, nonetheless, copious. Therefore, vegetable accompaniments other than the grilled tomato are nonessential. A well-made green salad with the dish or as a separate course with one or more cheeses and a crusty loaf of bread would be ample. A proper wine for this dish would be a dry red California or French wine. Something not too costly nor elegant.

Poulet Grillé a l'Américaine
(Chicken with mixed grill)

1 3-pound chicken, split for broiling	4 links sausages
Salt and freshly ground pepper to taste	2 red, ripe tomatoes
	4 large mushroom caps
Peanut, vegetable, or corn oil, for brushing	1 tablespoon Dijon mustard
	1 tablespoon white wine
4 slices bacon	4 to 8 tablespoons bread crumbs.

1. Preheat the broiler to high. You will use both the broiler and the oven, preheated to 450 degrees, to cook the dish.

2. Sprinkle the chicken, including the liver, with salt and pepper. Brush all over with oil.

3. Arrange the chicken halves skin side down on a baking dish. Cover each half with two slices of bacon.

4. Arrange the liver separately on the baking dish. Arrange the sausages on the same dish.

5. Split the tomatoes in half. Slice off the stems of the mushrooms. Arrange the tomatoes cut side up and the mushrooms stem side up on a separate dish. Sprinkle the tops with salt and pepper and brush the tops with oil.

6. Place the dish with the chicken under the broiler about four to five inches from the source of heat. Broil about 2 to 3 minutes or until the bacon is crisp. If necessary, turn the sausages and liver to prevent burning. Use your judgment. Broil the tomatoes and mushrooms about 2 to 3 minutes. Turn the mushrooms and continue broiling 2 to 3 minutes. Remove and keep warm.

7. When the bacon is crisp, remove it. Turn the chicken and other pieces. Broil the chicken skin side up until it is nicely browned, about 2 to 3 minutes.

8. Leave the chicken skin side up and place in the oven. Turn the sausages and liver as necessary.

9. When the chicken, sausages, and liver have baked 15 minutes, remove the lausages and liver. Transfer them to the dish with the tomatoes and mushrooms.

10. Continue baking the chicken. When the chicken has baked 5 minutes longer, turn each half skin side down. Blend the mustard and wine. Brush the top side with the mustard mixture. Sprinkle each half with 1 or 2 tablespoons of bread crumbs. Continue baking 10 minutes.

11. Turn the chicken halves skin side up. Brush with mustard mixture and sprinkle each half with 1 or 2 tablespoons of bread crumbs. Return to the oven and bake 5 minutes, at the end of which time return the dish of tomatoes, mushrooms, sausages, and liver to the oven to reheat.

12. Bake 5 minutes longer and serve.

Yield: Four servings.

THERE ARE MANY INESCAPABLE ASSOCIATIONS IN the world of food, and if you ask any Frenchman to associate words with foods, the name chicken would inevitably bring to mind the quotation of my fellow countryman, Henri the Fourth:

"Je veux qu'il n'y ait si pauvre paysan en mon royaume qu'il n'ait tous les dimanches sa poule au pot." I want there to be no peasant in my kingdom to be so poor that he cannot have a chicken in his pot every Sunday.

Chicken may not be the most aristocratic of foods, but it is certainly the most versatile, whether it is simply cooked as a poule au pot or turned into a fine ragout with a rich Burgundy sauce.

If, in this book, there seems to be a preponderance of chicken dishes, it is for a very good and logical reason. Chicken is quite simply—in the long run—the most available of foods, season in and season out. And, in addition to its incredible number of uses, it may well be the food least likely to have pitfalls in the ways in which it is cooked.

If there is one danger in cooking chicken, it is probably that it may be undercooked, although as many tourists have discovered in my homeland, there are those who prefer chicken—when spit-turned, for example—a bit underdone, but that's a question of taste.

The fact is that there is a good deal of latitude in the cooking conditions of chicken. If the cooking time is, to choose a random example, thirty minutes and the time is extended five or ten minutes, chances are the dish will still be admirable. To put it another way, the cooking time for most chicken dishes—as opposed to those made with fish, for example—is about as flexible as any meat or seafood dish that comes to mind.

In the recipe outlined here, the chicken is first placed under the broiler, turned to broil on the second side, then baked until done. The broiling, actually, is to give texture to the skin of the fowl before finishing the dish with oven heat. This dish is an all-in-one affair in which, for the last few minutes, the chicken is baked with pre-cooked vegetables. Actually the preparation of the vegetables demands a little more time and effort than does the chicken. Therefore, it is best to prepare the vegetables and get them ready to cook before proceeding to the chicken.

Poulet Grillé à la Moutarde
(Chicken grilled with mustard)

1 **4-pound chicken, split for broiling** **Salt and freshly ground pepper to** **taste**	2 **tablespoons peanut oil** **Sautéed vegetables, see recipe**
2 **tablespoons imported mustard** **such as Dijon or Düsseldorf**	1 **tablespoon red wine vinegar** 2 **tablespoons finely chopped** **parsley.**

1. Preheat the broiler.

2. Sprinkle the chicken halves with salt and pepper. Arrange the halves in one layer on a baking dish and brush on all sides with mustard.

3. Arrange the chicken, skin side down, on the dish and sprinkle the top with oil.

4. Place under the broiler and cook 10 minutes. Turn the halves and broil 10 minutes longer.

5. Pour off all the fat from the baking dish. Turn the chicken pieces.

6. Reduce the oven heat to 400 degrees.

7. Scatter the sautéed vegetables around the chicken and place the chicken in the oven. Bake 10 minutes.

8. Place the chicken in the baking dish on the stove. Add the vinegar to the pan liquid, cooking a few seconds over high heat. Sprinkle with parsley.

Yield: Four servings.

Légumes Sautés
(Sautéed vegetables)

¾ pound very small potatoes, peeled
1 large carrot, about ¼ pound, trimmed and scraped
4 small white onions, peeled

Salt to taste
2 tablespoons butter
12 mushrooms, about ⅓ pound
Freshly ground pepper to taste.

1. If the potatoes are not very small, cut them in half. Put them in a skillet with water to cover.

2. Cut the carrots into two-inch lengths. Cut each length into quarters. Cut the onions in half.

3. Add the carrots and onions to the potatoes. Add salt to taste and bring to the boil. Let boil 10 minutes and drain.

4. Add the butter to a skillet and when quite hot but not brown, add the vegetables. Cook over relatively high heat, shaking the skillet and stirring the vegetables. Add the mushrooms and sprinkle with salt and pepper. Continue cooking, shaking the skillet and stirring, about 7 or 8 minutes.

Yield: Four servings.

LTHOUGH I HAVE BEEN IN THE UNITED STATES for more than thirty years, one thing that is a constant source of wonder is the number of people who tell me that they had never known the flavor of tarragon during their childhood. In most home gardens in France, it is as common as parsley and chives. As a child I grew up eating omelets aux fines herbes, which always contained tarragon, and also enjoyed tarragon-flavored roasts and a variety of mayonnaise dressings with tarragon. One of the best-known (and one of the best) tarragon-flavored dishes is chicken with tarragon, which comes in many versions.

Actually it is a quickly and simply made dish that contains only six major ingredients, one of which is white wine used to "deglaze" the pan once the chicken is cooked. And a bit of water to dilute the concentrated pan juices destined to be served as a sauce.

Rice is a natural accompaniment for this dish and that could be cooked according to package directions (although it is preferable to cut down on the water recommended by most packagers).

Another excellent seasonal accompaniment for chicken with tarragon is a simply made dish of zucchini cooked with olive oil and lemon. The important thing about this dish is the haste with which it is cooked. You must avoid cooking the zucchini until it becomes soft; it must retain a slightly crunchy "bite" to keep its character.

Poulet à l'Estragon
(*Chicken with tarragon*)

1	2- to 2½-pound chicken, split in half as for broiling	2	tablespoons finely chopped shallots
	Salt and freshly ground pepper to taste	2	teaspoons finely chopped fresh tarragon or half the amount dried
2	tablespoons butter	½	cup dry white wine
		¼	cup water.

1. If the backbone is still attached to one of the chicken halves, hack it away or have this done by the butcher at time of purchase. This will hasten the cooking. Reserve the backbone. Also, it is best to sever the joint that connects the thigh bones with the legs. Do not cut through. Leave the thighs and legs otherwise attached.

2. Sprinkle the chicken with salt and pepper.

3. Heat the butter in a heavy skillet large enough to hold the whole chicken. Add the chicken skin side down. Surround it with the gizzard, liver, heart, neck, and backbone.

4. Cook about 10 minutes until golden brown on the skin side and turn. Cook about 5 minutes. Remove the chicken briefly.

5. To the skillet add the shallots and cook briefly. Add the tarragon and wine. Cook, stirring to dissolve the brown particles that cling to the bottom of the skillet. Stir in the water.

6. Return the chicken to the skillet skin side up and cover. Cook about 15 minutes. Continue cooking, basting often, about 5 minutes longer or until chicken is thoroughly tender and nicely glazed.

Yield: Four servings.

Courgettes au Citron
(*Zucchini with oil and lemon*)

---

2 or 3 zucchini, about 1¼ pounds
3 tablespoons olive oil

Salt and freshly ground pepper to taste
Juice of half a lemon.

1. Trim off the ends of the zucchini. If large, quarter them and cut each quarter into two-inch lengths. If smaller, cut them in half and cut each half into two-inch lengths.

2. Heat the olive oil in a skillet and add the zucchini, salt, and pepper. Cook, shaking the skillet and stirring the vegetable around until it starts to take on color.

3. Add the lemon juice and cover. Cook about 3 minutes. When ready, the vegetable should be crisp.

Yield: Four servings.

THERE IS A COMMON BELIEF THAT MOST OF THE traditional and classic dishes of French cooking require hours and days of preparation to bring about their ultimate goodness but this is, in hundreds of cases, totally fallacious. One of the great and best-known dishes in French culture (actually it is more a specialty of the Anjou region than any other) is a fricassée of chicken or veal.

Basically a fricassée consists of cooking chicken or veal in butter while browning it very lightly, if at all. A touch of onions and mushrooms is cooked with the chicken before the addition of cream. When the dish was recently prepared in my kitchen, a few sprigs of fresh tarragon were added to give it a different turn of flavor and it is an excellent combination. A touch of dried tarragon could be effectively substituted for the fresh herb.

The word fricasser has a few interesting uses, incidentally, in the French language. You can friscasser a fortune, which is to say, squander it. Copious kissing is sometimes referred to as a "fricassée de museaux" or a fricassee of cheeks. And a scandalous, poorly written article or pot-boiler is called a fricassée.

In the kitchen, the total cooking time for a well-made fricassée of chicken for a party of four is less than half an hour. And the use of the word party is deliberate. This is the sort of dish you could serve with pleasure to a special and friendly gathering.

A simple dish of rice and a salad would serve well with this meal. If, however, you wanted to serve a platter of rice with a bit of difference, you might offer your guests a rice that is both flavored and colored with a small spoonful of turmeric.

To plan such a menu, it would be best to start the preparation with the cooking of the chicken. When it is put on for its final simmering, you should start the rice. Incidentally, if the fricassée is not served the moment it is ready, little will be lost if it is set aside briefly and reheated.

Fricassée de Poulet à l'Estragon
(*Fricasse of chicken with tarragon*)

---

1 **3½-pound chicken, cut into serving pieces**	1 **carrot, scraped, quartered, and cut into 1-inch lengths**
Salt and freshly ground pepper to taste	¼ **pound mushrooms, rinsed and drained**
3 **tablespoons butter**	1½ **cups water**
2 **tablespoons flour**	1 **cup heavy cream**
⅓ **cup finely chopped onion**	1 **tablespoon finely chopped fresh tarragon or 1 teaspoon dried.**
1 **small clove garlic, finely minced**	
5 **sprigs fresh tarragon with leaves and stems, or use 1 tablespoon dried**	

1. Sprinkle the chicken with salt and pepper.

2. Heat the butter in a large heavy skillet large enough to hold the chicken in one layer. Cook chicken pieces, turning occasionally, without browning. After about 5 minutes, add the chopped onions, garlic, and tarragon sprigs.

3. Sprinkle with flour, stirring to distribute the flour evenly. Add the water and carrots. Cover and cook about 15 to 20 minutes.

4. Remove the chicken pieces and carrots to a serving dish and keep warm. Remove the tarragon sprigs if they are used. Let the sauce cook down, stirring often, about 5 minutes.

5. Add the cream, salt and pepper to taste. Simmer about 3 minutes. Stir in the chopped tarragon and serve with rice.

Yield: Four servings.

Riz au Tumerique
(*Turmeric rice*)

---

2 tablespoons butter	1 tablespoon powdered turmeric
2 tablespoons finely minced onion	1½ cups chicken broth
1 small clove garlic, finely minced	1 bay leaf.
1 cup rice	

1. Melt half the butter in a saucepan and add the onion and garlic. Cook until wilted and add the rice and turmeric. Stir to coat.

2. Add the broth and bay leaf. Cover and bring to the boil. Cook exactly 17 minutes. Uncover and stir in the remaining tablespoon of butter.

Yield: Four servings.

ONE OF THE CLUES TO FIRST-CLASS QUICK OR 60-minute cooking—or any other successful cookery for that matter—is logic and organization. A case in point is the main dish outlined below: Cornish game hen bonne femme, an American bird cooked in a traditional French manner. It has, by the way, all the components necessary for a main course—chicken, potatoes and mushrooms.

As far as organization is concerned, if you read through the recipe—and you should read through recipes before you start to cook—you will discover that the cooking of the dish is divided into two parts. The Cornish hens are baked for twenty minutes. During this period potatoes and mushrooms are cooked in a bit of butter. These two operations could and should occur simultaneously to diminish the total cooking time.

Incidentally, this dish brings up another interesting point: Can one say with authenticity exactly how many a particular dish will serve? The answer is, not really. Who are the guests and what is the nature of their appetites? When this recipe was tested, three people at the table were content to dine on half a bird each. A fourth devoured a whole bird. To arrive at the number of servings in this case you have to estimate the appetites of those you are feeding. Thus, the following recipe may serve as many as eight light eaters, or suffice for only four very hungry guests.

Cornish game hens bonne femme (the name means "good wife" and implies that the dish is bourgeois in concept) would go very well with nothing more than a tossed green salad and purchased first-quality ice cream or fresh fruit with cheese.

Cornish Game Hens Bonne Femme
(Roast game hens with potatoes and mushrooms)

4 rock Cornish game hens about 1 pound each
Salt and freshly ground pepper to taste
4 tablespoons butter
1 onion, cut into quarters or 8 very small peeled white onions

¾ pound potatoes
¼ pound mushrooms, about 8
¼ cup water
½ teaspoon chopped rosemary, fresh or dried.

1. Preheat the oven to 425 degrees.
2. Rub the game hens inside and out with salt and pepper. Truss them, if desired. (It helps them to hold their shape.) Place them breast side down in a buttered heatproof baking dish and dot with 2 tablespoons of butter. Scatter the gizzards and necks around the hens. Reserve the livers. Add the quartered onion or onions and place the dish on a low flame on top of the stove. This is done only to expedite the cooking time in the oven, and to get the baking dish hot. Place in oven and bake 20 minutes.

3. Meanwhile, peel the potatoes and cut them into half-inch cubes. Drop them into cold water in a saucepan. Bring to the boil.

4. As the potatoes come to the boil, rinse the mushrooms and pat dry. Cut them into quarters and set aside.

5. When the potatoes reach the boil, drain them. Heat remaining 2 tablespoons of butter in a skillet and add the potatoes. Cook, shaking the skillet and tossing the potatoes so that they brown evenly, about 5 minutes. When lightly brown, add the mushrooms, salt and pepper to taste. Cook about 10 minutes, tossing and shaking the skillet.

6. At this point the hens should have completed their first 20 minutes of cooking. Turn the hens on their backs. Sprinkle the livers with salt and pepper and add them to the baking dish. Continue baking about 10 minutes.

7. Scatter the potatoes and mushrooms around the hens and continue cooking about 15 minutes, basting often. Remove the hens. Lift them up and let the cavities drain before they are removed. Add the water and rosemary to the vegetables in the pan. Bring to the boil on top of the stove, stirring. The hens may be served whole or cut in half. Serve the mushrooms and potatoes and the pan sauce with the hens.

Yield: Four to eight servings.

A BIT OF PSYCHOLOGY. IT CAN SCARCELY BE STATED too often that in the interest of good cooking—whether it requires less than an hour or the better part of a weekend—organization is a primary consideration. It is, of course, more vital in doing what must be called "hasty" cookery.

Assemble the ingredients for a dish, chop what must be chopped, shred what must be shredded, measure what must be measured, and relax. This will make you flexible, and flexibility yields to dexterity. With all the ingredients at your disposal, ready for a skillet or pot, you can work on alternate dishes with facility.

Take Rock Cornish game hens cooked in a casserole with a light vinegar sauce. The actual cooking time of the birds is slightly more than half an hour. After the small hens are browned all over, there is little to do as they cook other than add more ingredients from time to time. During that half hour, you can turn your attention to a vegetable dish.

When in season, green beans are a tender and fresh vegetable. The beans should, as always, be cooked until they are just tender, retaining a "bite" in texture when ready to serve. They are excellent when served with only melted butter, a touch of parsley, lemon, and salt and pepper to taste.

Cornish Game Hens au Vinaigre
(Game hens with a delicate vinegar sauce)

4 1-pound Cornish game hens with giblets	1 whole clove garlic, unpeeled but lightly crushed
Salt and freshly ground pepper to taste	1 cup coarsely chopped onion
2 tablespoons butter	1 bay leaf
½ pound mushrooms, left whole or quartered	2 sprigs fresh thyme or ½ teaspoon dried thyme
	2 tablespoons red-wine vinegar
	½ cup chicken broth

1. Sprinkle the cavity of the game hens with salt and pepper. Truss the birds and rub the outside with salt and pepper.

2. Heat the butter in a heavy casserole or Dutch oven. Add the game hens. Do not crowd them or they will not brown properly. Brown all over, about 15 minutes, and add the giblets. Cook 5 minutes longer.

3. Add the mushrooms and garlic. Cook briefly and add the onion. Cook 5 minutes.

4. Add the bay leaf and thyme. Cover and cook 10 minutes.

5. Add the vinegar and broth. Cover and cook 10 minutes longer.

6. Untruss the birds and discard the strings. Drain the cavity juices back into

the pan. Discard the garlic and bay leaf. Serve the game hens hot with the mushrooms and the boiling-hot pan liquid.

Yield: Four servings.

Haricots Verts avec Beurre Persillé
(*Green beans with parsley butter*)

½ **pound tender, very fresh green beans**	3 **tablespoons melted butter**
Salt and freshly ground pepper to taste	2 **tablespoons chopped parsley**
	Juice of half a lemon.

1. Cut off and discard the tips of the beans. Break the beans into two-inch lengths. Drop them into boiling salted water and return to the boil. Simmer about 7 minutes or until crisp-tender. Do not overcook. Drain.

2. Sprinkle with salt, pepper, butter, parsley and lemon juice. Toss well and serve hot.

Yield: Four servings.

FOR ANYONE WHO CARES ABOUT NEW EXPERI-
ences in eating, one of the more obvious pleasures of travel
is the sampling of dishes not altogether common in one's own
kitchen or milieu. On a trip to Italy, particularly in Tuscany, we dined several
times on various birds stuffed with a blend of prosciutto and rosemary, a most
agreeable combination of flavors and certainly not common in the French repertory.

We had a picnic in the company of friends who contributed their share of
home-cooked dishes. One of the best was cold roast quail with rosemary and
prosciutto. Cooked ham of the domestic sort could certainly be substituted, but
the filling would lose part of its full, assertive taste.

Sometimes the stuffings are made with pieces of prosciutto rolled around
sprigs of rosemary; sometimes the two are chopped together. The combination
makes a fine filling for Cornish game hens. The results are pleasant to say the
least.

One of the best accompaniments for the dish is a simply made rice baked
with the livers of the game hens and chopped mushrooms.

For accounting purposes, let it be said that game hens stuffed with prosciutto
and rosemary is one of those deadline dishes when you play the game of 60-
minute gourmet. It is, indeed, possible to prepare and cook the dish in an hour,
but you won't have many seconds to spare when the roast birds and the rice are
cooked and ready to serve.

The birds require about forty-five minutes cooking time, the rice about
twenty minutes or less. Therefore you should start the chickens and get them
into the oven before you turn to cook the rice.

Cornish Game Hens with Prosciutto

4 Cornish game hens, about 1 pound each	Salt and freshly ground pepper to taste
¼ pound prosciutto or other ham	4 tablespoons butter
2 teaspoons dried rosemary leaves	4 thin slices fatback
	¼ cup chicken broth.

1. Preheat the oven to 425 degrees.
2. Set aside the hens' gizzards, necks, hearts, and livers. The livers will be
used for a rice dish to accompany the birds.
3. Chop the prosciutto and rosemary. The mixture should be coarsely
chopped. Add pepper and blend. Stuff the cavity of each bird with equal portions of the mixture. Truss the chicken with string. Sprinkle the birds with salt
and pepper to taste.
4. Rub a metal baking dish with 1 tablespoon of butter. Arrange the birds on
their backs on the baking dish. Dot each with the remaining butter. Place one
slice of fatback over each bird to cover. Scatter the necks, gizzards, and hearts

around the birds. Place the dish on top of the stove and heat until butter is sizzling.

5. Place the dish in the oven and bake 15 minutes.

6. Remove the pieces of fatback and turn the chickens on their sides. Bake 15 minutes, basting occasionally.

7. Turn the chickens to their other sides and cook, basting occasionally, 10 minutes longer.

8. Turn the birds on their backs and return the slices of fatback over the birds and bake 5 minutes longer, basting often.

9. Remove the baking dish from the oven and tilt it. Skim off and discard most of the surface fat from the pan liquid. Add the chicken broth and bring to the boil, basting all the while.

10. Untruss the chickens and serve, if desired, each bird with one piece of fatback and the pan gravy. Serve with rice.

Yield: Four servings.

Foies de Volaille et Champignons au Riz
(Rice with liver and mushrooms)

---

2 tablespoons butter	1 cup raw rice
¼ cup finely chopped onion	4 livers from the Cornish game
¼ pound fresh mushrooms, cut into	hens, chopped, about ¼ cup
small cubes, about 1½ cups	1⅓ cups fresh or canned chicken
Salt and freshly ground pepper	broth.
to taste	

1. Preheat the oven to 425 degrees.

2. Heat half the butter in a saucepan and add the onion. Cook, stirring occasionally, until wilted. Add the mushrooms and cook, stirring, about 3 minutes. Add salt and pepper to taste. Add the rice and stir.

3. Add the broth and bring to the boil. Cover closely and place the saucepan in the oven. Bake 17 minutes.

4. Remove and fluff the rice and mushrooms. Heat the remaining tablespoon butter in a small skillet and when quite hot, add the chopped livers, salt and pepper to taste. Cook about 45 seconds. Scrape the liver and butter into the rice and stir to blend.

Yield: Four servings.

THERE IS SOMETHING INFINITELY REWARDING ABOUT working with inexpensive foods for the simple reason that saving money is a cheering challenge. I have noted before that chicken, over any period of time—and it is historically true as well—is probably the least expensive of all meats. I can also add that value for value, flavor for flavor, chicken livers are the least expensive part of the chicken.

I happen to dote on chicken livers in a thousand different forms, from that New York standby, chopped chicken livers, to a toast spread with a purée of Cognac-flavored chicken livers to a pâté or terrine. Some of the best sauces I know of often call for a final purée of chicken livers to give body and flavor.

One of the most admirable uses for chicken livers is to sauté them quickly in hot oil over moderately high heat, turning them often until they are crisp and browned on all sides. The word quick is advisable when cooking chicken livers; otherwise they become exceedingly dry inside. Ideally, they should remain moist when cooked in whole pieces.

Chicken livers take well to a great variety of sauces including those flavored with Madeira, port, or sherry wine. One of the simplest, however, is a sauce with a distinctly American flavor, though it is said to have a French origin. That is a sauce créole.

Quite frankly, I've never been able to discern anything characteristically French about a créole sauce. It does to a degree resemble the tomato sauces of Provence but only in its uses of bay leaf and thyme.

The bases for a créole sauce are—in addition to tomatoes—chopped onion, celery, and sweet pepper, sometimes referred to in this country as a "bell" pepper. That onion-celery-green pepper base is quite foreign to any French cooking with which I am familiar but I find it refreshing to the taste and delectable. The important thing about making the sauce is that it not be overcooked, which most home cooks (and a good many chefs) tried to do. When the sauce is ready, the vegetables should retain some of their crisp texture. The best of all accompaniments for chicken livers with sauce créole is rice. To make such a menu, prepare the rice, which can stand briefly after cooking. The moment it starts cooking, prepare the sauce. The livers should be cooked at the last minute before serving the sauce over.

Foies de Volaille à la Créole
(Chicken livers in creole sauce)

1¼ pounds fresh chicken livers	1 dried, hot red pepper, optional
2 tablespoons olive oil	Salt and freshly ground pepper
¾ cup finely chopped onion	to taste
¾ cup finely chopped celery	⅔ cup peanut, vegetable, or corn
¾ cup finely chopped, cored,	oil
seeded sweet green pepper	1 tablespoon butter
2 cups imported peeled tomatoes	½ teaspoon dried rosemary.
1 bay leaf	

1. Pick over the livers and cut away connecting membranes. There should be about 2 cups.

2. Heat the olive oil in a saucepan and add the onions, celery, and green pepper. Cook, stirring, until onion wilts.

3. Add the tomatoes, bay leaf, hot pepper, salt and pepper. Bring to the boil. Cook about 10 minutes.

4. Have ready a strainer placed in a drain pan.

5. Heat half the peanut oil in a large skillet. When it is hot and almost smoking, add the livers. Cook over high heat, turning the livers as necessary until the livers are crisp and brown on all sides, about 2 to 3 minutes. Drain in the sieve.

6. Add the remaining oil and cook the second batch of livers in exactly the same way. Drain. Wipe out the skillet.

7. Heat the butter in the skillet and add the livers and rosemary. Cook, tossing and stirring, about 15 seconds. Serve the livers with the créole sauce spooned over. Serve with rice.

Yield: Four servings.

Riz au Four
(Baked rice)

2½	tablespoons butter	3	sprigs parsley
2	tablespoons minced onion	1	sprig fresh or ¼ teaspoon dried
½	teaspoon minced garlic		thyme
1	cup uncooked rice	½	bay leaf.
1½	cups chicken broth		

1. Preheat the oven to 400 degrees.

2. Melt half the butter in a heavy saucepan and cook the onion and garlic, stirring with a wooden spoon, until the onion is translucent. Add the rice and stir briefly over low heat until the grains are coated with butter.

3. Stir in the stock, making sure there are no lumps in the rice. Add the parsley, thyme, bay leaf. Cover with a close-fitting lid and place in the oven.

4. Bake the rice exactly 17 minutes. Remove the cover and discard the parsley and thyme sprigs. Using a two-pronged fork, stir in the remaining butter. If the rice is not to be served immediately, keep covered in a warm place.

Yield: Four servings.

Note: Like most dishes, this rice is best if served as soon as it is baked, but it may be made as much as half an hour in advance as long as it is kept tightly covered and warm.

THERE IS ONE SORT OF COOKERY WHICH, WHEN well done, is exceptionally tasty, and hasty to boot. These are foods cooked en brochette (as even American menus have it) or on skewers.

One personal preference for such cookery is chicken livers interlarded on skewers with bacon and brushed with oil, perhaps oil that has been blended with finely chopped fresh or dried rosemary. This is an herb that adapts itself very well to the flavor of chicken liver.

The technique for such cookery is simple. When the skewered foods are brushed with oil, they are placed under the broiler (say, about six inches from the source of heat) and they are broiled, turning once or twice, and basting a bit if desired. When the foods have broiled for about ten minutes altogether, the broiler is turned off and the oven turned to a medium-hot heat until ready to serve.

Such foods may or may not be served with a sauce. Even hot melted butter would be satisfactory. On the other hand, a somewhat spicy deviled sauce such as a quickly made sauce of deviled sliced mushrooms is an excellent complement to such a dish. That sauce can be made literally in seconds, during the time that the skewered foods are cooked.

It might be added that chicken livers are generally, throughout the course of a year, one of the best bargains on the butcher's counter. One-and-one-half pounds are more than ample to serve four hungry people.

One of the best accompaniments for chicken livers en brochette is a Parmesan rice, a simply made risotto. The total preparation and cooking time for the rice is less than half an hour. To prepare such a meal, skewer the livers with bacon. Start cooking the rice. As the rice cooks and when the livers are placed under the broiler, make the mushroom sauce, and in a jiffy the meal is ready to serve.

Foies de Volaille en Brochette
(*Chicken livers on skewers*)

1½ pounds chicken livers, about 20 livers	1 tablespoon finely chopped rosemary or half a teaspoon dried
6 strips thick sliced bacon	
Salt and freshly ground pepper to taste	2 tablespoons peanut, vegetable, or corn oil.

1. Preheat the broiler.

2. Cut the chicken livers in half. Cut away and discard the thin connecting fibers. There should be about forty chicken liver pieces.

3. Cut each strip of bacon into eight squares. This will produce forty-eight squares.

4. Use four skewers. Arrange an equal number of chicken livers alternately with squares of bacon on the skewers. Begin and end with a square

of bacon. Arrange the skewers on a broiler rack. Sprinkle with salt and pepper on all sides.

5. Blend the rosemary and oil. Brush all sides with rosemary oil.

6. Place under the broiler about six inches from the source of heat. Broil about 5 minutes.

7. Turn the skewers over and broil 5 minutes longer. Turn off the broiler. Turn oven heat to 400 degrees. Let livers cook 5 minutes longer. Serve with deviled mushroom sauce.

Yield: Four servings.

Sauce Duxelles à la Diable
(Deviled mushroom sauce)

---

2 tablespoons butter	⅓ cup chicken broth
2 tablespoons finely chopped onion	1 tablespoon imported mustard such as Dijon or Düsseldorf
¼ pound mushrooms, thinly sliced, about 2 cups	1 teaspoon Worcestershire sauce
2 tablespoons red wine vinegar	Salt and freshly ground pepper to taste.

1. Melt half the butter and add the onion. Cook, stirring, until wilted. Add the mushrooms and cook until they give up their liquid. Cook until the liquid evaporates.

2. Add the chicken broth and vinegar and simmer about 3 minutes. Do not let the broth evaporate. Add the mustard and Worcestershire, salt and pepper. Swirl in the remaining butter. Do not return to the heat. Reheat before serving.

Yield: Four servings.

Riz au Parmesan
(Rice with Parmesan)

---

3 tablespoons butter	1½ cups chicken broth
¼ cup finely chopped onion	Salt and freshly ground pepper to taste
½ teaspoon finely minced garlic	2 tablespoons grated Parmesan cheese.
1 cup rice	

1. Melt 2 tablespoons of butter in a heavy saucepan and add the onion and garlic, stirring until onion wilts.

2. Add the rice and stir. Add the broth, salt and pepper to taste. Bring to the boil and cover. Cook over low heat about 20 minutes.

3. Stir in remaining butter and the Parmesan cheese.

Yield: Four servings.

THE FAME OF LUXURY RESTAURANTS RESTS SE-
curely on sauces and bases made with costly ingredients. And
while these may have required hours, even days, of sim-
mering, sieving, and subsequent preparation, there are scores of exceptions.

One exception, a dish that is easily made, is molded rice pilaf stuffed with
sautéed chicken livers and served with a tomato and mushroom sauce. Start the
rice. As it cooks, the sauce should be put on to cook. The livers should be
cooked quickly at the last minute. A commendable second course is a salad of
broccoli and avocado.

Pilaf Foies de Volaille
(Chicken liver pilaf with tomato and mushroom sauce)

3	tablespoons butter	1	sprig parsley
2	tablespoons finely chopped onion	2	dashes Tabasco sauce
1	cup Carolina rice	1	pound chicken livers
1½	cups chicken broth	½	cup vegetable, peanut, or corn
	Salt and freshly ground pepper		oil
	to taste	2½	cups tomato and mushroom
½	bay leaf		sauce (see recipe).
1	sprig thyme or ½ teaspoon dried		
	thyme		

1. Preheat the oven to 450 degrees.

2. Heat 1 tablespoon of butter in a small casserole and add the onion. Cook,
stirring, until wilted. Add the rice and stir briefly. Add the broth, salt, pepper,
bay leaf, thyme, parsley, and Tabasco, and bring to the boil.

3. Cover and place the dish in the oven. Bake exactly 17 minutes and
remove from the oven. Remove the bay leaf, parsley, and thyme and stir in a
tablespoon of butter. Set aside, covered.

4. As the rice cooks, prepare the chicken livers. Trim off any tough veins.
Quarter the chicken livers and set them aside.

5. Heat half the oil in a skillet, and when it is hot and almost smoking, add
half the chicken livers. Sprinkle with salt and pepper. Cook quickly, tossing
and shaking the skillet and turning the livers so they cook evenly. Take care not
to overcook the livers. Drain quickly in a sieve.

6. Heat the remaining oil, and when it is very hot, add the remaining livers,
salt and pepper. Cook quickly, as before, and drain.

7. Wipe out the skillet and add the remaining tablespoon of butter. Add all
the livers and toss quickly, about 30 seconds or so. Set aside.

8. Butter a 3-cup mold and add about one-third of the rice. Using a metal
spoon, press the rice against the bottom and sides of the mold, leaving a cavity
in the center to hold most of the livers. Add about three-quarters of the livers,
and spoon about ½ cup tomato sauce over them. Cover with the remaining rice.
Cover with a piece of buttered wax paper and, press down compactly with the
fingers to mold the ingredients firmly. Remove the wax paper. Invert the mold

onto a plate. Carefully lift up the mold, leaving the mound of rice on the plate. Arrange the remaining livers around the rice, and spoon a little hot tomato sauce over. Serve the remaining sauce on the side.

Yield: Four servings.

Sauce aux Tomates et Champignons
(*Tomato and mushroom sauce*)

4 medium-size mushrooms, about
  ¼ pound
1 tablespoon butter
2 tablespoons finely chopped onion
1 teaspoon finely minced garlic

Salt and freshly ground pepper to
  taste
2 cups canned tomatoes with
  tomato paste
½ teaspoon chopped rosemary
¼ cup chicken broth.

1. Thinly slice the mushrooms. There should be about 1½ cups.
2. Heat the butter and add mushrooms, onion, and garlic. Sprinkle with salt and pepper and cook, stirring, about 5 minutes.
3. Add the tomatoes, rosemary and chicken broth. Add salt and pepper, and simmer, stirring occasionally, about 10 minutes.

Yield: About two-and-a-half cups.

Salade de Brocoli et Poires d'Avocat
(*Broccoli and avocado salad*)

1 small bunch broccoli
  Salt
1 large avocado
  Half a lemon
1 teaspoon prepared mustard, such
  as Dijon or Düsseldorf

2 tablespoons grapefruit juice (or
  use lemon juice to taste)
3 tablespoons olive oil
  Freshly ground pepper to taste.

1. Cut the broccoli tops into "flowerets." If the pieces are quite large, split them at the bottom and cut in half. Rinse and drain. Use the coarse or tough stems for soups or other uses.
2. Drop the broccoli pieces into boiling salted water and drain. Run briefly under cold water and drain again. Chill.
3. Cut the avocado in half. Peel each half and remove the seed. Cut each half into eight lengthwise strips. Sprinkle with the juice of the half a lemon to prevent discoloration. Arrange alternate pieces of broccoli and avocado on each of four serving plates.
4. Blend the remaining ingredients and pour over the broccoli and avocado. Serve immediately.

Yield: Four servings.

THERE ARE SOME FOODS WHOSE SUCCESS AT TABLE depends to a great extent on how rapidly they are cooked. These are foods that must be seared quickly, over very high heat, and tossed and stirred simultaneously, so they cook evenly all over.

Chicken livers, one of the best bargains in any meat counter, are another of those foods whose excellence at table depends on such a technique.

The role of chicken livers in this country seems, unfortunately, limited. They are much coveted for appetizers such as chopped chicken livers and chicken liver pâtés, and they are widely accepted in omelets and with shirred eggs, but in many homes they are still an oddity.

The fact is that chicken livers adapt well to many seasonings and methods of cookery. They are marvelous in risottos and rice pilafs. Chicken livers go well with sage, and we recently devised a dish that includes not only that herb but also a touch of cognac.

With the livers, I would propose a noodle dish from my childhood. Although I am a native of Burgundy, my mother often prepared noodles Alsatian style. These noodles are tossed with what is otherwise known as polonaise topping— bread crumbs, sieved egg, and parsley cooked rapidly in butter. Just how a Polish topping found its way onto a dish called Alsatian-style is anybody's guess.

As usual, it would be wise to prepare and assemble all the ingredients for the chicken livers and noodles before starting to cook.

Foies de Volaille à la Sauge
(*Chicken livers with sage*)

4   tablespoons butter
¾   cup finely chopped onion
1   pound chicken livers
¼   cup peanut, vegetable, or corn oil

Salt and freshly ground pepper to taste
1   teaspoon ground sage, more or less to taste
2   tablespoons cognac.

1. Melt 2 tablespoons of butter in a saucepan and add the onion. Toss and stir, then cover. Cook 10 minutes without browning. The onions should be quite soft.

2. Pick over the chicken livers and remove any tough veins. Quarter the livers.

3. Heat the oil in a skillet, and when it is quite hot add the livers. Sprinkle with salt and pepper and cook over high heat 2 to 3 minutes, shaking the skillet and tossing the livers so that they cook on all sides. Drain in a colander.

4. Heat the remaining 2 tablespoons of butter in a skillet, and when it is very hot add the livers and onions. Sprinkle with sage and cook, stirring, about 3 or 4 minutes. Sprinkle with cognac and ignite it. Serve piping hot with noodles.

Yield: Four servings.

Nouilles à l'Alsacienne
(*Noodles with crumb and egg topping*)

½   pound fine noodles
    Salt to taste
5   tablespoons butter
    Freshly ground pepper to taste

1   hard-cooked egg, peeled and put through a fine sieve
½   cup fine, fresh bread crumbs
¼   cup finely chopped parsley.

1. Cook the noodles in salted water until tender. Drain and add 1 tablespoon of butter, salt and pepper to taste. Toss.

2. Quickly add the remaining 4 tablespoons of butter to a skillet, and when it is hot and bubbling add the egg and bread crumbs. Cook shaking the skillet and stirring, over high heat about 30 seconds. Add the parsley. Toss and pour over the noodles. Toss and serve.

Yield: Four servings.

THERE IS, OF COURSE, A GOOD DEAL OF DIFFER-
ence between food preparation in a professional kitchen and
that in a home. One of the most obvious reasons is the num-
ber of hands and the number of hours that can be employed in well-staffed restaurants in the preparation of what are known in French as les fonds de cuisine
or the bases for cookery. These would include an assortment, some of which
require hours of simmering, the tedious task of putting the sauces through sieves
and so on.

There was a time, I think, when professional chefs were reluctant to offer
recipes to the public because they knew that with rare exceptions those bases of
cookery would not be used in the home kitchen. Many chefs now realize that
there are compromises that can be made so that a finished product in the home,
while not made according to the "classic" pattern, may yield results that
duplicate the professionally prepared dish to an admirable degree by using short
cuts.

One of the best sauces in a professional kitchen is that known as a sauce
madère or Madeira wine sauce. Traditionally, it is made with one of the long-
simmered brown sauces. You will find if you prepare the chicken livers in the
Madeira wine sauce outlined here, that an eminently edible variation of that
sauce can be made with mushrooms, a touch of tomato paste, chicken broth,
and, of course, Madeira. For a thickening, however, use arrowroot instead of
flour, (and if you don't have arrowroot, use cornstarch). Flour would make the
sauce starchy and heavy.

One more word of caution. Although the recipe has numerous steps, the
making of the dish is not at all complicated. The total cooking time for the dish
is half an hour or less and much of that time is used for simmering the sauce.
Plain rice or noodles with one chopped fresh herb or another make an ideal accompaniment. Parsley is indicated here, but chopped fresh dill would also be
excellent.

Foies de Volaille et Champignons
(Chicken livers and mushrooms in Madeira wine sauce)

The sauce:
½ pound fresh mushrooms
2 tablespoons butter
  Salt and freshly ground pepper to
  taste
2 tablespoons finely chopped
  shallots
⅓ cup plus 1 tablespoon Madeira
  wine
1 cup chicken broth

2 teaspoons tomato paste
1 teaspoon arrowroot or cornstarch
  The livers:
2 pounds very fresh chicken livers
4 tablespoons flour
  Salt and freshly ground pepper to
  taste
½ cup peanut, vegetable, or corn oil
2 tablespoons butter.

1. Thinly slice the mushrooms. There should be about 3 cups.

2. Heat the butter in a skillet and add the mushrooms and cook, stirring and shaking the skillet, until wilted. Add salt and pepper to taste. Cook about 5 minutes. Add the shallots and toss.

3. Add the ⅓ cup of Madeira wine and cook about 1 minute. Add the broth. Cook about 2 minutes and add the tomato paste. Simmer about 5 minutes.

4. Blend the arrowroot with the remaining tablespoon of Madeira wine and add it, stirring. Simmer 10 minutes, stirring occasionally. Set the sauce aside briefly.

5. Meanwhile, put the livers, one at a time, on a flat surface and trim and cut away every trace of thread-like veins and connecting tissues.

6. Blend the flour with salt and pepper. Coat the chicken livers in the seasoned flour.

7. Heat ¼ cup oil in a heavy skillet. When it is hot but not smoking, add half the livers. Cook over high heat, shaking the skillet and turning the livers. Cook quickly so that the livers are slightly crisp on the outside. Cook about 1½ to 2 minutes in all.

8. Pour the livers and oil in which they cooked into a colander to drain well. Pour the cooked livers into the sauce and stir to coat.

9. To the skillet add the remaining ¼ cup of oil. Add the remaining livers. Cook as before until crisp outside. Drain and add to the first batch. Stir in the 2 tablespoons butter. Heat and serve with buttered noodles with herbs, or with rice.

Yield: Four servings.

Nouilles Persillées
(Noodles with parsley)

½ **pound wide or medium noodles**
   Salt to taste
2 **tablespoons butter**

   Freshly ground pepper to taste
1 **tablespoon chopped parsley.**

1. Cook the noodles in boiling salted water to cover.

2. Drain well and return to the kettle. Add the butter, salt and pepper to taste, and toss. Add the parsley and serve hot.

Yield: Four servings.

Eggs

I
T ALMOST GOES WITHOUT SAYING THAT THE UL-
timate hastily made main course is an omelette nature or a
plain omelet. You simply beat eggs in a small bowl with salt
and pepper, add them to a smooth-bottom omelet pan in which butter is heated,
and, a second later, you turn it out onto a dinner plate.

There are, to my mind, two preferred pans for making an omelet. The first is
a heavy metal pan that has been well cured. "Cured" in this case means treated
in such fashion as to prevent sticking. The metal should be free of blemishes
and have, through use or the heating of oil in it, a totally smooth or "sliding"
surface. To cure a metal pan—whether aluminum or iron or whatever—before
its initial use, put it on the stove and add oil almost to the brim. Heat the oil,
taking constant care to prevent flames, until it is quite hot. Let stand overnight
or several hours and pour out the oil. Wipe the pan. Do not wash it. You
should only wash the pan if it has not been used for several weeks or if the
coating should happen to give a rancid taste to your omelets.

The second preferred pan is one with a Teflon coating. This would probably
be my first recommendation for a novice omelet maker. To make the omelets,
once the eggs are added, place the pan so it sits flat on the heating unit. As you
shake the pan, let it remain flat on the unit, all the while stirring with a fork
held so that the tines are parallel to the bottom of the pan. Do not scratch the
bottom. As outlined in the recipe below, cook the omelet over high heat, shaking and stirring for seconds or until eggs start to set. Quickly tilt the pan and
tap it firmly against the burner. This should make the omelet slide about one
inch in the direction away from the handle. This will "curve" the omelet.
Using the fork, "roll" the omelet downward away from the handle. Quickly
shift the pan handle to the left hand, hold a plate in the right, tilt the pan and
invert the omelet onto the plate.

The catalogue of omelet fillings is vast. One of the best for a "main course"
omelet is a simply made poached chicken. This may be made in advance of use
and reheated just before the omelets are to be made and served. Asparagus,
buttered and flavored with nutmeg, would make an excellent seasonal accompaniment to omelets.

Omelette à la Reine
(Poached chicken omelet)

---

12 eggs	4 teaspoons butter
Salt and freshly ground pepper to	Omelet filling such as poulet
taste	poché (see recipe).

1. Break 3 eggs into each of four small bowls. Add salt and pepper.
2. Make one omelet at a time. Beat the eggs until thoroughly blended. Heat
a small, well-cured omelet pan or one that is lined with Teflon.
3. Add 1 teaspoon of butter and when it is sizzling, add 3 beaten eggs.
4. Cook over high heat, shaking the pan and stirring with a fork held paral-

lel to the bottom of the pan. When the eggs start to set, tilt the omelet pan and tap it against the stove burner. This should make the omelet slide about one inch in the direction away from the handle. This will "curve" the omelet.

5. Add a spoonful or so of the omelet filling to the center.

6. Using the fork, carefully and neatly fold the part of the omelet nearest the hand over the filling to partially enclose it.

7. Shift the handle of the omelet pan to the left hand. Hold a plate in the right. Tilt the pan so that the omelet is inverted onto the center of the plate. Garnish each end of the omelet with another small portion of the filling.

Yield: Four omelets.

Poulet Poché
(Poached chicken)

¾ pound skinless, boneless chicken breasts	2 thin slices onion
1 cup water	1 small bay leaf
Salt to taste	1 sprig fresh thyme or half a teaspoon dried thyme.
1 parsley sprig	

Combine all the ingredients in a saucepan and bring to the boil. Cover and simmer 5 minutes. Remove from the heat and let stand until ready to use. Cube the chicken if desired. Reserve the broth.

Yield: About two cups cubed chicken.

Asperges au Beurre de Muscade
(Asparagus with nutmeg butter)

---

12 to 16 spears of fresh asparagus	Juice of half a lemon
Salt to taste	⅛ teaspoon freshly grated nutmeg.
3 tablespoons butter	

1. Line up the asparagus side by side on a flat surface. Using a heavy knife, cut off the tough bottoms of the asparagus. Discard the bottoms.

2. Using a swivel-bladed vegetable scraper, scrape the sides of the asparagus, starting about two inches from the tips. Rinse and drain if necessary.

3. Bring enough water to the boil in a skillet to cover the asparagus when added. Add salt to taste. Cook 2 to 4 minutes, depending on the size of the asparagus. Do not overcook; they will continue to cook even when drained.

4. Meanwhile, heat the butter and add the lemon juice, salt, pepper, and nutmeg in a saucepan. Remove the saucepan from the heat and swirl the sauce around to blend it. Pour over the asparagus and serve.

Yield: Four servings.

OMELETS ARE ONE OF THE SIMPLEST DISHES IN THE world to make. All it takes is a decent pan, fresh eggs, and a good dash of self-confidence.

I outlined earlier, in some detail, the steps for making an omelet. Here, I have added a list of necessary equipment, and, for more adventurous cooks, two more of my own favorite omelets.

These are large omelets designed to serve two or more people at a gathering. One of them was a great favorite during the days when I served as chef at Henri Soulé's Pavillon. It is made with creamed chicken, a light tomato sauce, and cheese, and serves four to six.

Another omelet, which also serves four to six, is a classic Spanish omelet, which is to say, it is not folded in the traditional manner, but is a whole, round flat omelet turned out onto a serving dish.

For making an omelet, the utensils include, in addition to the omelet pan, one or more small mixing bowls for eggs; another fork for the butter; warm plates for the omelets. Also a spoon for adding the fillings unless, as in the case of a cheese or herb omelet, the fingers will suffice.

The ingredients for a plain omelet include eggs, salt and pepper, and, if desired, a bit of cream. Ingredients for a filled omelet include of course, the fillings, such as grated cheese or mixed herbs, or fillings that are cooked and ready to be added.

Just before you start cooking the omelets, break three eggs for each omelet into as many individual bowls as needed for the number of omelets to be made. Add salt and pepper to taste and about two teaspoons of heavy cream. You may also beat the eggs to expedite making the omelets.

Omelette Pavillon
(Omelet with chicken, tomato, and cheese)

7 tablespoons butter	Salt and freshly ground pepper to taste
3 tablespoons flour	
1 cup chicken broth	1 cup finely cubed cooked breast of chicken
½ cup heavy cream	
3 tablespoons finely chopped onion	1 egg yolk
2 cups peeled, seeded, chopped tomatoes	¼ cup grated swiss, Gruyère, or Fontina cheese
2 sprigs fresh thyme or ½ teaspoon dried thyme	10 eggs
1 bay leaf	3 tablespoons grated Parmesan cheese.

1. Heat 2 tablespoons of butter in a saucepan and add the flour. Stir with a wire whisk until blended. Add the chicken broth and cook, stirring vigorously with the whisk. Add the cream and bring to the boil. Simmer about 10 minutes.

2. Meanwhile, heat another tablespoon of butter in a saucepan and add the onion. Cook, stirring, until wilted, and add the tomatoes, thyme, bay leaf, salt and pepper. Simmer, stirring occasionally, about 10 minutes.

3. Heat another tablespoon of butter and add the chicken. Cook, stirring about 30 seconds. Add 3 tablespoons of the cream sauce. Bring to the boil and remove from the heat. Set aside.

4. To the remaining cream sauce add the egg yolk and stir to blend. Add salt and pepper to taste and the grated Swiss cheese. Heat, stirring, just until the cheese melts. Set aside.

5. Beat the eggs with salt and pepper. Add 6 tablespoons of the tomato sauce. Heat the remaining 3 tablespoons of butter in an omelet pan or a Teflon skillet, and when it is hot add the eggs. Cook, stirring, until the omelet is set on the bottom but moist and runny in the center. Spoon creamed chicken down the center of the omelet and add the remaining tomato sauce. Quickly turn the omelet out into a baking dish.

6. Spoon the remaining cream sauce over the omelet and sprinkle with grated Parmesan cheese. Run the dish under the broiler until golden brown.

Yield: Four to six servings.

Omelette Espagnole
(Spanish omelet)

2	or 3 red or green sweet peppers	1	tablespoon finely minced garlic
2	or 3 Bermuda onions	1	cup peeled, chopped tomatoes
2	tablespoons olive oil	10	eggs
	Salt and freshly ground pepper to	3	tablespoons butter
	taste		Vinegar, optional.

1. Core and seed the peppers. Cut the peppers into very fine julienne strips. There should be about 2 cups.

2. Peel the onions and cut them in half. Thinly slice the onions. There should be about 2 cups.

3. Heat the oil in a saucepan and add the onions and peppers. Add salt and pepper and cook briskly, stirring, about 5 minutes. Add the garlic and tomatoes and cook 15 minutes.

4. Beat the eggs until frothy and add salt and pepper. Add 1¼ cups of the tomato sauce and beat lightly.

5. Heat the butter in an omelet pan or in a Teflon skillet and add the egg mixture. Cook, shaking the pan and stirring with a fork. Let the omelet set on the bottom. The omelet should remain moist and runny in the center. When cooked, place a large serving plate over the pan and quickly invert the omelet onto the plate. Spoon the remaining tomato sauce into the center of the omelet as a garnish. This omelet is normally served hot, but it is good cold. In Burgundy, it is frequently eaten with a dash of vinegar on each serving.

Yield: Four to six servings.

IT HAS BEEN NOTED THAT AN EGG, MORE THAN any other food, is probably the ultimate item for a hastily made and excellent main course. Given a few additional and inspired ingredients, such as spinach, sour cream, mushrooms, ratatouille (freshly made or leftover), ham, cheese, and so on, an egg can quickly be turned into an omelet for a feast.

Omelets, of course, take many forms. The classic and best known is the folded version, which must be made in seconds or it will become tough and rubbery. Then there is a flat omelet, with its various ingredients, which is cooked until set and served without folding.

In Spain, two basic methods are taught for making an omelet—à la Francesa, which is rolled and oval-shaped, and à la Espanola, which is flat.

In my childhood one of the favorite dishes was a flat omelet, a hearty, delectable preparation made with home-cured ham cut into small cubes and thinly sliced potatoes cooked in oil until crisp, with onions. The ham and seasonings were added and the eggs cooked, stirring and lifting gently with a spatula, until set. It was all turned out onto a platter and served sliced. If any of this omelet was left over, it was often saved and served cold for the outings in the country.

This makes for a substantial main course and an excellent accompaniment is quickly cooked asparagus served with a vinaigrette sauce. The significant thing to remember in making the flat omelet is to use a smooth-surfaced pan so that the omelet does not stick when transferred to a platter.

Omelette Paysanne
(A flat potato and ham omelet)

2	Idaho potatoes, about ¾ pound	1	cup cooked ham cut into ½-inch dice
3	tablespoons peanut, vegetable, or corn oil	4	teaspoons butter
	Salt and freshly ground pepper to taste	10	eggs
½	cup halved, very thinly sliced onion	2	tablespoons finely chopped parsley
		1	teaspoon finely chopped tarragon
		2	teaspoons finely chopped chives.

1. Peel the potatoes and slice them as thinly as possible. Drop into cold water to prevent discoloration. Drain and pat dry.

2. Heat a skillet and add the oil. When it is very hot, add the potatoes. Do not break the slices. Sprinkle with salt and pepper.

3. Cook, making sure the potatoes do not stick. Brown well about 10 minutes and add the onions. Continue cooking about 1 minute. Add the ham and dot with 3 teaspoons of butter. Shake skillet and gently turn over ingredients so that they cook evenly.

4. Beat the eggs with a wire whisk. Add salt, pepper and herbs. Pour the eggs over the ham and potato mixture.

5. Gently stir the mixture from the bottom, allowing the egg mixture to flow to the bottom. Cook over high heat. Lift up the edges of the omelet and let the remaining butter flow beneath the omelet. Shake the skillet to make certain the omelet is loose.

6. Invert a large plate over the skillet and quickly invert the skillet, letting the omelet fall into the plate. This omelet is best served hot, but it is also delicious at room temperature.

Yield: Four servings.

Asperges Vinaigrette
(*Asparagus vinaigrette*)

24	asparagus spears	¼	cup peanut, vegetable, or corn oil
	Salt to taste		
1½	teaspoons wine vinegar	1½	teaspoons finely chopped shallots or green onions
1½	teaspoons imported mustard, preferably Dijon or Düsseldorf	1½	teaspoons finely chopped parsley.
	Freshly ground pepper to taste		

1. Use a potato peeler and scrape the asparagus spears to within about two inches of the top. Cut off and discard the tough bottoms of the spears to make their lengths uniform. Place them in a skillet, add cold water to cover and salt. Bring to the boil and simmer until tender yet firm, al dente, so to speak.

2. Place the vinegar, mustard, salt and pepper in a mixing bowl and stir rapidly with a wire whisk. Gradually add the oil, stirring constantly. Stir in the shallots.

3. Drain the asparagus spears well while they are still hot. Arrange six spears on each of four serving dishes. Spoon the sauce over the tops of the asparagus, which should be lukewarm or at room temperature. Sprinkle the parsley over the tips and serve.

Yield: Four servings.

ONE OF THE ODDEST COOKING MYTHS, MORE PREV-
alent in this country than in France, is the notion that a soufflé
is the most fragile of foods. And, therefore, one of the most
difficult to prepare. There seems to be a belief that it will collapse like a
pierced balloon if the oven door is opened or if there is a jarring of the oven rack.

That is nonsense and so is that old wives' tale that a soufflé must be served
at some magic moment of its readiness. The fact is that tastes in texture vary
where soufflés are concerned. I happen to like soufflés that are quite moist (although cooked) in the center. There are those who prefer a "drier" interior texture, a point that comes about through prolonged cooking. While it is true that
a soufflé must be taken from the oven and served immediately (preferably
within seconds), a soufflé can remain in the oven for five minutes or so between the moment when it could be pronounced "ready to serve" and the time
when it must be taken from the oven or be overcooked.

The basics of making a soufflé are simple. Take a cheese soufflé, for example, the best known and probably the best liked of all main course soufflés.
It consists simply of making a simple white sauce to which cubed or grated
cheese is added. Egg yolks (plus cornstarch mixed with water) are added to
give it body. And stiffly beaten egg whites are folded in. This is perhaps the
"tricky" part for most home cooks. The best method for folding in the whites
is as follows:

Stir in half the beaten whites with a whisk. Fold in the remaining egg whites
and pour into a prepared dish. Bake and serve.

Soufflés have many uses in menu planning, of course. They can be served as
a first course, main course, or dessert. The one I outline here—a cheese
soufflé—can be served by itself as a first course or main course. To some tastes
it may seem insubstantial as a main course; therefore, I have offered it along
with ham in a cream sauce to be served with the soufflé. After the soufflé is put
in the oven, there is ample time to prepare the ham in cream sauce. Serve with
a mixed green salad and a crusty loaf of bread.

Soufflé au Fromage
(Cheese soufflé)

¼ pound Swiss or, preferably, Gruyère cheese	Salt and freshly ground pepper to taste
2 cups milk	⅛ teaspoon freshly grated nutmeg
3 tablespoons plus 2 teaspoons of butter	Pinch of cayenne pepper
6 large eggs	2 teaspoons cornstarch
4 tablespoons flour	1 tablespoon water
	¼ cup finely grated Parmesan cheese.

1. Preheat the oven to 375 degrees.

2. Grate the cheese or cut it into tiny cubes. There should be about ¾ cup.
Set aside.

3. Bring the milk just to the boil without boiling.

4. Use 2 teaspoons of butter to grease a 5-cup soufflé dish. Set the dish aside.

5. Separate the egg yolks and whites. Put the whites into a mixing bowl.

6. Melt 3 tablespoons of butter in a saucepan. Add the flour, stirring with a wire whisk. When blended and smooth, add the hot milk, stirring rapidly with the whisk. Add the salt, pepper, nutmeg, and cayenne and cook, stirring rapidly, about 5 minutes.

7. Blend the cornstarch and water and add it, stirring briskly.

8. Remove from the heat and add the yolks, stirring rapidly. Pour and scrape the mixture into a large mixing bowl. Add the grated Parmesan cheese. Stir to blend.

9. Beat the whites until stiff. Add half the whites to the sauce and fold them in with the whisk. Add the remaining whites and grated or cubed cheese. Fold this in with a plastic or rubber spatula. Fold over and around, top to bottom, until the whites are incorporated.

10. Pour and scrape the soufflé mixture into the prepared bowl. Place in the oven and bake 20 minutes. Serve, if desired, with the ham in cream sauce.

Yield: Four servings.

Jambon à la Crème
(Ham in cream sauce)

½ **pound boiled ham in one piece**
2 **tablespoons plus 1 teaspoon butter**
2 **tablespoons flour**
1 **cup milk**

⅛ **teaspoon finely, freshly grated nutmeg**
   Salt and freshly ground pepper to taste
1 **tablespoon finely chopped shallots**
3 **tablespoons dry sherry wine.**

1. Cut the ham into half-inch or slightly smaller cubes. There should be slightly more than 2½ cups. Set aside.

2. Heat 2 tablespoons of butter in a saucepan and add the flour, stirring with a wire whisk. When flour and butter are blended, add the milk, stirring rapidly with the whisk. Add the nutmeg, salt and pepper to taste. Let cool, stirring occasionally, about 5 minutes.

3. Meanwhile, heat the teaspoon of butter and add the ham. Cook briefly, stirring, and add the shallots. Cook and stir briefly. Add the sherry. Heat through.

4. Add the cream sauce and turn off the heat. Serve with cheese soufflé, on toast, or put to any desired use.

Yield: Four servings.

Fish

I T IS MY BELIEF THAT ALMOST EVERY CHEF IN THE world could express a preference for the type of cooking he finds more gratifying than any other. The reasons why would be as varied as the dishes he admired as a child; the dishes which personally gratify his own appetite, or the kind of cookery to which he was first subjected as a professional.

I prefer fish cookery to all others, for two reasons. In the ultimate sense, I prefer fish to many meats. Also, I was a poissonier, or fish cook, during my formative years in restaurants.

Curiously, in this country at least, home cooks seem to find fish to be the most complicated of foods to cook. It isn't, although more care must be used in preparing it because it can be overcooked in seconds. I have often been asked to give recipes for the basic techniques of cooking fish, and they are included here. In a sense this might be considered a primer for the basic fish dishes, but that by no means implies a lack of sophistication. Some of the simplest dishes can be foods for the gods.

The techniques and recipes offered here include a plain broiled fish in which fish fillets are simply turned in butter, seasoned and placed under the broiler for from two to eight minutes, with no turning required.

The cooking time will depend on the thickness of the fish. There is also a basic recipe for cooking fish in a skillet. The fish is simply bathed briefly in milk, coated with flour, and cooked hastily over moderately high heat, turning once.

Remember, in any of these, simply choose a fresh fish and take care not to overcook it.

Poisson Grillé
(Plain broiled fish)

4 skinless, boneless fish fillets, about 1¼ pounds (flounder, sole, or cod will do)	Salt and freshly ground pepper to taste
	2 tablespoons butter
	¼ teaspoons paprika.

1. Preheat the broiler to high.
2. Sprinkle the fish with salt and pepper to taste. Set aside.
3. Select a heatproof serving dish large enough to hold the fish in one layer and add the butter. Heat under the broiler until the butter melts.
4. Add the fish fillets and turn them in it to coat in the butter. When ready for the broiling, leave the fish pieces skinned side down. Hold a small sieve over the fish and add the paprika. Sprinkle the paprika over the fish and place under the broiler, about five inches from the source of heat. The cooking time will depend on the thickness of the fish. A very thin fish fillet such as that of a small

flounder will cook in 2 to 4 minutes. A one-inch thick slice of boneless, skinless cod will require 8 minutes.

Yield: Four servings.

Poisson Meunière
(A basic sauté of fish)

---

4   skinless, boneless fish fillets, about 1¼ pounds (flounder, sole, cod)
    Salt and freshly ground pepper to taste
3   tablespoons milk
¼   cup flour

¼   cup peanut, vegetable, or corn oil
4   tablespoons butter
    Juice of half a lemon
4   slices lemon
2   tablespoons finely chopped parsley.

1. Sprinkle the fish fillets with salt and pepper to taste.
2. Pour the milk into a flat dish.
3. Dip the fillets in the milk and then dredge in flour, shaking to remove excess.
4. Heat the oil in a skillet large enough to hold the fillets in one layer. Add the pieces of fish and cook about 1½ minutes or longer until golden brown on one side. The fish should be cooked over a fairly high or moderately high heat. It must cook fast.
5. Turn the pieces of fish and cook until golden brown on the other side, from 1 to 2 minutes.
6. Transfer the fish to a serving dish and pour off the fat from the skillet.
7. Add the butter to the wiped-out skillet and cook over moderately high heat until the butter is foamy and then starts to brown. Sprinkle the fish with lemon juice, pour the butter over the fish. Garnish each piece of fish with a slice of lemon and chopped parsley.

Yield: Four servings.

IT IS ANOTHER OF THOSE SUPERFICIALLY EVIDENT facts about hasty cooking—"gourmet" or otherwise—that fish in general, and fillets of fish in particular are tailored to the task. Although I grew up in a small town in Burgundy, a good distance from the ocean (about 350 kilometers, as we reckoned it), we could always buy fresh fish. The fish—there were great varieties—were, shipped in iced barrels and hampers by train from Boulogne-sur-Mer, a seaport on the English Channel.

My father and I doted on fresh fish, and I would go with him—both of us on bicycles—to meet the train when it arrived. If we were fortunate we would have first choice of the haul—channel sole, turbot, herring, whiting and a great variety of shellfish including mussels and oysters, all depending on the season.

Both my mother and grandmother were fine fish cooks. They were not much schooled in the fancy sauces I learned later in Paris restaurants, but everything they turned out was excellent in its simplicity.

I am quite certain that in those days my mother never gave a second thought to how long a dish would take to prepare and cook. Cooking was simply a part of living, a thing that gave her pleasure day by day. And although it had nothing to do with time, one of the dishes I liked best could be conjured up in much less than an hour.

There was no question of preheating an oven. The stove in my home served a double purpose. It was fired with wood and charcoal and was used both for cooking and heating the small living where we lived most of our existence. Our oven, in winter at least, was always preheated.

When we arrived home with the fish, my father would fillet them. She would roll them like turbans, sprinkle with butter, shallots, bread crumbs and a little white wine and heavy cream, and twenty minutes later we sat down to dine. With that dish we always had steamed potatoes and a good loaf of homemade bread. And a nice white Burgundy—in my case watered down, as happened with all Burgundy children.

Filets de Poisson au Four
(Baked fish fillets)

---

8 skinless, boneless fillets of flounder or sole, about 1¾ pounds	**4 teaspoons finely chopped shallots**
Salt and freshly ground pepper to taste	**¼ cup dry white wine**
	¼ cup heavy cream
3 tablespoons butter	**¼ cup fine fresh bread crumbs**
	1 tablespoon finely chopped parsley.

1. Preheat the oven to 400 degrees.
2. Sprinkle the fish fillets lightly with salt and pepper. Roll each of the fillets compactly.
3. Grease a baking dish large enough to hold the fish rolls in one layer. Use

1 tablespoon of butter. Sprinkle the bottom of the dish with salt, pepper and 3 teaspoons of shallots. Arrange the fish rolls over this bed, seam side down.

4. Pour wine and cream over the fish.

5. Sprinkle the fish evenly with salt, pepper, bread crumbs, parsley, and the remaining teaspoons of shallots.

6. Melt the remaining 2 tablespoons butter and pour over all. Place in the oven and bake 20 minutes or until fish rolls are cooked and the crumbs are lightly browned.

Yield: Four servings.

Pommes de Terre au Paprika
(*Paprika potatoes*)

1 pound "new" red, waxy potatoes or 2 large Idaho potatoes Salt to taste	1 tablespoon butter ½ teaspoon paprika.

1. Peel the potatoes. If they are new potatoes, there should be at least eight. Leave them whole. If they are large Idaho potatoes, quarter them, which is to say cut each potato into four equal-size pieces.

2. Place the potatoes in a saucepan and add water to cover and salt to taste. Bring to the boil and simmer until tender, 15 or 20 minutes, depending on size. Do not overcook.

3. Drain and add the butter and paprika, shaking the saucepan until the potatoes are coated.

Yield: Four servings.

BROILED FOODS, FISH IN PARTICULAR, ARE IDE-ally suited to good but hasty cookery. And yet home cooks seem more perplexed by broiling techniques than almost any other. It's true that broiling may embrace the simplest yet most confusing of cooking procedures. To broil properly, numerous variables are involved—including source of heat, intensity of heat, and the thickness of the food to be cooked.

Here are two recipes for broiled fish, the first a "perfectly" broiled fillet that will have a naturally browned surface. To prepare this dish I often use tilefish, a little-known fish that is becoming increasingly available and popular in this country along the Atlantic Coast. I could also use striped bass, flounder, or whatever.

To aid in browning, the fish—which is placed on a buttered baking dish—should be brushed often with butter as it cooks. For this particular dish I used melted butter with a little anchovy paste for flavor. To prevent the fish from drying out, it is essential that it be cooked under very high heat. In this case the flame is at its highest point.

The fish is best cooked relatively close to the flame or other source of heat—say two-and-one-half to three inches away. There is probably less danger of the fish burning than one would think, but mind it carefully as it cooks. Cooking time will depend on the thickness of the fillets. Tilefish fillets, slightly less than an inch thick, require about twelve to fifteen minutes to cook. If your fillets are half that size, they should cook in about half that time, given a minute or two one way or the other.

A second method of broiling fish is considered here. In this one, the cook "cheats" a bit and gives the surface of the fish a light dusting with a mixture of bread crumbs and paprika. This, most assuredly, will aid in "browning."

The fillets are placed on a buttered baking dish, then sprinkled with the bread crumb and paprika mixture. The fillets are then placed under a hot broiler, not quite full flame, and they are broiled about six inches from the source of heat. In this case, the heat must be slightly less intense than otherwise stipulated and the fish broiled at a greater distance from the source of heat. If the broiler heat is too high or if the crumb-covered food is too close to the heat, the crumbs will burn.

Filets de Poisson Grillés au Beurre d'Anchois
(Broiled fish fillets with anchovy butter)

2	pounds fish fillets such as tilefish, sea bass, fluke, and so on	1	teaspoon anchovy paste
			Lemon wedges
5	tablespoons butter		Parsley sprigs optional.
	Salt and freshly ground pepper to taste		

1. Preheat the broiler to full heat.

2. Some fillets of fish have a small bone line running the length of the center. If there is, use a sharp knife and cut on both sides of this line to remove and discard it. Cut the fish fillets into four to six pieces of approximately the same size.

3. Generously butter a baking pan with about 1 tablespoon of butter. Sprinkle with salt and pepper.

4. Arrange the fish pieces over the pan.

5. Melt the remaining 4 tablespoons of butter and stir in the anchovy paste. Brush the top of the fish with some of this.

6. Run the fish under the broiler, about two and one-half to three inches from the source of heat. As the fish cooks, brush it occasionally with more of the anchovy butter. Cook 12 to 15 minutes. Transfer the fish to a hot platter or hot individual serving dishes. Serve with lemon wedges and, if desired, garnish with parsley sprigs.

Yield: Four servings.

Filets de Poisson Grillés
(Broiled fish fillets)

---

4 fish fillets, about ½ pound each	1 cup fresh bread crumbs
8 tablespoons butter	1 teaspoon paprika.
Salt and freshly ground pepper	
to taste	

1. Preheat the broiler to high. Just before cooking the fish, reduce the broiler heat by a fraction.

2. Select a baking dish just large enough to hold the fish fillets in one layer. Grease the bottom of the dish with 1 tablespoon of butter. Sprinkle it with salt and pepper.

3. Arrange the fillets, skin side down, on the dish and sprinkle with salt and pepper to taste.

4. Scatter the bread crumbs on a piece of wax paper. Hold a small sieve over the crumbs. Put the paprika through the sieve and blend paprika and crumbs. Sprinkle the fish fillets with the crumbs and dribble the remaining butter over all. Broil about six inches from the heat until golden brown. Broil 10 minutes.

Yield: Four servings.

LIKE MOST PROFESSIONAL CHEFS, I TEND TO pride myself on the ability to detect the ingredients of almost any dish that is set before me. Plus the ability to recreate, in fairly accurate detail, a reproduction of that dish, within the confines of my own kitchen. Perhaps I should qualify that to add that I am speaking of foods of the Western world. Much of the cooking of the Orient is infinitely more complex in some preparations and many of the ingredients are—for better or for worse—foreign to my Western palate.

All that is said to preface a confession. Two or three years ago I was invited into the home of friends to feast on a meal, one of the dishes of which had very fresh flounder as its base. It was a simple dish of broiled fish but the flavor was a bit piquant and there was a golden brown topping. The only two ingredients of which I was absolutely certain were, in addition to the fish and the parsley garnish, the flavor of lemon and mustard.

I must admit that I was a bit flustered, and volunteered the thought that the topping of the fish was perhaps a hollandaise flavored with the mustard. I was both amused and abashed when the hostess—an excellent cook—told me that she had simply smeared the fish with a mustard mayonnaise before putting it under the broiler. That's all there was to it. The fish with its mustard coating had been placed about three or four inches from the source of heat and allowed to broil for a minute or so until the topping became a golden brown.

This is conceivably the most easily made and quick dish appearing in this book.

Because of the speed with which that dish—it can well serve as a main course—is prepared and cooked, there is ample time to spend on accompanying vegetable. An excellent choice is zucchini, sliced and cooked in a skillet with assorted fresh herbs if available, including parsley, chives, dill, tarragon, and basil. If the fresh are not available, use a small amount of dried herbs.

Filets de Flet à la Moutarde
(Broiled flounder fillets with mustard)

8 small; skinless, boneless flounder
fillets, about 1 pound
Salt and freshly ground pepper to
taste
1 tablespoon peanut, vegetable, or
corn oil

2 tablespoons mayonnaise,
preferably homemade although
bottled mayonnaise may be used
1 tablespoon imported mustard such
as Dijon or Düsseldorf
2 teaspoons finely chopped parsley
4 lemon or lime wedges.

1. Preheat the broiler to high.

2. Place the fillet halves on a flat surface. Sprinkle with salt and pepper and brush with oil.

3. Arrange the fillets on a baking sheet or dish. Blend the mayonnaise, mustard, and parsley. Brush it evenly over the fillets.

4. Place the fillets under the broiler, about three or four inches from the source of heat. Broil about 1 minute or until golden brown on top and the fish is just cooked through. Serve with lemon wedges.

Yield: Four servings.

Courgettes aùx Herbes d'Été
(Zucchini with summer herbs)

1½	pounds zucchini	1	tablespoon chopped parsley
4	tablespoons olive oil	1	tablespoon chopped chives
	Salt and freshly ground pepper to	1	tablespoon chopped dill
	taste	1	teaspoon chopped tarragon
2	tablespoons butter	1	tablespoon finely chopped fresh
2	teaspoons chopped garlic		basil.

1. Rinse the zucchini and pat dry. Trim off the ends but do not peel. Cut the zucchini into thin slices about an eighth of an inch thick. There should be about 6 cups.

2. Heat the oil in a skillet and when it is quite hot add the zucchini. Cook over relatively high heat, shaking the skillet, tossing and stirring gently with a spatula to turn the slices. Add salt and pepper to taste. Cook about 5 to 7 minutes. Drain in a sieve. Do not wipe out the skillet.

3. To the skillet add the butter. When melted and hot return the zucchini. Add the garlic and herbs. Add salt to taste. Toss and serve hot.

Yield: Six servings.

IT WOULD BE DIFFICULT TO THINK OF ANY MAIN course that offers itself more readily—and tastefully—to hasty cooking in a so-called gourmet style than a well-made fish soup. There are literally countless thousands of ways to make a palatable, indeed an eminently edible and hearty, fish soup. Techniques and ingredients for making these soups differ, of course, from country to country and region to region.

Along the Mediterranean, fish soups are almost invariably based on olive oil, garlic, onions, tomatoes, and such herbs as thyme or bay leaf. The fish bear such names as rascasse, saint-pierre, congre, rouget, rouquier, and the end result is robust.

The classic example is bouillabaisse. In Paris, fish soup tends to be based on butter and cream and to be made with a more delicate fish. Some fish soups incorporate the elements of both the Paris and Mediterranean areas, including both tomatoes and cream.

A basic fish soup, quickly and easily made, is offered here. Almost any white-fleshed, non-oily fish can be used—obviously the fresher the better. Although scallops are included in this recipe, they are not essential. Instead of scallops, you might simply increase the quantity of the basic fish used. Recipes are and should be flexible.

The soup, by the way, is made more substantial and given a more interesting texture by the addition of croutons—crisply broiled slices of French bread, rubbed lightly with garlic and sprinkled with a little olive oil before cooking. These, too, are optional.

The recommended way to proceed with this recipe is to prepare all the ingredients in advance. The most time-consuming thing is the preparation of the fish and vegetables, the onion, garlic, green pepper, leeks, potatoes, and parsley. These foods must be chopped, cubed, or sliced. The remainder of the ingredients come out of bottles or tins. The croutons may be prepared after the soup has been put on to simmer.

The menu could include, as a second course, the usual salad with cheese and, if desired, a final course of fresh fruit or a purchased or previously made dessert.

Soupe de Poisson
(*Fish soup*)

3 tablespoons olive oil
¼ cup finely chopped onion
1 teaspoon finely chopped garlic
½ cup chopped green pepper
½ cup chopped leeks, optional
½ cup finely chopped carrots
1 hot red pepper, crumbled
1 bay leaf
2 teaspoons fresh thyme sprigs or
½ teaspoon dried thyme
1 cup dry white wine

1 cup chopped fresh or canned tomatoes
⅓ pound potatoes
1 cup water
1¼ pounds white-fleshed, non-oily fish such as cod, tilefish, or a combination of two or more fish
½ pint bay scallops
1 cup heavy cream
¼ cup finely chopped fresh parsley
Salt and freshly ground pepper
16 toasted croutons (see recipe).

1. Heat the oil in a kettle and add the onion, garlic, green pepper, leeks, and carrots. Cook, stirring often, until the onions are wilted.

2. Add the crumbled red pepper, bay leaf, thyme, wine, and tomatoes. Bring to the boil.

3. Peel the potatoes and cut them into half-inch cubes. Drop into cold water briefly. Drain. Add the potatoes to the soup.

4. Cover closely and cook 10 minutes.

5. Add the water. Uncover and cook 5 minutes.

6. Add the fish and scallops and simmer 2 or 3 minutes. Do not overcook or the fish will fall apart. Add the cream and bring to the boil. The soup must be piping hot.

7. Gently stir in the parsley and add salt and pepper to taste. Add one or two croutons to each serving and serve the remainder on the side.

Yield: Four servings.

Croûtons

Half a loaf of French bread
1 clove garlic, peeled and left whole

¼ cup olive oil.

1. Rub the outside crust of the bread all over with garlic.

2. Cut the bread into sixteen thin slices. Arrange the slices on a baking sheet and sprinkle with oil.

3. Broil until golden on one side. Turn and brown lightly on the other side.

Yield: Sixteen croutons.

IF YOU WERE TO COMPARE THE TIME AND EFFORT required to produce a dish with the pleasure that dish offers those who dine on it, chances are that a fish would win with honors. There may be nothing (outside of an omelet or a hamburger, perhaps) more gratifying to the palate in autumn or winter, and the only labor—if you could call it that—is involved in the preparation of the fish and a few vegetables, herbs, and spices.

Another of the incredible things about fish soups are the endless variations in flavors and textures that can be utilized in their preparation. The kinds of fish and shellfish that can be used could fill volumes. The choice of herbs and spices has the broadest latitude, for most fish soups adapt well to a multitude of aromatics.

Many well-meaning acquaintances tell me that the best fish soups invariably contain tomatoes, which is far from the truth. Some of the most highly refined fish soups of France, particularly in Paris, are cream soups, often without a trace of tomato in any form.

There is one recipe for a much admired fish soup printed here. It contains neither tomatoes nor cereals, although it does suggest the addition of toasted croutons that are faintly redolent of garlic and olive oil. I used blackfish, a fish that is apparently abundant but little known in American waters. It is excellent for fish soups—fine flavor, fine texture. The soup can be made in approximately forty-five minutes, preparation and cooking included. The soup, a salad, and cheese could make an elegant meal.

Soup de Poisson avec Palourdes
(French fish soup with clams)

1½ pounds fillets of firm, white-fleshed fish such as blackfish or striped bass

12 littleneck clams

1 teaspoon finely chopped garlic

¾ cup finely chopped onion

1 leek, trimmed, rinsed well, and cut into ½-inch cubes

½ cup chopped heart of celery

¾ cup carrot cut into small cubes

⅔ cup cubed sweet red or green pepper

1 teaspoon loosely packed stem saffron

1 small hot, green or red pepper, optional
Salt and freshly ground pepper to taste

1 sprig fresh thyme or ½ teaspoon dried thyme

1 bay leaf

1 cup dry white wine

3 cups water

¾ cup potatoes cut into small cubes

2 cups heavy cream

8 bread croutons (see recipe)

¼ cup finely chopped parsley.

1. Cut the fillets into one-and-one-half-inch cubes or slightly smaller. Set aside.

2. Rinse the littlenecks well and set them aside.

3. Heat the oil in a kettle and add the garlic and onion. Cook until the onion is wilted and add the leek, celery, carrot, sweet pepper, saffron, hot pepper, salt, pepper, thyme, and bay leaf.

4. Cook about 1 minute and add the wine and water. Cover and cook 5 minutes.

5. Add the potatoes and cover. Cook about 10 minutes.

6. Add the fish and clams and cook about 5 minutes or until the clams open. Add the cream, bring to the boil and simmer about 2 minutes.

7. Top each serving with two croutons and sprinkle with chopped parsley.

Yield: Four servings.

Croûtons

1 loaf French or Italian bread, seeded or not	1 large clove garlic 2 tablespoons olive oil.

1. Preheat the broiler.

2. Rub the outside of the bread loaf with garlic. Cut eight slices of bread, each slice about a half-inch thick or slightly less.

3. Arrange the slices on a baking sheet and brush on one side with oil. Broil until golden brown, turn the slices and brown the other side.

Yield: Eight croutons.

ONE OF THE MOST IMPORTANT THINGS IN LEARNING to cook—and in knowing how to cook—is flexibility. It's the ability to adapt and alter a recipe to circumstance, to the need of a day. You can't or shouldn't be hidebound by rule, and many times personal judgment is vital whether it pertains to baking times or to the use of an herb or spice.

Ingredients can be altered within reason. A quarter cup of parsley, let us say, can be substituted for a third of a cup without a great deal of flavor loss. Some ingredients, while they obviously may add something to a recipe or else they wouldn't be called for, can be eliminated without critical damage. Chicken stock or other broth may be substituted for white wine, for example, provided the quantities are minimal. Bottled clam broth diluted with water can be substituted for fresh fish broth, and so on.

There are, on occasion, certain ingredients that add such special character to a dish that they are really worth going out of one's way to find. In the fish soup listed here (which requires a total cooking time of half an hour or less), that special ingredient is chopped leeks. They can be omitted and the soup will be highly edible. But if you can find leeks (and they will keep for weeks if properly refrigerated) by all means add them.

This soup is very much a main course unto itself, containing as it does potatoes and other vegetables. And the fish when properly selected from a reputable fish dealer—will be fresh and delicious.

Leeks are available, incidentally, at many supermarkets and grocery stores and certainly in markets that specialize in fresh garden produce.

Soupe de Poisson Jardinière
(Fish soup with vegetables)

1¾ pounds skinless, boneless fish fillets such as striped bass or blackfish

3 cups fish broth (see recipe), or use water or a combination of half bottled clam juice and water

1 cup chopped onion

2 cups chopped sweet green or red peppers, preferably one of each

2 cloves garlic, finely minced

1½ cups chopped leeks, both white and green part

2 cups cored, skinned, cubed tomatoes

1 cup peeled potatoes cut into ½-inch cubes

¼ cup olive oil

1 teaspoon loosely packed saffron, optional

1 hot dried red pepper, optional
Salt and freshly ground pepper to taste

1 bay leaf

2 sprigs fresh thyme or ½ teaspoon dried thyme

1 cup dry white wine

½ cup heavy cream

2 tablespoons anise-flavored liqueur such as ricard or pernod, optional

¼ cup finely chopped parsley

8 slices French bread croutons (see recipe), optional.

1. Cut the fish into one-and-one-half-inch cubes. There should be about 4 cups. Set aside.

2. If the fish broth is to be used, prepare it. Otherwise use water, or water and clam broth as indicated.

3. Prepare the onion, peppers, garlic, leeks, tomatoes, and potatoes and set them aside in separate batches. Add cold water to the potatoes to prevent discoloration. Set aside.

4. Heat the oil in a casserole and add the onion. Cook until wilted. Add the peppers and garlic, saffron, and leeks and cook, stirring, about 1 minute.

5. Add the hot red pepper, salt, pepper, bay leaf, and thyme. Cook about 3 to 5 minutes.

6. Add the tomatoes and cook, stirring, about 1 minute. Add the wine and potatoes and cover. Cook 10 minutes.

7. Add the fish broth, if used, or the optional water or clam broth mixed with water. Add the fish. Cook 5 minutes.

8. Add the cream and bring to the boil. If desired, add the liqueur. Serve piping hot in individual bowls. Serve sprinkled with chopped parsley and two croutons for each serving.

Yield: Four servings.

Fumet de Poisson
(*Fish broth*)

In a large saucepan or small kettle, combine about 1½ pounds fresh fish bones (with the head but without gills) and 3 cups of water. Bring to the boil and simmer about 15 minutes. Turn the fish once during the cooking. Drain.

Yield: About three cups.

Croûtons

Rub the outside of one section of French bread (large enough to make eight slices) with a peeled clove of garlic. Cut into eight slices. Brush each slice with ½ teaspoon of olive oil. Place under the broiler, turning once, until crisp and golden.

Yield: Four servings.

OME THINGS SEEM MADE FOR EACH OTHER LIKE
Moët and Chandon, Lea and Perrins and Cross and Black-
well. That lengthy list would also include a couple of plen-
tiful foods from American waters, shad and shad roe. Separately either would
make good feasting. Cooked together with a bit of shallots, a touch of heavy
cream, and a final sprinkling of chopped parsley and/or chives, this is food to
appease the appetite of the most sluggish connoisseur. And the entire kitchen
proceedings—minus the eating, of course—can be accomplished in far less
than an hour.

In fact, the actual cooking time is approximately twenty minutes, leaving
ample time for the preparation of the sundry accompaniments. Speaking of
things that go together, steamed potatoes are in order for this dish, although
steamed rice would be an agreeable substitute. A chilled salad of Belgian endive plus sliced tomatoes and a simple oil and vinegar dressing would be ideal.
In the days and weeks prior to the arrival of the first honestly vine-ripened
tomatoes, it may be best to choose cherry tomatoes, which seem to have more
flavor than the run-of-the-mill hothouse varieties.

When this dish was prepared in my own kitchen, we sat down to dine with a
nice, chilled bottle of Burgundy at hand, specifically a Chassagne-Montrachet.
A bottle of Mosel or Rhine wine, however, would not have been out of place,
nor a good, light dry California wine.

Alose à la Crème
(Shad and shad roe in cream)

2 boned shad fillets, about 2 pounds	2 tablespoons finely chopped shallots
2 pairs shad roe	1 cup heavy cream
Salt and freshly ground pepper to	Juice of half a lemon
taste	2 tablespoons finely chopped parsley
4 tablespoons butter	or chives.

1. Cut the fillets in half lengthwise. Sprinkle the fillets and roe on all sides
with salt and pepper.

2. Heat the butter in one or two heavy skillets and add the shad and roe in
one layer. Sprinkle the shallots between the pieces of fish and roe. Add ½ cup
of heavy cream and cover. Bring to the boil and cook 10 to 15 minutes.

3. Uncover and remove the fish to a serving platter. Split the roe in half and
top each portion of fish with a piece of roe.

4. Add the remaining ½ cup of heavy cream to the skillet and bring to the
boil. Put the sauce through a fine sieve into a saucepan. Bring to the boil and
simmer 5 minutes. Add lemon juice and salt and pepper to taste. Pour the sauce
over the fish and roe and serve sprinkled with parsley. Serve with steamed potatoes.

Yield: Four servings.

Pommes Vapeur
(*Steamed potatoes*)

1 **pound red, new, waxy potatoes**
   Salt to taste

2 **tablespoons butter, optional**
   Freshly ground black pepper to taste.

1. Rinse and drain the potatoes and put them in a small kettle or deep saucepan.

2. Cover with water and add salt to taste. Bring to the boil and simmer 20 minutes or until tender. Drain and when cool enough to handle, peel.

3. Heat the butter in a heavy saucepan and add the potatoes. Sprinkle with salt and pepper to taste. Cover and heat thoroughly.

Yield: Four servings.

FROM MY APPRENTICESHIP AS A CHEF IN PARIS more than forty years ago, one of the things I remember most profoundly is the occasional trip to the old markets at Les Halles with my mentor and guide, the chef of the Restaurant Drouant, at that time one of the most celebrated restaurants in the city.

He was a man obsessed with the quality of fresh produce, and we would arrive before dawn, going from produce stall to produce stall, walking between what seemed like mountains of scarlet-red radishes, snow white and deep green leeks, new celery and green hills of parsley, thyme, and chervil. We would visit the displays of freshly slaughtered veal and beef and spend a long time at the fish merchants.

Through him I had it pounded into my brain that food is best when purchased and cooked in its purest and most recenlty gathered or harvested state. And this applies, of course, to the home as well as the restaurant.

I thought of this while visiting the fish market in Amagansett, L.I., where they had on display several dozen mackerel that had just come in from the sea. I used four of them to make a fine supper for four in much less than an hour, and you could not have dined on fish much fresher than that. There are those who complain that they don't like mackerel because it has an oily flavor. Not if they are newly caught.

The recipe here is for mackerel Portuguese-style, which is to say with tomatoes and sweet peppers, and, optionally, a touch of saffron. It is an easy dish to prepare. It requires about thirty minutes of baking time. As the fish cook, there is ample time to prepare such side dishes as you may require. Plain boiled potatoes—known in French as pommes vapeur—are excellent with it.

The menu could include as a second course the usual salad with cheese and, if desired, a final course of fresh fruit or previously made dessert.

Maquereaux Portugaise
(Mackerel with tomato and pepper sauce)

4 very fresh mackerel, about ½ pound each, cleaned, gills removed but with head and tail left on
¼ cup olive oil
2 teaspoons finely minced garlic
1 onion, sliced wafer thin, about 1 cup
½ teaspoon red pepper flakes
1 cup sliced, seeded sweet green pepper

Salt and freshly ground pepper to taste
1 bay leaf
½ teaspoon leaf saffron, loosely packed, optional
2 large red, ripe, unblemished tomatoes, cored and coarsely chopped, about 3 cups
4 anchovies, chopped.

1. Preheat the oven to 450 degrees.

2. Using a pair of kitchen scissors, trim off the back and side fins of the fish if this has not been done by the fisherman. Rinse well and drain.

3. Heat 3 tablespoons of oil in a skillet and add the garlic. Cook briefly and add the onion. Cook until wilted and add the pepper flakes and cook until onion starts to brown lightly. Add the green peppers, salt and pepper and continue cooking, stirring occasionally, until the peppers start to brown lightly. Add the bay leaf, saffron, and tomatoes. Cook, stirring occasionally, about 5 minutes.

4. Grease an oval baking dish (a dish measuring about 10 by 16-inches was used to test this recipe) with the remaining tablespoon of oil. Arrange the fish side by side in the dish. Sprinkle with salt and pepper. Pour the sauce on top and sprinkle with salt and pepper. Dot with the chopped anchovies. Place in the oven and bake 30 minutes.

5. Run quickly under the broiler and serve hot or cold.

Yield: Four servings.

Pommes Vapeur
(*Steamed potatoes*)

---

1   **pound red, new, waxy potatoes**   **Freshly ground black pepper to**
    Salt   **taste.**
2   **tablespoons butter, optional**

1. Rinse and drain the potatoes and put them in a small kettle or deep saucepan.

2. Cover with water and add salt to taste. Bring to the boil and simmer 20 minutes or until tender. Drain and when cool enough to handle, peel.

3. Heat the butter in a heavy saucepan and add the potatoes. Sprinkle with salt and pepper to taste. Cover and heat thoroughly.

Yield: Four servings.

LIKE MOST CHEFS, I HAVE A SPECIAL CRAVING AT times for certain foods. And like many people who come from Mediterranean countries, I have seasonal cravings for the fish known in America as whiting, in France as merlan and in Italy as merluzzo. The whiting of America is both relatively abundant and relatively inexpensive.

Whiting has a special appeal because its texture is tender and it has a sweet flavor that enhances other flavors with which it is associated. It is a highly versatile fish and is easily cooked.

The cooking time of whiting depends, of course, on the size of the fish and the manner in which it is cooked. One of the simplest and best preparations is called merlan au plat avec herbes, in which the whiting is baked with a coating of bread crumbs and a light cooking liquid made with dry white wine and butter.

The menu recommended here calls for baked zucchini with tomatoes as an accompaniment. As outlined here, the dish is similar to a Mediterranean ratatouille, but the cooking process is simplified. The ingredients are lightly broiled and then finished in the oven.

The pattern for proceeding here would be to heat the oven and prepare the bread crumbs for the fish. As the bread bakes prepare the ingredients for the vegetable accompaniment. Assemble it, start it to broil and as it cooks begin preparation of the fish.

Place the vegetable dish in the oven. Assemble the fish dish. Place it in the oven and bake simultaneously with the vegetables. The vegetables may cook a bit longer than the time indicated. Or they may be removed from the oven and kept warm until the fish is done.

Merlan au Plat avec Herbes
(Breaded baked whiting with herbs)

4	whiting, about ½ pound each	2	tablespoons finely chopped
3	slices French bread		parsley
1	tablespoon finely minced shallots	¼	cup butter
1	tablespoon finely minced onion	½	cup dry white wine.

1. Preheat the oven to 400 degrees.

2. Arrange the bread slices on a baking dish. Bake until golden brown and as crisp as Melba toast. Let cool. Rub through a sieve or process until fine in a blender or food processor. There should be about ⅓ cup of crumbs.

3. Combine the crumbs, shallots, onions and parsley.

4. Butter a baking dish large enough to hold the fish in one layer with 1 tablespoon of butter. Sprinkle about 3 tablespoons of the crumb mixture over the bottom. Arrange the fish over the crumbs. Sprinkle with remaining crumbs and dot with remaining butter.

5. Pour the wine around the fish and bake 30 minutes. Baste and bake 5 minutes longer.

Yield: Four servings.

Courgettes au Four avec Tomates
(Baked zucchini with tomatoes)

---

1   zucchini, about ½ pound
2   medium-size tomatoes, about ½ pound
1   medium-size green pepper, cored, seeded, and chopped

1   cup finely chopped onion
    Salt and freshly ground pepper to taste
¼   cup olive oil.

1. Preheat the oven to 400 degrees.
2. Trim off the ends of the zucchini and core the tomatoes. Cut each into ten half-inch slices. Arrange them, edges slightly overlapping, alternating the zucchini with tomato.
3. Sprinkle with green pepper, onion, salt and pepper. Sprinkle evenly with oil.
4. Broil about 5 minutes. Take care that the vegetables do not burn on top.
5. Place in the oven and bake about 25 minutes. Serve hot.

Yield: Four servings.

GIVEN A CHOICE OF FISH FILLET OR WHOLE FISH, the average American would undoubtedly settle for the fillet. In a sense, where the character and flavor of most fish is concerned, this is unfortunate, because fish cooked with their bones intact are generally more distinctive. It is no fantasy: The nearer the bone, the sweeter the meat.

The bone structures of fish vary considerably, and certain fish—shad, for example—possess an elaborabe configuration of bones that makes filleting highly desirable. One of the finest fish to swim in American waters is whiting, a classic example of a fish that is best when cooked and served with bones intact. There is one major bone structure from gills to tail, and this can be removed with a single motion. The diner is left with a fine white mass of sweet-tasting, solid, tender flesh on which to feast.

Whiting (I am thinking mainly of small whiting, one fish per person) is a fish of such delicate nature that it doesn't really need much embellishment outside of a few drops of lemon juice. And whiting is a cinch to prepare. The fish is dipped in milk, coated with flour and deep fried in four or five minutes. It is then drained quickly and served.

This gives the cook ample time to concentrate on other materials or side dishes. Because of its admirably clean taste, a fish like whiting is best complemented with a vegetable dish with considerable contrast in flavors, such as provencale ratatouille or its American equivalent, eggplant créole with the traditional blending of celery, onions, and green peppers. This, too, is an easy concoction to make. It demands, once the ingredients are blended, twenty-five minutes cooking time. For this menu it is best to have the eggplant cooking, then cook the fish.

Friture de Merlan au Citron
(Deep-fried whiting with lemon)

4 medium-size whitings, about 1¾ pounds cleaned weight (without heads)	½ cup flour Fat for deep frying Lemon halves and parsley sprigs for garnish.
½ cup milk Salt and freshly ground pepper to taste	

1. Using a pair of heavy kitchen shears, cut off the fins from the back and sides of the fish. Rinse the fish well in cold water and drain.

2. Put the fish in a dish and add milk. Salt and pepper to taste. Remove them from the milk and dredge immediately in flour.

3. Heat the oil for deep frying and cook the fish 4 to 5 minutes. Drain on ab-

sorbent paper towels. Serve hot, garnished with lemon halves and parsley sprigs. Serve with boiled potatoes if desired.

Yield: Four servings.

Aubergines à la Créole
(*Eggplant in creole sauce*)

---

1 **eggplant, about 1¼ pounds**	1 **or 2 teaspoons finely chopped**
1 **green pepper, cored and seeded**	**garlic**
1 **tomato, about 1 pound, cored**	1 **cup celery, diced**
¼ **cup peanut, vegetable, or corn**	**Salt and freshly ground pepper**
oil	**to taste**
1 **cup onion, coarsely chopped**	1 **bay leaf.**

1. Peel the eggplant and cut it lengthwise into one-inch slices. Stack the slices and cut them into one-inch strips. Cut the strips into one-inch cubes. There should be about 5 cups.

2. Cut the green pepper into one-inch pieces. There should be about ½ cup.

3. Cut the tomato into one-inch cubes. There should be about 2½ to 3 cups loosely packed.

4. Heat the oil in a deep, heavy skillet and add the cubed eggplant, onion, garlic, and celery. Add salt and pepper to taste.

5. Cook, stirring often, about 3 to 5 minutes and add the green pepper. Cook, stirring occasionally, about 2 minutes. Add the tomato, bay leaf, salt and pepper. Cover closely and cook 25 minutes.

Yield: Four servings.

THERE IS A DISH THAT DOVETAILS NICELY WITH AN old American custom. It is the New England tradition of offering guests fresh salmon, peas, and new potatoes in celebration of the Fourth of July.

In this case, however, there is a slight departure from tradition. The custom, particularly around Boston and in Connecticut, is to serve a whole steamed salmon with peas and potatoes.

A whole salmon properly steamed (poached is more like it) requires a good deal of time and effort. The preparation proposed here is for grilled salmon, and the procedure is no more complicated and time-consuming than marinating the fish fillets in a mixture of oil, dill, salt, and pepper before cooking briefly on a preheated grill.

To tell the truth, the inspiration for this dish is of Scandinavian origin, notably gravlax, although the curing time is dispensed with. This is another of those dishes whose preparation and cooking time, start to finish, is so rapid that the better part of scheduling is to concentrate on the vegetable accompaniment—in this case, potatoes in a light cream sauce with fresh or frozen peas. The potatoes must be cooked in their jackets before the dish is finished. The cooking time is about twenty minutes.

When the potatoes are peeled and sliced into rounds, they are cooked briefly with milk and cream and seasonings. If fresh peas are to be blended with the potatoes, they should be cooked separately. If the peas are really fresh from the garden, the cooking time could almost be measured in seconds. If the peas are frozen, however, they can simply be added to the potatoes at the last minute and cooked until piping hot throughout.

If you really wanted to complete a Fourth of July meal, New England-style, you would end the meal with strawberry shortcake, but that, of course, would require more time.

Saumon Grillé á la Danoise
(Grilled dilled salmon fillets)

---

2 pounds boneless fillets, preferably with the skin left intact
¼ cup peanut, vegetable, or corn oil
3 tablespoons finely chopped dill

Salt and freshly ground black pepper to taste
4 tablespoons melted butter
4 thin slices lemon for garnish
Parsley sprigs for garnish.

1. Cut the salmon into four pieces of approximately the same size and weight. Put the pieces in a dish and add the oil, dill, salt and pepper. Blend well.

2. Refrigerate briefly, turning the pieces in the marinade several times.

3. Preheat the broiler.

4. Arrange the pieces of fish in one layer on an unheated broiler tray. Place

the fish under the broiler about two or three inches away from the source of heat.

5. Broil about 4 minutes or just until the pieces are cooked through. It is not necessary to turn the pieces. Brush with melted butter. Garnish with lemon slices and parsley sprigs.

Yield: Four servings.

Pommes de Terres et Pois à la Crème
(Potatoes with peas in cream)

---

4 potatoes, about 1¼ pounds	Freshly ground pepper to taste
Salt to taste	⅛ teaspoon freshly grated nutmeg
1 cup milk	2 cups fresh or frozen green peas
½ cup heavy cream	¾ cup chopped scallions.

1. Put the potatoes in a saucepan with water to cover and salt to taste. Bring to the boil and simmer 20 minutes or longer or until tender without being mushy.

2. When cool enough to handle, peel the potatoes and cut them into quarter-inch rounds. There should be about 4 cups.

3. Put the slices in a saucepan and add the milk and cream.

4. Place on the heat and add salt, pepper, and nutmeg. Bring to the boil and simmer over high heat about 5 minutes.

5. Meanwhile, if fresh peas are to be used, cook them in boiling salted water until tender. Drain and add them to the potatoes in cream. Add the scallions and stir. Cook about 1 minute.

Yield: Four servings.

DURING THE SUMMER THERE ARE FEW FRENCH RES-
taurants throughout the country that do not have cold poached
fish served with one kind of sauce or another on the menu. It
is warm weather fare, the kind of dish that is ideal for cooking.

It requires a minimum of care, for poached fish must be cooked for a short
period or it loses its texture. But more about that later.

It is possible, naturally, to cook a fish in only water with salt and peppercorns. It is far preferable, however, to cook the fish in an easily made cooking
liquid called a court bouillon. This consists of water and wine blended with
herbs and spices plus one or two vegetables, such as carrots and onions.

The best thing about poached fish in terms of care and time is that once the
fish is brought to the boil there is nothing more to be done until it is cooked.
Simply let is simmer gently for a short, specified time. The three-pound striped
bass called for here will cook perfectly in 10 minutes.

One of the best of all sauces to go with a poached fish is a sauce verte or
green sauce that can be whipped up in seconds using a food processor or
blender. For a summer menu, a tomato and hard-cooked egg garnish is very
much in order. To extend the menu you might want to cook a few potatoes
(cook them separately but simultaneously with the fish) and add a cold sliced
cucumber salad.

Bar Rayé Poché
(*Poached striped bass*)

1	3-pound striped bass, with head on but gills removed	1	bay leaf
24	cups water	10	peppercorns
1	cup dry white wine		Salt to taste
½	cup carrot rounds	1	hot red pepper
¾	cup coarsely chopped onion		Lemon wedges for garnish
8	sprigs fresh parsley		Sauce verte (see recipe)
1	teaspoon dried rosemary		Tomato and hard-cooked egg garnish (see recipe).

1. Rinse the fish well and pat dry. Set aside.

2. Combine all the remaining ingredients except the lemon wedges, sauce
verte, and tomato and hard-cooked egg garnish in a fish poacher or other oval
casserole or pot large enough to hold the fish. Bring to the boil and simmer 10
minutes.

3. Carefully lower the fish into the liquid. If desired, the fish may be
wrapped in cheesecloth to facilitate its removal, but if a fish poacher with a
rack is used, this is not necessary.

4. Bring the liquid to the boil and simmer gently exactly 10 minutes. Remove the cooker from the heat and let stand until ready to serve. The fish may
rest in the liquid for up to half an hour without detriment.

5. To serve, place the fish on a serving dish and carefully remove and discard the skin. Garnish with lemon wedges and serve separately the sauce verte and tomato and hard-cooked egg garnish.

Yield: Four servings.

Sauce Verte
(*Green sauce*)

⅓ cup coarsely chopped parsley, loosely packed
⅓ cup coarsely chopped raw onion
2 tablespoons coarsely chopped chives
1 teaspoon chopped fresh tarragon

1 clove garlic, finely minced
½ cup olive oil
3 tablespoons wine vinegar
1 tablespoon imported mustard such as Dijon or Düsseldorf
1 hard-cooked egg, quartered.

1. Combine the parsley, onion, chives, tarragon, garlic, olive oil, vinegar, and mustard in the container of a food processor or electric blender. Blend until herbs are finely chopped. Do not overblend, however. The ingredients should retain some texture.
2. Add the egg and blend briefly until coarsely blended.

Yield: About one-and-a-quarter cups.

Garniture d'Oeufs Durs
(*Garnish of hard-cooked egg*)

1 large, red-ripe tomato
  Salt to taste
2 hard-cooked eggs, peeled

  Freshly ground pepper
  Mayonnaise, optional.

1. Remove the core and cut away a small slice from the bottom of the tomato. Cut the tomato into eight wedges and sprinkle with salt.
2. Quarter the eggs. Arrange four pairs of two tomato wedges, centers touching. Arrange quartered eggs neatly in the center to fit. Serve with salt and pepper on the side. And, if desired, serve with a spoonful of mayonnaise on each serving.

Yield: Four servings.

ONE OF THE OBVIOUS ADVANTAGES OF LIVING IN coastal areas is the relative abundance of fresh fish. Perhaps the most abundant fish is that sold over the counter as "sole." The truth of the matter is that the sole found in American markets may well be fluke or flounder, gray sole or lemon sole, among others. Just why the word sole became a sort of catch-all is not known, but the ultimate consideration in buying sole, as any other fish, is its fresh quality.

Fillet of sole is admirable for hasty cooking, for overcooked fish becomes dry and fibrous. One of the most appetizing preparations for sole is sole grenobloise, which is to say in the style of Grenoble, France. The fish is first cooked meunière (lightly coated with flour and sautéed quickly). It is then given a grenobloise garnish, which is lemon and capers.

Since capers have a character all of their own and they are a bit assertive, the dish is best complemented by a vegetable dish of substantial flavor, and an excellent idea for this is cherry tomatoes provençale, in which you use a touch of garlic and parsley. That, plus the classic accompaniment for fish meunière or any of its variations, buttered, boiled, or steamed potatoes.

The best method of approaching such a menu is to get all the ingredients prepared before starting to cook. Both dishes, once the ingredients are assembled and made ready, can be cooked in a very few minutes.

Filets de Sole Grenobloise
(Sautéed sole with capers and lemon)

4	individual servings fish fillets, about 1¼ pounds total weight	1	tablespoon drained capers
¼	cup milk	1	tablespoon finely chopped parsley
	Salt and freshly ground pepper to taste	½	cup flour
		½	cup peanut, vegetable, or corn oil
1	small lemon	¼	cup butter.

1. Place the fillets in a dish large enough to hold them in one layer. Pour the milk over them and add salt and pepper. Turn the fish in the milk so that they are coated on all sides.

2. While they stand, peel the lemon, cutting away and discarding all the white pulp as well as the yellow skin. Cut the lemon into thin slices and discard the seeds. Cut the slices into small cubes. Set aside.

3. Drain the capers and chop the parsley and set aside.

4. Scatter the flour over a large pan and add salt and pepper to taste. Blend well.

5. Heat the oil and 1 tablespoon of butter in a large skillet.

6. As the oil heats, remove the fillets from the milk but do not drain. Coat the fish on all sides in seasoned flour, shaking to rid the fillets of excess flour.

7. When the oil is quite hot but not smoking, add the fillets (this might have

to be done in two steps) and cook until nicely browned on one side. Turn and brown on the other. The total cooking time for each fillet should be from 4 to 5 minutes. As the fillets are cooked, transfer them to a warm platter.

8. Heat the remaining butter in a small skillet and cook, shaking the skillet until butter foams up and takes on an appetizing hazelnut-brown color. Remove from the heat. Add the cubed lemon and capers. Pour this evenly over the fillets. Sprinkle with chopped parsley and serve.

Yield: Four servings.

Tomates Cerises à la Provençale
(*Cherry tomatoes with garlic and parsley*)

---

24 red, ripe, unblemished, and firm cherry tomatoes	**1** teaspoon finely chopped garlic
2 tablespoons olive oil	**2** tablespoons finely chopped parsley.

1. Remove the stems from the tomatoes. Rinse and pat tomatoes dry.

2. Heat the oil in a skillet large enough to hold the tomatoes in one layer. Add the tomatoes and cook, shaking the skillet so that the tomatoes are distributed and cook evenly. Cook about 1 or 2 minutes, just until tomatoes are heated through. Do not overcook or the skins will split and the tomatoes will become mushy.

3. Sprinkle with garlic, toss briefly, and serve sprinkled with parsley.

Yield: Four servings.

I T IS THE UNDERSTATEMENT OF THE DECADE TO say that American cooking habits have undergone mind-boggling changes within recent memory. Home cooks have traditionally never been noticeably keen about deep-frying in the kitchen but, if the sale of electrically operated deep-frying units is any indication, then that technique is gaining widespread currency from the East Coast to the West.

To my mind, this is all to the good, for there are thousands of hastily made dishes in French cookery that call for deep-frying, not the least being that universally admired contribution from the French kitchen, pommes frites, otherwise known as french fries.

One of the best of all deep-fried dishes bears the name of fillets of sole en goujon and sometimes referred to as goujonnettes de sole.

A gougon is a very small European fish that abounds in fresh water. It resembles a minnow-size catfish and sports a tiny moustache. The fillet of sole dish consists of cutting the fillets into thin strips about the size of goujons.

The technique for cooking the goujonnettes is simple. The pieces are dipped first in flour, then in egg and finally in bread crumbs. They are deep-fried and served, generally with a hollandaise-type mustard sauce or a tartar sauce.

The cooking time for the sole pieces is less than ten minutes. Therefore, to prepare a meal with goujonettes as the main course, bread the raw strips of sole and refrigerate them. Prepare the sauce and then deep-fry the fish. Buttered boiled or steamed potatoes go well with the dish and they may be put on to cook before breading the fish and preparing the sauce. Serve with a tossed green salad.

Goujonnettes de Sole
(Deep-fried strips of sole)

---

6 fillets of flounder or sole, about 1¼ pounds	2 tablespoons water
1 whole egg	¼ cup flour
Salt and freshly ground pepper to taste	3 cups fresh bread crumbs
	4 cups oil or enough for deep-frying
	Mustard sauce (see recipe).

1. There is a small bone line down the center of each fillet. Place the fillets on a flat surface and cut down the center, making two parallel slices on either side of the bone line. Remove and discard the bone line.

2. Cut each fillet half on the diagonal into half-inch thick strips.

3. Combine the egg, salt, pepper, and the water and beat well with a whisk. Pour the mixture into a flat dish for dipping.

4. Sprinkle the fish strips with salt and pepper and dredge in the flour. Each piece should be coated with flour, but toss to remove excess flour.

5. Transfer the fish strips to the egg mixture. Toss to coat and transfer the strips to the bread crumbs. Toss to coat each individual piece.

6. Pick up each piece of fish, one at a time, and roll on a flat surface using one palm.

7. Heat the oil in a skillet or wok and when it is very hot, add the sole pieces, about twelve pieces at a time. Stir gently as they cook. Do not overcrowd the pieces in the oil or they will not brown evenly and properly. Total cooking time is about 2 minutes per batch. It takes longer to cook a larger batch than it does to cook a dozen or so pieces at a time. Continue cooking until all the pieces are used. Drain on paper towels and serve with mustard sauce.

Yield: Four servings.

Sauce Moutarde
(*Mustard sauce*)

2 eggs	1 tablespoon prepared mustard, preferably Dijon or Düsseldorf
2 dashes Tabasco sauce	
8 tablespoons cold butter	Salt and freshly ground pepper to taste.
Juice of half a lemon	

1. Put the eggs in a heavy saucepan and add the Tabasco sauce.

2. Pour about one inch of water into a skillet large enough to hold the saucepan comfortably. Bring the water to the simmer.

3. Beat the eggs off heat. Cut the butter into six pieces and add two pieces to the eggs. Set the saucepan in the hot water. Stir constantly with whisk. The important thing about this sauce is it must not become too hot or the eggs will curdle.

4. When the butter melts, remove the skillet from the heat but continue beating constantly. Add another piece of butter and beat until melted. Continue adding butter, one piece at a time, beating constantly until all butter is used. When thickened and smooth, remove the saucepan from the skillet. Add the lemon juice, mustard, salt and pepper.

Yield: Four servings.

SOME OF THE FINEST DINING IN THE UNITED STATES can occur right in the middle of winter because some of the finest, freshest fish come from the cold winter waters of the Atlantic.

And since most fish cookery is designed for hasty cooking, a hot platter of halibut, cod, or other seasonal fish is timely.

It is odd that in French cooking so many of the best-received dishes stem directly from the countryside rather than from the cities. Fish boulangère could be counted as one of those dishes. Boulangère means in the style of the baker's wife. It is called that because the dish is baked and one of its characteristics is a final sprinkling of the baker's bread crumbs before it is put in the oven.

Fish boulangère—it is delicious made with fresh halibut or cod fillets—consists of fillets folded and baked with potatoes and onions sliced wafer-thin.

It is a simple dish, for after the fillets are surrounded by the vegetables and sprinkled with crumbs and butter, it simply requires half an hour of baking.

In essence, halibut or cod boulangère could easily serve as a meal in itself, but, personally, I prefer it with another vegetable such as vichy carrots or perhaps with a well-dressed green salad made a trifle piquant with the addition of a good grade of imported mustard.

The preparation of such a meal is simplicity itself. Once the dish is in the oven, there is a half-hour for preparing salad greens, salad dressing, or whatever else strikes your fancy.

Flétan Boulangère
(Halibut baked with bread crumbs)

1¼	pounds potatoes, peeled and sliced as thinly as possible, about 4 cups		Salt and freshly ground pepper to taste
1	onion, about ⅓ pound, peeled and sliced wafer thin	¼	cup chopped parsley
12	tablespoons butter	1	clove garlic, finely minced
4	halibut or cod fillets, about 2½ pounds	½	cup bread crumbs
		½	cup dry white wine.

1. Preheat the oven to 425 degrees.
2. Prepare the potatoes and keep covered with cold water.
3. Prepare the onion rings and set aside.
4. Rub the bottom of an oval baking dish with 6 tablespoons of butter.
5. Fold each halibut fillet over itself and arrange down the center of the baking dish. Sprinkle with salt and pepper.
6. Drain the potatoes and put them in a bowl. Add the onions, parsley, garlic, salt and pepper to taste. Blend well.

7. Arrange the vegetable mixture around the fillets. Dot with remaining butter. Sprinkle the fish with bread crumbs. Add the wine.

8. Bring the dish to a boil on top of the stove and place in the oven. Bake 30 minutes. As the fish bakes, tilt the baking dish and spoon the liquid over the fish.

Yield: Four servings.

Carottes Vichy
(*Steamed carrots*)

1 pound carrots	1½ teaspoons sugar
1 cup water	Salt and freshly ground pepper
2 tablespoons butter	to taste.

1. Trim and scrape the carrots and cut them into very thin rounds.

2. Put the carrot rounds in a deep casserole and add the water. It should barely cover the carrots. Add the butter, sugar, salt, and pepper.

3. Cook about 10 minutes and uncover. Cook over high heat about 15 to 20 minutes or until all the water has evaporated. Toss and stir the carrots so that they cook evenly. Cook until the carrots are nicely glazed and lightly browned.

Yield: Four servings.

OUT ON MY TWENTY-FOOT FISHING VESSEL WE fished one day, a neighbor and I. The bluefish were running and the catch was above average. My friend asked a question about food I'd never considered before.

"Which fish," he asked, "is the one most admired throughout the world?"

Not bluefish, certainly. Many people find it too oily. Not striped bass. That's found mostly in American waters (I read recently that striped bass were first introduced into the Pacific in the late 1800s). Tuna, of course, may be the most popular fish in the world (think of tuna fish sandwiches and casseroles), but—outside of the Japanese kitchen—it is not the universal choice of connoisseurs.

The most admired fish in the world is probably salmon. Smoked salmon—from Ireland, Scotland, or Nova Scotia—is one of the world's greatest delicacies and is, along with caviar and foie gras, one of the hors d'oeuvre riches. Poached salmon, broiled salmon, and grilled salmon are admired throughout the world where salmon is available. In Hawaii, salmon is admired in the form of lomi-lomi—salted salmon massaged with the fingers (lomi means massage) and blended with onions and tomatoes. Salmon doesn't even exist in Hawaiian waters.

One of the best salmon dishes is a Japanese creation in which slices of salmon are coated with bread crumbs and deep-fried. This is not only a delectable creation but it requires a very few minutes to prepare—the initial breading and hasty cooking in hot oil. In fact, the fish must be cooked quickly or the flesh will become dry. The salmon is often garnished with thin slices of lemon and pickled ginger stems, which are not essential to the success of the dish. The pickled ginger is widely available in Japanese supermarkets and grocery stores, however.

When this dish is served in Manhattan restaurants, the inevitable accompaniment is lettuce with a tomato-flavored mayonnaise. This is due, of course, to the recent American influence on one corner of the Japanese kitchen. No need to go into the aesthetics of that, but the two dishes seem to complement each other.

Saumon Frit à la Japonaise
(Fried salmon steaks in bread crumbs)

1 pound skinless, boneless salmon fillets	⅓ cup flour
	2 cups fresh bread crumbs
1 large egg	Fat for deep frying
3 tablespoons water	Lemon slices for garnish
Salt and freshly ground pepper to taste	Pickled ginger sprouts (hajikami), available in Japanese groceries, optional.

1. Cut the salmon into four pieces of approximately the same size and weight.

2. Beat the egg with water, salt, and pepper.

3. Dip the salmon pieces in flour to coat well. Shake off excess. Dip the flour coated pieces in egg to coat well.

4. Dip the pieces in bread crumbs until coated all over. Place the pieces on a flat surface and tap with the flat side of a knife to help the crumbs adhere. Set aside.

5. Heat the oil and when it is quite hot, add the salmon pieces. Cook 2 to 3 minutes. Do not overcook or the fish will dry out. Drain on absorbent towels. Serve, garnished with lemon slices and pickled ginger sprouts.

Yield: Four servings.

Mayonnaise aux Ciboules
(*Scallion mayonnaise*)

1 small egg yolk	1 teaspoon vinegar
2 teaspoons imported mustard such as Dijon or Düsseldorf	¾ cup peanut, vegetable, or corn oil
Salt and freshly ground pepper to taste	¼ cup chopped scallions
	1 tablespoon tomato ketchup.

1. Put the egg yolk in a bowl and add the mustard, salt, pepper, and vinegar.

2. Beat with a whisk until well blended. Gradually add the oil, beating constantly. Add the scallions and ketchup and stir to blend.

Yield: About one cup.

Shellfish

MOST COOKS TEND TO CATALOGUE DISHES IN their mind in two categories—those for the everyday table and those for the special occasions. In many cases—dishes requiring elaborate and tediously prepared dough; dishes with costly ingredients such as truffles and foie gras—such divisions are justified. There some dishes, however, so easily made and of such special character they can serve well as one or the other.

For years, at least as long as I can remember, the Spanish rice and seafood dish has been considered very much a dish for special functions. And, of course, in its most elaborate form—garnished with cut-outs of pimentos, egg, and so on—it can be time-consuming. That is not to pretend that the dish recommended here is an absolute authentic paella. It is, however, an excellent dish of seafood with rice, which is what a paella essentially is.

And it is certainly easily made within the space of sixty minutes. It helps, of course, if the seafood can be purchased ready-cleaned and ready for the kettle—the shrimp peeled, the mussels scrubbed, the clams washed, and so on—and the best fish dealers, in most metropolitan centers, sell their shellfish in such fashion.

Other than that, the only steps that are time-consuming are the chopping of a few vegetables such as onion, garlic, green peppers, and tomatoes, and the cooking of rice, which any reasonably intelligent ten-year-old child can do with small effort.

Rice requires less than twenty minutes cooking time—if it is cooked longer than that it becomes mushy and unpalatable. In this recipe seasoned rice is cooked separately from the shellfish; and not the least important thing about prepared seafood where rapid cookery is concerned, it must be cooked in haste for maximum flavor and texture. Thus, while the rice cooks, the seafood preparation should be in progress, the two operations timed to be ready for serving simultaneously. More or less. Once the rice is cooked less than its alloted time, it can be removed from the heat and allowed to stand for several minutes or longer without detriment to its texture.

Fruits de Mer au Riz
(Mixed shellfish with rice)

The rice:
2 tablespoons olive oil
¼ cup finely chopped onion
¼ cup diced green pepper
1 clove garlic, finely minced
½ teaspoon loosely packed saffron stems
1 cup rice
1¼ cups water
Salt and freshly ground pepper to taste

The seafood:
¼ cup olive oil
1 cup finely chopped onion
2 cloves garlic, finely minced

1 hot, dried red pepper, optional
1½ cups diced, peeled, fresh or canned tomatoes
1½ cups dry white wine
1 teaspoon dried oregano
Salt and freshly ground pepper to taste
18 small littleneck clams, the smaller the better, rinsed well
1½ quarts, well-scrubbed mussels, about six cups
½ pound shrimp, shelled and deveined
½ pound sea scallops, halved or quartered.

1. To begin, prepare and measure out all the ingredients for the rice. To save time, chop an extra cup of onions and 2 extra cloves of garlic for the seafood mixture. Set these aside.

2. Heat the 2 tablespoons of oil for the rice in a saucepan and add ¼ cup of onion, green pepper, and 1 clove of garlic and cook until wilted. Add the saffron and cook about 2 minutes longer.

3. Add the rice, water, salt, and pepper and cover closely. Cook about 17 minutes or just until the rice is tender. As the rice cooks prepare the seafood. Remember that when the rice is cooked, remove it from the heat. It can stand several minutes, covered, without damage.

4. In a kettle, heat the ¼ cup oil and add the 1 cup of onion and 2 cloves of garlic. Stir and cook until wilted. Add the red pepper, tomatoes, wine, and oregano. Add salt and pepper. Cover and cook about 10 minutes.

5. Add the clams and mussels to the kettle and cover again. Cook about 3 minutes and add the shrimp, scallops, salt and pepper to taste. Cover and cook about 5 minutes.

6. There are several ways to serve this dish. Use a large, deep serving dish and make a border of rice with a "well" in the center. Add the shellfish with their juices to the center and serve. Or you may blend the rice and the shellfish and serve as a paella.

Yield: Four servings.

T HERE IS NO DOUBT THAT TASTES IN FOOD ARE
sometimes cyclical. During the 1930s when I was an apprentice and then a young chef at the Resturant Drouant in Paris,
there were numerous dishes that appeared on Paris menus that contained or cen-
tered on cooked oysters. And then for a long time cooked oysters were seldom
heard of on French menus.

There is a story, although I don't believe a word of it, that when Georges
Auguste Escoffier was the reigning chef of Europe and presided over the
kitchen of the Ritz, he was asked by a wealthy American lady who lived at the
hotel to prepare a turkey with an oyster stuffing for one of her holiday meals. He
refused on the grounds that turkey or any other kind of fowl and oysters were
incompatible if not "cannibalistic."

Within recent memory, however, I have noticed that more and more cooked
oysters are appearing on the menuus of some of the most famous restaurants
both in this country and abroad.

Actually, cooked oysters—if they are not overcooked—are quite special, and
I like to use them in a dish contrived with smoked salmon and a julienne of
vegetables with a light white wine and cream sauce. The oysters and salmon
are served on a bed of fine noodles, and it is recommended as an easily made
dish for special occasions.

As a vegetable accompaniment, I propose a lukewarm salad of green beans
vinaigrette with chopped fresh dill.

The order of cooking would be to prepare all the ingredients for the creamed
oyster dish and set them aside until the last moment. The water should be kept
at the simmer in a kettle to cook the noodles. The noodles cook in about five
minutes.

Prepare the salad and keep the same separate and warm. Start cooking the
oysters with salmon and as they cook drop the noodles into the water to simmer
five minutes or less. Assemble the foods in a logical manner.

Huîtres et Saumon Fumé á la Crème avec Nouilles
(Creamed oysters and smoked salmon with noodles)

2	pints shucked, raw oysters	½	cup oyster liquor or bottled clam
4	pieces of fresh leeks, each about		juice
	2 inches long	1½	cups heavy cream
2	carrots	6	tablespoons butter
4	large mushrooms	2	tablespoons finely chopped
½	pound smoked salmon		shallots
½	cup dry white wine	½	pound fine noodles
	Salt and freshly ground pepper		Juice of 1 lemon.
	to taste		

1. Empty the oysters into a sieve placed over a mixing bowl. Let drain. Reserve the oyster liquor.

2. Cut the pieces of leeks in half. Rinse and drain well. Cut the pieces lengthwise into very thin strips (julienne). There should be 1 cup, loosely packed. Set aside.

3. Scrape and cut the carrots into two-inch lengths and cut each length into very thin strips like the leeks. There should be about 1 cup. Set aside.

4. Cut the mushrooms into thin strips. There should be about 1 cup. Set aside.

5. Cut the salmon into one-inch squares or diamond-shaped pieces. Set aside.

6. Combine the carrots, leeks, and mushrooms in a saucepan and add the wine. Add a little salt and pepper. Add the oyster liquor if there is any; otherwise, add the clam juice.

7. Simmer partly covered about 5 minutes and add the cream. Add any more liquor that may have accumulated from the oysters. Cook about 5 minutes.

8. Heat 2 tablespoons of butter and add the shallots. Cook briefly and add the oysters and salmon pieces. Sprinkle with pepper; no salt. When sizzling, cover and cook 30 seconds, no longer. Strain any liquid that accumulates and add to the vegetables. Continue to add any liquid that accumulates.

9. Cook the noodles in boiling salted water about 3 to 5 minutes or until tender. Drain quickly and add 2 tablespoons of butter. Add salt and pepper and stir.

10. To the vegetable mixture, swirl in the remaining butter and the juice of one lemon.

11. Spoon equal amounts of noodles onto each of four to six hot plates. Spoon equal portions of oysters and salmon over the noodles and spoon the sauce over all. Serve hot.

Yield: Four to six servings.

ONE OF THE MOST WIDELY QUOTED DEBATES OR EX-
positions on food was written many years ago by the American food researcher Waverly Root in his much-praised book
"The Foods of France." About ten pages of that detailed and scholarly work
were dedicated more or less to the question of whether you can make an honest
bouillabaisse, the famed fish soup or stew, in any area far distant from Marseilles. His theory was that there are certain fish indigenous to the waters
around Marseilles that simply prohibit a dish that properly bears that name any-
where else.

Using the same line of reasoning, it can be argued that chowders made in the
United States are not true chowders. For the fact is that the name was origi-
nated by the early French settlers in this country who prepared a fish and potato
dish known in France as chaudières.

The Americanization of chowders is such that today the versions served here
bear little resemblance to anything you might find on a native table of Brittany.
Of whatever origin, chowders have a delectable and well-founded place in
American culinary history. What's more, they have a time-honored place
whether they are made of fish, seafood, potatoes, corn, green beans, lima
beans, or whatever.

Quite honestly, I don't know of any American dish more gratifying than a
well-made chowder to be served on a cold, midwinter day.

One of my favorite recipes for the dish is also the simplest. It contains the
basics—potatoes and onions and fish. That is the way I prepare it in my home
kitchen. And as often happens, I have discovered another element in my refrigerator that could be considered optional—a pint of shucked oysters. Added to
this dish, they are a natural. If you add the oysters, by the way, take care that
they are only heated through, or they toughen quickly through excess heat.

A hot loaf of French bread stuffed with herbs and heated through is an excellent accompaniment.

Chaudrée aux Fruits de Mer
(Fish and oyster chowder)

---

1 pound potatoes, scraped	Salt and freshly ground pepper
½ pound onions, peeled	to taste
1½ pounds skinless, boneless	1 bay leaf
flounder or other fish fillets	2 cups milk
2 tablespoons butter	1 cup heavy cream or 1 additional
1 pint shucked oysters with their	cup of milk
liquor	⅛ teaspoon cayenne pepper.
1 cup water, approximately	

1. Cut the potatoes into half-inch-thick slices. Stack the slices and cut them
into quarter-inch-wide strips. Cut the strips into half-inch cubes. As the pota-

toes are cut drop them into cold water to prevent discoloration. There should be about 2 cups.

2. Chop the onions. There should be about 1½ cups finely chopped.

3. There may be a small bone line running down the center of each fillet. If so, cut on either side of this bone line and discard it. Cut the fish into one-inch cubes.

4. Heat the butter in a small casserole or large saucepan. Add the onions and cook, stirring often, until wilted. Add the oyster liquor and enough water to make 1 cup. Add the potatoes. There should be enough liquid to barely cover the potatoes. Bring to the boil.

5. Add salt, pepper, and bay leaf. Cover and simmer until potatoes are tender, about 12 minutes or longer. Do not overcook.

6. Add the milk, 1 cup heavy cream, and the fish. Add the cayenne, salt and pepper. Bring just to the boil and stir gently. Add the oysters and turn off the heat. Heat through, but do not cook further. Serve in hot bowls with herbed French bread.

Yield: Four servings.

Pain Rôti aux Herbes
(Herbed French bread)

---

1 loaf French bread
4 to 8 tablespoons butter

½ cup finely chopped parsley
1 tablespoon finely chopped garlic.

1. Preheat the oven to 400 degrees.

2. Split open the bread lengthwise.

3. Melt the butter and add the parsley and garlic. Spoon the mixture down the center of the bread and reshape it. Wrap in foil and place in the oven. Bake 30 minutes.

Yield: Four servings.

ONE OF THE BASICS IN FOOD PREPARATION—PERhaps the most important basic, in fact—is the balance of flavors in any given recipe. In a salad dressing, for example, the ratio of oil to vinegar or lemon juice is vital. The same can be said for nuances in flavors and what "marries" well with what. It is an indisputable fact that some flavors complement certain foods better than others. As you learn more about cooking, you realize that nutmeg complements cheese dishes, that the flavor of rosemary teams well with veal and chicken and liver, that garlic and oil go well in robust tomato sauces, and so on.

One of the oddest and most admirable liaisons in tastes—and the reasons for it I can't explain—is that of spinach and oysters. Nowhere is this more evident than in New Orleans, where oysters Rockefeller is almost the principal municipal dish. The variations on that dish (all of them called oysters Rockefeller) seem limitless, and the list of ingredients is fairly lengthy.

In my own home I have prepared an uncommonly simple and delicious oyster-and-spinach creation that is not much more difficult—nor time-consuming—than preparing a cheese or mushroom omelet. The spinach filling—or topping—consists of only seven ingredients, two of which are salt and pepper. The added fillip is—as it often is with oysters Rockefeller—a dash of the anise-flavored liqueur called ricard or pernod. The principal point to be made is that the oysters on the half shell, the basis of the dish, must be heated as briefly as possible, without cooking, or they will toughen.

These oysters are well complemented with a simple dish of buttered noodles that are given more interest, perhaps, with added slivers of cooked carrots and poppy seeds. And even the carrots are optional.

Huîtres à la Florentine avec Pernod
(Oysters with spinach and pernod)

24	oysters on the half shell	3	tablespoons finely chopped shallots
1	10-ounce package fresh spinach, or use 1 pound fresh spinach in bulk	1	cup heavy cream
¼	cup dry white wine		Salt and freshly ground pepper to taste
		1	tablespoon pernod or ricard.

1. Have the oysters opened and loosened from the half shells. Leave them on the half shells. Set aside.

2. Preheat the oven to 425 degrees.

3. If bulk spinach is used, break off and discard any tough stems and blemished leaves. In any case, wash the spinach well in cold water.

4. Add the spinach to a basin of boiling water and cook about 1 minute. Drain and run under cold water to chill. Squeeze to extract excess moisture. Chop the spinach with a knife, or use a food processor.

5. Arrange the oysters close together in a large baking dish. Sprinkle with equal amounts of the wine. Place in the oven and bake about 5 minutes, no longer. They should barely be heated through.

6. Put the shallots in a skillet.

7. Remove the oysters from the oven and carefully pour on the shallots the liquid that has accumulated on the half shell around the oysters. Cook briefly and add the cream. Cook down over high heat, stirring, to about ¾ cup.

8. Add the spinach and stir. Add salt and pepper and pernod. Spoon the sauce over the oysters and serve immediately.

Yield: Four servings.

Nouilles avec Carottes et Graines d'Oeillette
(Noodles with carrots and poppy seeds)

2 carrots, trimmed and scraped	3 tablespoons butter
Salt to taste	1 tablespoon poppy seeds
½ pound medium noodles	Freshly ground pepper to taste.

1. Cut the carrots into quarter-inch slices. Stack the slices into quarter-inch strips. Cut the strips into one-inch lengths. There should be slightly less than 1 cup. Set aside.

2. Drop the carrots into boiling salted water and simmer about 3 minutes or until crisp tender. Drain.

3. Drop the noddles into boiling salted water and simmer until tender. Return the noodles to the saucepan and add the butter and carrots. Add the poppy seeds and stir. Add salt and pepper to taste.

Yield: Four servings.

I N COOKING, AS IN MOST THINGS IN LIFE, EVERY-
thing is relative—including flavors and cooking times. In that
this book is dedicated to the proposition that excellent foods
can be prepared in less than an hour, it is evident that some dishes cook far
more quickly than others. It is also obvious that the end results of some dishes
may be more sophisticated than others, more elegant than others, and better
suited to the finest of wines. And guests who have been chosen with special
care.

It seems to me that of all the recipes printed in this book, none can exceed
the dish outlined here for sheer elegance. Similarly, I can't recall a dish of
whatever genre that requires less time and preparation in the kitchen. The dish
in question is a quick sauté of scallops and leeks, finished with cream and
delicately flavored with the perfume of Marseilles, the anise-flavored drink
known as pastis—pernod or ricard.

If anyone cares, this is a dish, made in far less than sixty minutes, that would
certainly qualify as the much-touted nouvelle cuisine.

This is the kind of dish that should be served on special occasions. And I
might add, without apology, that it is calorie-laden. The recipe serves four people generously and six people adequately, and it calls for from one and a half to
two cups of heavy cream. In my own kitchen I prefer the larger amount.

The ideal accompaniment for scallops and leeks in cream is baked rice,
which requires more time to cook—exactly seventeen minutes in the oven—
than the time it takes to cook the main course. Therefore, it would be wiser to
prepare the rice and then go about the main course. Besides which, the rice,
once baked, can stand for several minutes without damage to its flavor and texture.

Coquilles St. Jacques et Poireaux avec Pernod
(Scallops and leeks with pernod)

1 quart scallops, preferably bay scallops	2 tablespoons dry white wine
6 tablespoons butter	2 cups heavy cream
3 leeks, chopped, about 3½ cups	3 tablespoons finely chopped shallots
Salt and freshly ground pepper to taste	2 tablespoons pernod or ricard or other anise-flavored liqueur.

1. Although bay scallops are best for this dish, sea scallops may be used. If
sea scallops are used, cut them into quarters.

2. Heat 2 tablespoons of the butter in a skillet and add the leeks. Sprinkle
with salt and pepper. Cook, stirring occasionally, about 2 minutes.

3. Sprinkle with wine and cook about 1 minute. Add the cream and cook,
stirring often, about 5 minutes.

4. As the sauce cooks down, in a separate skillet heat 2 tablespoons of butter

and add the shallots, salt, and pepper. Cook about 1 minute, stirring. Add the scallops.

5. Sprinkle with pernod or ricard and heat. Combine the two mixtures. Bring to the boil and swirl in the remaining 2 tablespoons of butter.

Yield: Four to six average servings.

Riz au Four
(*Baked rice*)

3	tablespoons butter	Salt and freshly ground pepper
⅓	cup minced onion	to taste
1½	cups uncooked rice	2 sprigs thyme or ½ teaspoon
2¼	cups water	dried thyme
2	sprigs parsley	½ bay leaf
		Tabasco sauce to taste.

1. Preheat the oven to 400 degrees.

2. Melt half the butter in a saucepan and add the onion. Cook, stirring, until wilted. Add the rice and stir to blend.

3. Add the water, stirring to make certain there are no lumps in the rice. Add the remaining ingredients. Cover with a close-fitting lid and when the water boils, place the pan in the oven.

4. Bake exactly 17 minutes. Remove the cover and discard the parsley, bay leaf, and thyme sprigs. Using a two-pronged fork, stir in the remaining butter. If the rice is not to be served immediately, keep covered in a warm place.

Yield: Four to six servings.

ONE OF THE RECURRENT QUESTIONS IN MY LIFE IS whether any "new" dishes have been created in the last century, and the answer, of course, is yes. If that question were phrased differently—Have any new principles of cookery been developed in the last hundred years?—the answer would probably be no. The creation of new dishes is limitless, and yet they are based on the same inevitable laws known to Antonin Carème and La Varenne. Techniques have been refined, but the principles remain the same. The so-called 60-minute dish that appears here has, to my knowledge, never been duplicated before the day it came out of my skillet. It came about because fresh scallops, one of the finest seafoods to be found in American waters (or the world, for that matter), had recently come into season and were available at the local fish market.

In the refrigerator on arrival home, there were the remaining ingredients inside—cream, white wine, shallots, butter, mushrooms, tomatoes, and parsley. You simply add them all together (a manner of speaking) and they turn out to be coquilles St. Jacques façon du chef—chef's fashion is a much used and easy method for naming dishes that are otherwise nameless.

Scallops, like many fish and seafoods, depend for their goodness and delicacy on rapid-fire cooking—a term not used loosely. You should cook them as quickly as possible over very high heat. Low heat and slow cooking will cause their valuable juices to flow from within them and thereby cause dryness and tastelessness.

Note, too, that you must never cook too many scallops at one time, which is to say they should never be crowded in a skillet. In fact, they should not even touch except as they are stirred or the skillet is shaken.

To go about preparing this less-than-60-minute meal with scallops, cook the recommended rice accompaniment. As it cooks, prepare the ingredients for the scallops. Cook the scallops at the very last minute before serving.

Coquilles St. Jacques Façon du Chef
(Scallops and mushrooms in cream sauce)

---

3 tablespoons butter	2 cups quartered or sliced fresh mushrooms
2 pints scallops	
Salt and freshly ground pepper to taste	12 cherry tomatoes
	¼ cup dry white wine
2 tablespoons finely chopped shallots	1 cup heavy cream
	1 tablespoon finely chopped parsley.

1. Heat 2 tablespoons butter in one large or two medium skillets. Take care that the scallops when added will not be crowded in either pan or pans. If they are too close together they will not "sear" properly and the juices will flow.

2. When the butter is quite hot and before it browns, add the scallops. Cook

over high heat, shaking the skillet and stirring. Sprinkle with salt and pepper. Cook about 1 or 2 minutes, until lightly golden all over. The less cooking time the better.

3. Using a slotted spoon, remove the scallops and keep them warm.

4. To the skillet add the shallots and cook briefly. Add the mushrooms and cherry tomatoes and cook, stirring often, about 1 minute. Add the wine and reduce the liquid by half.

5. Add the cream, salt and pepper to taste. Cook down over high heat about 3 minutes. Add the scallops. Swirl in the remaining tablespoon of butter. Sprinkle with chopped parsley and serve. Serve with rice.

Yield: Four servings.

Riz au Four avec Pignolats
(Baked rice with pine nuts)

2½	tablespoons butter	1	sprig fresh thyme or ¼ teaspoon
2	tablespoons minced onion		dried thyme
¼	teaspoon minced garlic	½	bay leaf
1	cup uncooked rice	⅛	teaspoon cayenne pepper or
1½	cups chicken broth		Tabasco sauce to taste
2	sprigs parsley	¼	cup toasted pine nuts.

1. Preheat the oven to 400 degrees.

2. Melt 1 tablespoon of the butter in a heavy saucepan and cook the onion and garlic, stirring with a wooden spoon, until the onion is translucent. Add the rice and stir briefly over low heat until all the grains are coated with butter.

3. Stir in the chicken broth, making sure there are no lumps in the rice. Add the parsley, thyme, bay leaf, and cayenne. Cover with a close-fitting lid and place in the oven.

4. Bake the rice exactly 17 minutes. Remove the cover and discard the parsley and thyme sprigs and bay leaf. Using a two-pronged fork, stir in the remaining butter and pine nuts. If the rice is not to be served immediately, keep covered in a warm place.

Yield: Four servings.

A N ACQUAINTANCE ONCE SAID THAT THE TIME TO start to cook is before you start to cook. The notion isn't all that nonsensical. A few mental gymnastics—anticipation of what must be done to prepare a meal—are highly in order.

With a little foresight, the body of the meal recommended here can be accomplished in less than half an hour.

The principal dish is scallops meunière, and these must be cooked in seconds or they will be overcooked and chewy and lose some of their natural flavor. They are to be served with pommes naturs or "natural" potatoes, which is to say simmered, drained and served as simply as possible with butter.

And again there are cherry tomatoes provençale, and these take the least effort of all. The stems are removed from the tomatoes and the tomatoes are cooked rapidly in butter and sprinkled with a touch of garlic.

A point to be made a hundred times is organization. Before you start to cook, chop what has to be chopped and measure what has to be measured. Bring out such pots and pans as are necessary for cooking—in this case two skillets (one for the scallops, one for the tomatoes) and a saucepan (for the potatoes).

Coquilles St. Jacques Meunière
(Scallops quick-fried in butter)

---

1 pint (1 pound) scallops	5 tablespoons peanut, vegetable, or
¼ cup milk	corn oil
Flour for dredging	4 tablespoons butter
Salt and freshly ground pepper to	Juice of half a lemon
taste	2 tablespoons finely chopped
	parsley.

1. Empty the scallops into a bowl and add the milk, stirring to coat. Let stand briefly.

2. Place the flour in a dish and add salt and pepper to taste. Blend well. Drain the scallops. Dredge them in flour and add them to a large sieve. Shake to remove excess flour. Scatter them onto a sheet of foil or wax paper so that they do not touch or they might stick together.

3. The scallops must be cooked over high heat without crowding. Heat 3 tablespoons of the oil and 1 tablespoon of butter in a large skillet. When the mixture is quite hot but not smoking, add half of the scallops, shaking and tossing them in the skillet so that they cook quickly and evenly until golden brown on all sides.

4. Use a slotted spoon and transfer the scallops to a hot platter. Add remaining 2 tablespoons of oil to the skillet and when it is quite hot, add the remaining scallops, shaking and tossing them in the skillet as before. When brown, transfer them to the platter with other scallops. Wipe out the skillet, add the

remaining butter and cook until lightly browned or the color of hazelnuts. Sprinkle over the scallops. Then sprinkle scallops with the lemon juice and chopped parsley.

Yield: Four servings.

Pommes Nature
(*Steamed potatoes*)

---

8 to 12 small, new, waxy potatoes or use 3 or 4 medium Idaho or Maine potatoes

Salt to taste
2 or 3 tablespoons melted butter.

1. Peel the potatoes. If the potatoes are small and new, leave them whole. If they are large, cut them into thirds or quarter them.
2. Place the potatoes in a saucepan, add water to cover and salt to taste. Bring to the boil and simmer until the potatoes are tender, about 10 to 15 minutes, depending on size.
3. Drain and pour melted butter over them. Serve hot.

Yield: Four servings.

Tomatoes Cerises à la Provençale
(*Cherry tomatoes with garlic*)

---

1 pint cherry tomatoes
2 tablespoons butter

Salt and freshly ground pepper to taste
1 clove garlic, finely minced.

1. Pluck off and discard the stems from the tomatoes.
2. Heat the butter in a skillet and when it is quite hot, add the tomatoes, tossing and shaking them in the skillet so that they cook evenly. Sprinkle with salt and pepper to taste and the garlic. Continue cooking briefly, just until the tomatoes are heated through. If they cook too long, they will become mushy in the center. It is better to undercook than overcook these tomatoes. Pour onto a platter and serve hot.

Yield: Four servings.

FOOD PATTERNS IN AMERICA ARE CURIOUS. THERE are wide taste differences between the North and South. Northerners can't understand the Southern passion for hominy grits and to many Southern palates, the bread known as a bagel is an oddity.

I think about these differences every time I indulge myself in one of the greatest foods from the sea. It would be hard to recall when I didn't prize mussels as one of the finest foods for feasting ever put in a kettle and steamed. Mussels, or moules as they are known in France, are choice fare. They are highly esteemed throughout Europe and for some reason are particularly associated with Belgium. Walk down any street in Brussels and you'll find yourself smelling the fine scent and aromatic, herbed steam from kettles of mussels which will be served in deep dishes with frites or French fried potatoes on the side.

Like many another food spoken of in this book, mussels depend for their inherent goodness on quick cooking. They should be cooked just until all the shells are open, no longer, or they will become poorly textured and lose part of their natural savor. Generally speaking, there are two liquids used for "steaming" mussels—dry white wine or just a touch of vinegar. Mussels give up a good deal of their own liquor as they cook and this is one of the finest broths known to any cook. Or to anyone who dines on them. A bit of water could also be used for the steaming but there will be a touch less flavor in the broth.

Mussels are, of course, more popular and available now than ever. A few years ago, most of the mussels cooked in this country were those used in restaurant kitchens. Or those sold to European immigrants and their descendants.

Fortunately, today almost all the best fish markets on much of the East Coast have an abundant supply of mussels.

Mussels, as the French and Belgians long ago discovered, are quite adequate for a meal unto themselves. Serve steamed mussels with a few crisp slices of garlic toast made with a crusty French or Italian loaf and olive oil, and the combination is a joy.

Moules Poulette
(Mussels in cream and egg sauce)

3 quarts cleaned, well-scrubbed mussels	½ cup dry white wine
3 tablespoons butter	¼ cup finely chopped parsley
¼ cup finely chopped onion	1 bay leaf
2 tablespoons finely chopped shallots	4 sprigs fresh thyme or ½ teaspoon dried thyme
Salt and freshly ground pepper to taste	½ cup heavy cream
	1 egg yolk
	Garlic toast (see recipe).

1. Drain the mussels and set aside.
2. Heat 3 tablespoons of butter in a heavy kettle or deep skillet and add the onion and shallots. Cook, stirring, until wilted.
3. Add the mussels, salt, pepper, wine, parsley, bay leaf, and thyme. Cover closely and bring to the boil. Cook about 10 minutes, shaking and tossing the mussels in the kettle to redistribute them. Cook mussels only until they are opened.
4. Beat the cream and yolk together until well blended.
5. Turn the heat off under the kettle and add the cream to the mussel liquid, stirring. Cover and let stand briefly.
6. Serve the mussels and liquid in hot soup bowls and sprinkle with parsley. Serve with garlic toast on the side.

Yield: Four servings.

Toast à l'Ail
(*Garlic toast*)

---

12 slices French bread
2 tablespoons olive oil

1 large clove garlic.

1. Preheat the broiler.
2. Brush the bread slices on both sides with oil.
3. Arrange the slices on a baking sheet and broil first on one side, then the other, until golden brown.
4. Remove the toast. Rub on both sides with garlic.

Yield: Twelve slices.

THERE MAY JUST POSSIBLY BE SOME SAVANTS IN this world who can explain the phenomenon of flavors that marry other flavors. Why, for example, is lime better suited to tropical foods than lemons? It's true whether it's a langouste grilled on the beach or a tropical drink. Why do those flavors and foods indigenous to Provence—tomatoes, garlic, and thyme—seem so natural in a dish? And why does that Mediterranean drink, the anise-flavored pastis, seem made to add a final fillip to the fish soups of Marseilles?

The thought was logical as applied to the dish on this page, stuffed lobsters, the liver and coral scraped away and blended with butter, bread crumbs, and tarragon. Tarragon goes with lobster like a rich consommé with port wine, or fresh foie gras with a well-chilled sauternes. It is, to put it one way, a marriage made in culinary heaven. And it was not without reason that this was for many years one of the most admired and widely ordered items on the menu of Le Pavillon Restaurant, respected at the time as one of the greatest French restaurants in America. I must have prepared the dish a thousand and more times during my twenty-five years as a chef.

I am amused to think that not one customer among those who ordered the dish knew how incredibly easy the dish is to prepare. Truth to tell, the only difficult thing about the dish is in the initial preparation of the lobsters. There are those who seem a bit squeamish about splitting a lobster down the back. The fact is, however, this can easily be done by the fish merchant although it should be done not too far in advance of the lobster being taken into the kitchen and made ready for the broiler. Should you have this done outside the home kitchen, by all means caution the butcher to save every morsel of the coral and liver (the soft, greenish or darker mass found in the chest cavity of the crustacean).

It is no exaggeration to state that the tarragon filling for the lobsters can be made in approximately ten minutes. The baking time is less than half an hour, and you and your guests can feast like kings. Such a simple thing as corn on the cob can be an excellent match for the dish.

Homards Farcis à l'Estragon
(*Tarragon stuffed lobsters*)

---

4 **lobsters weighing from about 1½ to 1¾ pounds**	2 **tablespoons finely chopped fresh tarragon or half the amount dried**
¼ **pound butter cut into chunks**	⅓ **cup peanut, vegetable, or corn oil, approximately**
1 **cup bread crumbs**	**Lemon wedges for garnish**
Salt and freshly ground pepper to taste	4 **tablespoons melted butter.**

1. Preheat the oven to 500 degrees or its highest setting.
2. Split the lobsters in half and remove the intestinal tract and the small,

hard sac near the eyes of the lobsters. Arrange the halves, split side up on a baking dish.

3. Remove and reserve the coral and liver (all the soft, edible interior portions of the lobster except the meat). Add them to a mixing bowl. Cut off the claws of each lobster. Arrange these on a separate baking dish.

4. To the coral and liver add the butter, bread crumbs, salt, pepper. Beat the mixture with a spoon or whisk until finely blended. Beat in the tarragon.

5. Spoon the mixture inside the cavities of each lobster. Do not cover the tail meat. Sprinkle the tail meat with salt and pepper.

6. Drizzle over each lobster half 2 teaspoons of oil.

7. Place the pans in the oven and bake 20 to 30 minutes.

8. Serve hot with lemon wedges and spoon the melted butter over all.

Yield: Four servings.

Maïs en Épi au Beurre de Poivre Vert
(Corn on the cob with green peppercorn butter)

---

8 ears fresh corn, shucked	**1 teaspoon chopped green peppercorns, available in specialty shops where fine imported foods are sold.**
4 tablespoons butter at room temperature	

1. Drop the corn into boiling salted water. Cover. When the water returns to the boil, remove from the heat. Let stand 5 minutes or longer, until ready to serve.

2. Meanwhile, beat the butter with the green peppercorns. Drain the corn and serve with the peppercorn butter.

Yield: Four servings.

DURING MY MANY YEARS AS CHEF AT THE LATE Pavillon Restaurant in New York, I was as fascinated by the food preferences of le patron, Henri Soulé, as by the tastes of any of the clientele. Cost in that kitchen meant very little in those bygone years; there was always a count or a duke or an emperor with an appetite to be appeased by grouse or breast of guinea hen or fresh foie gras or turbot freshly flown in from France.

Oddly, Mr. Soulé shunned the luxury foods and ate very simply, generally in mid-afternoon after the last customer had departed. I remember well that one of his favorite dishes was one of the simplest to make. And it was rich. This was fresh crabmeat cooked in a cream sauce and served over lightly broiled Smithfield ham on toast. There was good reason why he admired this dish. The crab was in a cream sauce lightly flavored with sherry wine, and although rich, it was easy to digest, and the Smithfield ham (when I make the dish today I generally use thinly sliced prosciutto which is more widely available) offered a highly complementary contrast in textures and flavor.

This is the sort of dish that, many years ago, would have been thought of as chafing dish cookery. It is done with great haste and little effort. To prepare it, cream is cooked down with a touch of chopped shallots and dry sherry. The crabmeat (already cooked, of course) is sautéed quickly in a little butter and the two elements are combined. Once toast is made and the prosciutto run under the broiler for a matter of seconds, the dish is ready to assemble and serve.

As with many fish and seafood dishes, lightly cooked cucumbers make an excellent foil for the crab dish. These, too, can be prepared in haste.

It almost goes without saying that this is an expensive dish, the cost of crab in most areas being somewhat elevated. It is best to buy the fresh crab in one-pound tins rather than the frozen kind which is more costly—perhaps because of the package. Either version will do. And if you don't have prosciutto, use a good grade of cooked ham, preferably Smithfield.

Fondue de Crabe avec Prosciutto sur Canapé
(*Creamed crab with prosciutto on toast*)

1	pound fresh crabmeat	1	egg yolk, lightly beaten
2	tablespoons butter	1	teaspoon Worcestershire sauce
2	tablespoons finely chopped shallots	4	slices toast
5	tablespoons dry sherry wine	8	thin slices prosciutto or other ham.
1	cup heavy cream		

1. Pick over the crab to remove all traces of shell and cartilage, if necessary. Drain well.

2. Heat half the butter in a heavy skillet and add the shallots. Cook, stirring, until wilted. Add 4 tablespoons of the wine and cook down. Reduce the liquid to about half.

3. Add the cream and cook down about 5 minutes over high heat.

4. Meanwhile, heat the remaining butter and add the crabmeat. Add 1 table-spoon of wine and heat thoroughly. Remove from the heat.

5. Add a few spoons of the hot cream to the egg yolk and stir to blend. Return this mixture to the cream, stirring rapidly. Remove from the heat.

6. Spoon and scrape the sauce over the crabmeat.

7. Prepare the toast and keep warm.

8. Heat the prosciutto under the broiler.

9. Place ham slices on toast and top with the crabmeat in cream sauce.

Yield: Four servings.

Concombres Sautés
(*Sautéed cucumbers*)

---

1 or 2 cucumbers, about 1 pound	**Salt and freshly ground pepper**
2 tablespoons butter	**to taste**
	1 tablespoon finely chopped dill.

1. The new so-called "gourmet" or "burpless" cucumber is good for this. Trim off the ends of the cucumbers.

2. Cut the cucumbers into one and one-half inch lengths. Cut each length in half. Peel the cucumber and cut away the soft center, leaving batons. Set aside.

3. Heat the butter in a skillet and add the cucumber batons. Sprinkle with salt and pepper. Cook, tossing and stirring, so that the pieces cook evenly. Cook for a total of about 2 minutes. Sprinkle with dill and serve hot.

Yield: Four servings.

THE COOKING TIME FOR MOST STUFFED DISHES IS fairly extended and hard to embrace within the time space of an hour or less. One of the great, easily made and hastily cooked dishes, however, is stuffed sole fillets. In case you wonder, it is true that many fish are sold over the fishmonger's counter and labeled sole. It is confusing, for the list may consist of such things as grey sole, lemon sole, flounder, and so on.

The important thing in preparing the stuffed sole outlined here is the quality, which is to say, the freshness of the fish and the size of the fillets. To prepare the dish properly, you must ask your fishman to sell you small, skinless, boneless fish fillets and they must be approximately the same size. The reason for this is obvious. To prepare the dish you place the fillets on a flat surface and sprinkle with salt and pepper. You add a small mound of filling atop half the fillets. You then cover each of the "stuffed" fillets with a second fillet so that the contours of the fillets match all around.

The preparation of the stuffing is simplicity itself. You simply blend crabmeat (that has been picked over to remove all chance bits of shell and cartilage) with an egg yolk and seasonings plus a minimum amount of fresh bread crumbs to lighten the texture.

The cooking of the dish is nearly as quick as abracadabra. When the fillets have been filled and are ready, you arrange them on a buttered baking dish. You sprinkle dry white wine and a few chopped shallots all around the fish and bring the wine to a boil on top of the stove. This is to expedite the cooking. The dish is then placed under a preheated broiler and cooked just until the top of each fillet is golden and the fish flakes easily. The total oven time is about six or eight minutes.

This is a dish of such simplicity and ease that it allows more than ample time to prepare an accompaniment. Zucchini with summer herbs (you could use dried) is an excellent side dish for the fish.

Sole Farcie au Crab
(Sole or flounder stuffed with crab)

8   skinless, boneless fillets of sole or flounder, each of approximately the same size, about 1¼ pounds total weight
Salt and freshly ground pepper to taste ·

1   cup crabmeat, preferably lump crabmeat, picked over to remove all trace of shell and cartilage

1   egg yolk

2   tablespoons finely chopped parsley

1   tablespoon fine, fresh bread crumbs

4   tablespoons melted butter

2   tablespoons finely chopped shallots

½   cup dry white wine.

1. Preheat the broiler.

2. Place four fillets, skinned side up, on a flat surface. Sprinkle with salt and pepper.

3. Blend the crab, egg yolk, parsley, bread crumbs, salt, and pepper in a bowl. Center equal portions of this filling on the top of the fillets on the flat surface. Smooth the filling over, leaving a slight margin around it.

4. Sprinkle the remaining fillets with salt and pepper. Arrange them, skinned side down, over the filling. Press lightly around the sides.

5. Rub the bottom of a heat-proof baking dish with half the butter. Arrange the stuffed fish over it. Sprinkle the shallots around the fish.

6. Melt the remaining butter and brush 'the fillets with it. Pour the wine around the fillets.

7. Place the baking dish on the stove. Bring the wine to the boil and let simmer about 15 seconds. Place under the broiler about seven or eight inches from the source of heat. As it cooks, watch closely to prevent burning. Turn the baking dish so that the fish broils evenly. The total broiling time is about 6 to 8 minutes.

Yield: Four servings.

Courgettes aux Herbes d'Été
(*Zucchini with summer herbs*)

1	pound zucchini	1	tablespoon chopped parsley
3	tablespoons olive oil	½	tablespoon chopped chives
	Salt and freshly ground pepper	1	tablespoon chopped dill
	to taste	½	teaspoon chopped tarragon
1½	tablespoons butter	1	tablespoon finely chopped fresh
1	teaspoon chopped garlic		basil.

1. Rinse the zucchini and pat dry. Trim off the ends but do not peel. Cut the zucchini into thin slices about an eighth of an inch thick. There should be about 6 cups.

2. Heat the oil in a skillet and when it is quite hot, add the zucchini. Cook over relatively high heat, shaking the skillet, tossing and stirring gently with a spatula to turn the slices. Add salt and pepper to taste. Cook about 5 to 7 minutes. Drain in a sieve. Do not wipe out the skillet.

3. To the skillet add the butter. When melted and hot, return the zucchini. Add the garlic and herbs. Add salt to taste. Toss and serve hot.

Yield: Six servings.

ONE OF THE MOST INTRIGUING ASPECTS OF INTERnational cooking are the variations on themes. To my mind, there isn't a western country that does not have what we know in French as a sauce verte or green sauce.

Green sauce, the name, derives, of course, from the use of green herbs which give the color—and freshness—to the sauces. The green herbs generally contain chopped parsley, chives, scallions, and tarragon. In French, more often than not, we also include chervil (which flourishes in my garden on Long Island), but oddly the herb is not much known on these shores.

I thought of this once while dining at a very plain but excellent restaurant in Puerto Rico, La Fragua in San Juan. There we dined on an elegant dish of mero or pollock in green sauce, Spanish-style. This green sauce was unlike the traditional French green sauce. It was cooked quickly with the fish, which had been dusted in flour and cooked in the sauce.

Recently this dish was reproduced in my own kitchen, but substituting clams (the chef of La Fragua told me that clams are often served with the sauce) for the fish. The salsa verde in this case contains chopped garlic (the flavor should be somewhat pronounced), parsley, and scallions, plus white wine and a touch of hot red pepper.

This is a dish that must cook in seconds. The only time-consuming aspect is the opening of the clams, but this could be done by the market. These clams go well with rice cooked with green peppers. The rice, which cooks in less than twenty minutes, requires more time than the clams in preparation.

Almejas con Salsa Verde
(*Hot clams with green sauce*)

24 to 32 littleneck clams, the smaller the better	¾ cup fresh or canned clam juice
Freshly ground pepper to taste	⅛ teaspoon hot dried red pepper flakes
¼ cup oil	1 tablespoon arrowroot or
1 tablespoon finely chopped garlic	cornstarch
¼ cup finely chopped scallions	Salt to taste
½ cup plus 1 tablespoon dry white wine	¼ cup chopped parsley.

1. Open the clams on the half-shell, discarding the top shell. Leave the clam attached by its muscle to the bottom shell. Be sure to collect all the liquid that accumulates. There should be about ¾ cup.

2. Heat the oil in a large skillet and when it is very hot, add the garlic and clams on the half-shell. Cook, stirring, over very high heat about 30 seconds. No longer. If they cook longer, the clams will toughen. Add the scallions and ½ cup of wine. Add the clam juice and pepper flakes. Let boil.

3. Quickly blend the remaining tablespoon of wine and arrowroot and stir it

into the clams and sauce, stirring until thickened. Add a little salt. Sprinkle with parsley and stir. Toss and serve in small soup bowls or small bowls with rims. Serve with rice.

Yield: Four servings.

Riz aux Piments
(Rice with peppers)

---

1 tablespoon butter	1 cup rice
3 tablespoons finely chopped onion	1½ cups water
½ cup diced pimento or roasted, peeled sweet pepper	Salt to taste.

1. Heat the butter in a saucepan and add the onion. Cook until wilted and add the diced pepper, rice, water and salt.
2. Bring to the boil and cover closely. Cook exactly 17 minutes. Remove from the heat and keep warm until ready to serve.

Yield: Four servings.

IF I WERE TO NAME THE ONE INGREDIENT THAT IS more often than not elaborately overcooked in American kitchens—be they in private homes or in restaurants—it would certainly be shrimp. It is beyond my concept how any home cook and certainly any professional chef refuses to understand that only the briefest simmering, a minute or two, to keep their texture firm and intact—not soggy, flabby, and fibrous—is necessary.

It is not only their brief cooking time that should give shrimp a special appeal to those who would cook in a hasty time period. Shrimp happen to be one of the great food delicacies of the world. I can recall several happy occasions when in mid-summer we have dined on a shrimp feast with family and friends. Generally out of doors, at a table covered with newspapers to receive the shells, and with only a hot butter and lemon sauce in which to dip the shrimp—freshly steamed with beer and seasonings—as they were peeled.

Shrimps, cooked and left in the shell, can be prepared in a thousand different ways when cold. From a basic shrimp cocktail with a typical American cocktail sauce (ketchup, lemon juice, Worcestershire sauce, horseradish, and hot pepper sauce) to blendings with mayonnaise or vinaigrette sauces. One of the best of these sauces is the one known as rémoulade. This sauce, incidentally, is not the same as that in Louisiana or New Orleans cooking. That sauce, although tasty and excellent, is made with oil, lemon or vinegar, chopped celery, and green onions. The classic rémoulade has a mayonnaise base and contains chopped small sour pickles, chopped anchovy, capers, parsley, and tarragon.

Crevettes à la Bière
(Shrimp with beer)

3 pounds shrimps in the shell	1 bay leaf
4 cloves garlic, peeled	6 sprigs fresh parsley
6 allspice	2 sprigs fresh dill
1 hot, dried red pepper	1 12-ounce can beer.
Salt and freshly ground pepper to taste	

1. Combine all the ingredients in a heavy skillet and cover closely. Bring to the boil.

2. Let the shrimps simmer 2 minutes and remove from the heat. Serve in the shell, letting each guest peel his own. Serve hot with individual portions of melted lemon butter.

Yield: Eight servings.

Beurre au Citron
(*Lemon butter*)

¼ pound butter	Salt and freshly ground pepper to
Juice of half a lemon	taste
1 teaspoon Worcestershire sauce	1 clove garlic, unpeeled but lightly crushed.

1. Heat the butter until quite hot and almost bubbling.
2. Add the remaining ingredients and stir. Serve hot with shrimp steamed in beer.

Yield: About half a cup.

Crevettes Rémoulade
(*Shrimp in mayonnaise sauce*)

1½ pounds shrimp cooked in the shell (see recipe for shrimp cooked in beer)	1 tablespoon anchovy paste or chopped flat anchovy fillets
1 egg yolk	2 tablespoons finely chopped parsley
1 teaspoon imported mustard	2 teaspoons chopped fresh
2 teaspoons tarragon vinegar	tarragon or ½ teaspoon dried
Salt and freshly ground pepper to taste	Juice of half a lemon
1 cup peanut, vegetable, or corn oil	8 leaves Boston lettuce
1 tablespoon finely chopped capers	2 hard-cooked eggs, peeled and quartered
3 tablespoons finely chopped, drained cornichons (small, imported sour pickles)	8 cherry tomatoes.

1. Peel and devein the shrimp. Leave them whole or cut them in half. Set aside.
2. Put the yolk into a bowl and add the mustard, vinegar, salt, and pepper. Start beating with a wire whisk and gradually add the oil, beating vigorously with the whisk.
3. Squeeze the capers in a clean cloth to extract their liquid. Add the capers to the mayonnaise. Add the cornichons, parsley, and tarragon. Blend well.
4. Put shrimp in a bowl and sprinkle lemon juice over. Add the sauce and blend well.
5. Arrange two lettuce leaves on each of four plates. Spoon equal portions of the shrimp onto the lettuce. Garnish with hard-cooked eggs and cherry tomatoes.

Yield: Four servings.

THE FIRST ANECDOTE I EVER HEARD ABOUT AMERI-
can cooking after I came to this country in 1939 had to do
with that hastily made preparation called shrimp, lobster, or
crabmeat, Newberg. It is a story I have heard in several versions since then, but
basically it concerns a customer named Wenberg who dined often at the old
Delmonico's restaurant in Manhattan during the last quarter of the nineteenth
century. Some say he created a dish with cream and egg yolks and sherry
which he offered the chef and which subsequently was listed on menus as
seafood Wenberg.

For years, it was said, Mr. Wenberg enjoyed a considerable rapport with the
management and his name became famous and synonymous with the dish.
Then one day he became involved in a heated argument with the restaurant's
owner. He was banned from the premises and the dish was rechristened Newberg.

That history may be a bit of a fabrication, but the dish itself is excellent.
Much of its success depends on quick cooking. There are actually two ways of
making it, one with flour as a thickening agent, the other with only egg yolks
used to thicken. I prefer the latter.

Not too many decades ago, chafing-dish cookery was a fad in this country,
somewhat akin to fondue cookery today. It isn't surprising that the Newberg
dishes were among the best known of the chafing-dish creations.

Although lobster or crabmeat may be used in preparing this dish, I find that
shrimp are more conveniently cooked in the sauce from the raw state. In the
long run, the shrimp provide more flavor. Note that the cooking time for the
dish is reckoned in minutes, thus it will be best to start to prepare an accompaniment such as rice, which requires longer cooking, a few minutes in advance.

Crevettes ''Newberg''
(Shrimp in cream sauce)

2	tablespoons butter	1	tablespoon paprika
1½	pounds shelled and deveined shrimp (1¾ pounds with shells on)	1	tablespoon finely chopped shallots
	Salt and freshly ground pepper to taste	⅓	cup dry sherry wine
		1½	cups heavy cream
		2	egg yolks.

1. Melt the butter in a large, heavy skillet and add the shrimp. Cook briefly
and sprinkle with salt, pepper, and paprika.

2. Sprinkle with shallots and stir. Add the wine and stir. As soon as the
shrimp have lost their raw look, after a minute or so, transfer the shrimp to
another skillet and cover. Keep warm.

3. Reduce the pan liquid by half and add 1¼ cups of cream. Cook about 5
minutes over high heat.

4. Beat the yolks with the remaining heavy cream and add it to the cream sauce, stirring rapidly. Bring almost but not quite to the boil. Add the shrimp and reheat.

Yield: Four servings.

Riz avec Pois et Persil
(*Rice with parsley and peas*)

3	tablespoons butter		Salt and freshly ground pepper to taste
2	tablespoons chopped onion		Tabasco sauce to taste
1	cup raw rice	1	cup frozen peas
1½	cups water	2	tablespoons finely chopped parsley.
1	bay leaf		

1. Melt 2 tablespoons of the butter in a saucepan and add the onion. Cook until wilted. Add the rice and stir briefly.
2. Add the water, bay leaf, salt, pepper, and Tabasco.
3. Bring to the boil. Cover and simmer 20 minutes.
4. Meanwhile, combine the peas with the remaining butter, salt and pepper to taste. No liquid. Heat, shaking the saucepan to redistribute the peas so that they cook evenly, about 1 minute.
5. Add the peas and parsley to the rice and stir to blend.

Yield: Four servings.

ALTHOUGH PROFESSIONAL CHEFS IN FRENCH kitchens adhere fairly strictly to the precepts of Auguste Escoffier in classic cooking, there is a good deal of flexibility in the preparation of untraditional dishes. Many dishes develop, particularly in home kitchens, through the simple expedient of what happens to be at hand.

Once, because of experiments of a previous day, I found available two seemingly disparate ingredients: a pound of shrimp and a couple of chicken breasts.

The combination of seafood and meat, including poultry, is not all that common in French cookery, although the original chicken Marengo used crayfish, as well as a fried egg, as a garnish. Internationally, there are many dishes that combine the two: the veal Oskar of Sweden, garnished with crayfish or shrimp; the many dishes in Chinese cooking, including stir-fried kidneys with shrimp, and a Portuguese specialty that blends clams and pork.

As it turned out that recent morning, shrimp and chicken in a light curry sauce can be exceptionally palatable and quickly made. The dish is highly compatible with noodles combined with a fine julienne of carrots tossed with butter and a smattering of finely chopped dill (the carrot and dill being bonuses of the previous day).

The only time-consuming element in the preparation of the curry is peeling the shrimp and skinning and boning the chicken. The actual cooking time of the curry is considerably less than thirty minutes, leaving ample time to prepare the carrots and dill for the quickly cooked noodles.

With the curry, I would invariably serve cold beer, and no doubt, a tossed green salad.

Crevettes et Poulet au Kari
(Curried shrimp and chicken)

1	pound raw shrimp, peeled and deveined	1	tablespoon tomato paste
2	chicken breasts, about 1½ pounds	½	cup banana cut into ½-inch cubes
4	tablespoons butter	1	cup peeled apple cut into ½-inch cubes
½	cup finely chopped onion	2	cups chicken broth
¼	teaspoon finely chopped garlic		Salt and freshly ground pepper to taste.
½	cup finely diced celery		
2	tablespoons curry powder		

1. Peel the shrimp, rinse, and drain well. There should be about 2 cups. Set aside.

2. Pull away the skin of the chicken breasts. Cut the meat from the bones. Discard the skin and bones or use the scraps for soups. Cut the meat into one-inch cubes. There should be about 3 cups; set aside.

3. Heat half the butter in a small casserole and add the onion and garlic. Cook briefly and add the celery. Cook, stirring, about 1 minute. Sprinkle with

curry powder and stir. Add the tomato paste and stir. Add the banana and apple. Stir.

4. Add the broth and stir to blend. Add salt to taste. Simmer about 10 minutes.

5. Heat the remaining butter in a saucepan and add the chicken. Sprinkle with salt and pepper and cook, stirring occasionally, about 2 to 3 minutes. Add the shrimp and sprinkle with salt and pepper. Cook, stirring, about 2 minutes.

6. Meanwhile, pour the curry mixture into the container of a food processor or electric blender. If a blender is used, this may have to be done in two or more stages.

7. Pour the curry sauce over the chicken and shrimp. Bring to the boil and simmer about 2 minutes, stirring occasionally.

Yield: Four servings.

Nouilles à la Scandinave
(Noodles with carrots and dill)

1	small carrot, trimmed and scraped	5	tablespoons butter
½	pound fine noodles		Freshly ground pepper to taste
	Salt to taste	1	tablespoon chopped fresh dill.

1. Cut the carrot lengthwise into quarter-inch-thick slices. Stack the slices and cut them into quarter-inch-thick strips. Cut the strips into two-inch lengths. There should be about ⅔ cup.

2. Put the noodles on to cook in boiling salted water, to the desired degree of doneness.

3. Heat 2 tablespoons of the butter in a small skillet and add the carrots. Sprinkle with salt and pepper. Cook about 2 minutes, stirring.

4. When the noodles are ready, drain them quickly but thoroughly. Spoon them onto the carrots. Add the dill and remaining butter and toss quickly. Serve hot.

Yield: Four servings.

WE HAVE DISCUSSED THE VIRTUES OF SHRIMP FOR cooking à la minute. Shrimp should be cooked at relatively high heat, whether in a skillet or in the oven, so that they change from a grayish, translucent state to achieve a red outer coating and a snow white interior as rapidly as possible. The moment they become piping hot throughout, they are ready to be served, although a minute or two beyond that point will probably not make them unsavory.

I have had pointed out to me on several occasions various regional recipes across the United States that call for cooking shrimp half an hour or even longer. Like most things in cooking, I presume these recipes are designed for people who don't really care about food. They are, in my opinion, in much the same category as people who prefer their prize beef well-done.

Shrimp have a wholly admirable versatility. They adapt—in the best of taste—to a multitude of herbs, spices, and other seasonings.

Shrimp, like many fish soups of France, are totally complemented with the addition of a spoonful or so of the anise-flavored liqueur known as pernod or ricard. Either liqueur gives a curious and compelling flavor that is almost exotic and certainly welcome.

Shrimp in almost any form are also complemented by rice and that is recommended here. It is best to go about the preparation and cooking of the rice accompaniment before you tackle the shrimp.

Crevettes au Pernod
(Shrimp sauté with pernod)

1½ pounds shrimp	2 tablespoons pernod, ricard, or
3 tablespoons butter	other anise-flavored liqueur
2 tablespoons finely chopped shallots	¾ cup heavy cream
	Salt and freshly ground pepper to taste

1. Peel the shrimp but leave the last tail segment intact. Split the shrimp down the back. Wash the shrimp under cold running water to remove the black vein down the back. Drain well.

2. Heat the butter in a skillet and add the shrimp and shallots. Cook, shaking and stirring and tossing the shrimp in the skillet. Cook quickly until shrimp are pink all over, 3 or 4 minutes.

3. Add the pernod and stir. Using a slotted spoon, remove the shrimp to a warm dish. Add the cream to the skillet and cook over high heat about 1 minute. Add salt and pepper to taste. Return the shrimp to the sauce and cook just to heat through. Serve with rice.

Yield: Four servings.

Riz au Four
(*Baked rice*)

2½	tablespoons butter	1	sprig thyme or ¼ teaspoon dried	
2	tablespoons minced onion		thyme	
¼	teaspoon minced garlic	½	bay leaf	
1	cup uncooked rice	⅛	teaspoon cayenne pepper or	
1½	cups chicken broth		Tabasco to taste.	
2	sprigs parsley			

1. Preheat the oven to 400 degrees.

2. Melt 1 tablespoon of the butter in a heavy ovenproof saucepan and cook the onion and garlic, stirring with a wooden spoon, until the onion is translucent. Add the rice and stir briefly over low heat until all the grains are coated with butter.

3. Stir in the broth, making sure there are no lumps in the rice. Add the parsley, thyme, bay leaf, and cayenne. Cover with close-fitting lid and place in the oven.

4. Bake the rice exactly 17 minutes. Remove the cover and discard the parsley and thyme sprigs. Using a two-pronged fork, stir in the remaining butter.

Yield: Four servings.

COOK A GOURMET MEAL IN THE TIME OFTEN
required to cope with one dish? With inventiveness and a little
planning, there is no reason why a working wife, a bachelor,
or a husband who likes to cook cannot prepare an elegant meal in under an hour.

Regardless of time, an inventive and qualified chef has two distinct avenues
to follow: the classical and traditional or the improvisational. If he's adventurous, he'll indulge in both.

The age-old question is, of course, whether or not an established chef follows recipes when he or she cooks. The answer is no, but in a qualified sense.
In strictly traditional matters, most chefs still refer to Escoffier, who has been
called the Moses of classic French cookery.

The "quick" recipe has nothing to do with the classics, but, rather, is concerned with improvisation: I was challenged by a friend, who likes to serve
margaritas before dinner, to concoct a dish with the same ingredients as that
potent Mexican libation. My answer to the challenge was shrimp margarita. It
has the same ingredients as the drink, with just one exception—the Cointreau
or triple sec, either of which is too sweet, has been omitted.

One of the things essential for "compact" cookery, so to speak, is coordination. Plainly cooked rice—and not minute rice, which takes as much time as
regular rice and doesn't taste as good—can be cooked according to package directions while the shrimp is cooking. Guava shells are available in cans. Cooking in less than an hour, which most of the people I know do on a Monday-through-Friday basis—takes only a little foresight.

Crevettes ''Margarita''
(Shrimp with tequila)

¾ pound (about 20) raw shrimp	1 tablespoon finely chopped shallots
¼ cup lime juice	¼ cup tequila
Salt and freshly ground pepper to	¾ cup heavy cream
taste	1 tablespoon finely chopped cilantro
1 small, ripe, unblemished avocado	or Chinese parsley (see note),
2 tablespoons butter	optional.

1. Shell and devein the shrimp and "butterfly" them; that is, split them
partly down the back and flatten lightly. Place the shrimp in a bowl and add the
lime juice, salt and pepper. Let stand briefly until ready to cook.

2. Peel the avocado and cut it into half-inch thick slices. Discard the pit.
Use as soon as possible or the flesh will discolor.

3. Heat the butter in a skillet and when it is quite hot but not smoking, add
the shrimp, stirring rapidly, and cook about 2 minutes. Sprinkle with the shallots and cook, stirring, about 10 seconds. Add the tequila. Take care, for the
tequila may flare up. Add the cream and cook over high heat about 1 minute.
Add salt and pepper to taste. Add the avocado and cook just until the slices are

piping hot, no longer. Using a slotted spoon, transfer the shrimp and avocado pieces to hot serving dishes. Bring the sauce to a full rolling boil for about 30 seconds and add the chopped cilantro. Spoon the sauce over the shrimp and avocado. Serve with rice.

Yield: Four servings.

Note: Cilantro or Chinese parsley is available in markets that specialize in Chinese, Spanish, or Mexican greens.

Sauce Vinaigrette aux Herbes
(Vinaigrette sauce with herbs)

1 tablespoon imported mustard such as Dijon or Düsseldorf	1½ tablespoons red wine vinegar
Salt and freshly ground pepper	¼ teaspoon crushed oregano
to taste	½ teaspoon ground cumin
½ teaspoon finely chopped garlic	4½ tablespoons olive oil.

1. Place the mustard in a bowl and add the salt, pepper, garlic, vinegar, oregano, and cumin. Stir well with a wire whisk.
2. Gradually add the oil, stirring rapidly with the whisk. Serve over chilled salad greens.

Yield: About one-third cup.

OOKING IS AN ADVENTURE, AND ONE OF THE most intriguing aspects of it can be innovations that come about by blending foods on an international scale. One of the best and most hastily made Greek dishes is known as garides me feta—shrimp baked with feta cheese. There are many variations on the dish—dill is sometimes added or parsley or capers. Some cooks also add a dash of that potent white spirit, ouzo, which provides a nice and unexpected anise or licorice taste to the dish.

On a recent evening, it was decided that such a dish, with its distinctly Mediterranean flavor, would be compatible with an Italian pasta. It was. Shrimp with feta cheese and rigatoni are an excellent match.

Although a leafy green salad tossed with a neat blend of oil and vinegar, and salt and pepper would be suitable for a meal with this as a main course, cold green beans vinaigrette would be a highly palatable accompaniment, particularly when the first crop of green beans are on the market.

To prepare a meal in an hour's span with this salad and the shrimp dish as the main components, the beans should be put on to cook first. And timed. As the beans cook, proceed to the tomato sauce and shrimp. The rigatoni can be cooked during the final ten or fifteen minutes in which the shrimp with feta cheese are heating in the oven.

Although rigatoni is proposed for this menu, almost any short, tubular pasta could be used, pasta such as penne or ziti. Elbow macaroni would not be suitable, for the pieces of pasta are too small to complement the medium-size shrimp in the recipe.

Crevettes à la Mode Grecque avec Rigatoni
(Shrimp Greek-style with rigatoni)

5	tablespoons olive oil	1	teaspoon dried, crumbled oregano
1	teaspoon finely chopped garlic		
2	cups peeled, cubed tomatoes, preferably fresh, about 1 pound whole	1½	pounds medium-size fresh shrimp, about 48
½	cup dry white wine	⅛	teaspoon hot red pepper flakes
	Salt and freshly ground pepper to taste	⅓	pound rigatoni, ziti, spirals, and so on
¼	cup finely chopped fresh basil leaves	½	pound crumbled feta cheese.

1. Heat 2 tablespoons of the oil in a skillet and add the garlic. Cook briefly, stirring, and add the tomatoes. Cook about 1 minute and add the wine, salt, and pepper. Add the basil and oregano.

2. Cook over moderate heat about 10 minutes.

3. Meanwhile, peel and devein the shrimp, leaving the last tail segment on. Sprinkle the shrimp with salt and pepper.

[160]

4. Heat the remaining 3 tablespoons of oil in a large skillet and add the shrimp. Cook quickly, about 1 minuet, just until shrimp turn red. Stir as they cook. Sprinkle with red pepper flakes.

5. Preheat the oven to 400 degrees.

6. Spoon the shrimp and any pan juices into a small baking dish. Sprinkle the shrimp with the crumbled feta cheese and spoon the tomato sauce over. Place the baking dish in the oven and bake 10 minutes until piping hot.

7. Meanwhile, cook the rigatoni according to taste and drain. Do not overcook. Serve the hot rigatoni with the shrimp mixture spooned over.

Yield: Four servings.

Haricots Verts et Oignons Vinaigrette
(Green beans and onions vinaigrette)

½ pound green beans	1 teaspoon imported mustard such
Salt to taste	as Dijon or Düsseldorf
1 tablespoon finely chopped parsley	3 tablespoons olive oil
2 teaspoons red wine vinegar	Freshly ground pepper to taste
	12 thin red onion rings.

1. Trim or snap off the ends of the beans. If the beans have "strings," pull them off. Otherwise, leave the beans whole. Drop them into boiling salted water and cook until crisp-tender, about 5 minutes. Do not overcook.

2. Drain and run the beans briefly under cold running water. Drain again while the beans are still warm.

3. Put the parsley, vinegar, and mustard in a mixing bowl. Add the olive oil, salt and pepper to taste, stirring rapidly with a whisk.

4. Put the beans in a serving dish. Garnish with the onion rings. Spoon the sauce over and toss lightly.

Yield: Four servings.

THERE IS ONE ARTICLE OF FOOD, OFTEN FOUND ON menus and much admired in America, that is almost if not impossible to define with any sense of total accuracy. That food is scampi. It is generally agreed that they are prawns, another name that is used loosely in this country to describe large shrimp.

European encyclopedias sometimes state that scampi is the Italian word for what are known in Ireland as Dublin Bay prawns, and then add that the Italian version is twice as large as the Dublin Bay version.

For simplicity's sake it seems reasonable to conclude that any recipe calling for "scampi" or "prawns" in this country can be properly made with shrimp, the larger the better.

The most frequent preparation of scampi in Italian restaurants in America is a hastily made dish in which the shrimp (or prawns or scampi) are bathed in a blend of olive oil, garlic according to the chef's conscience, plus parsley and oregano. And, at times, a sprinkling of fresh bread crumbs to contribute a bit of texture.

Once the mixture is blended (the shrimp, oil, and seasonings) there only remains the necessity to arrange the shellfish in a single layer in a baking dish (along with the marinating ingredients) and to broil—without even turning them—until the shrimp have lost their raw, greyish-white look and turn bright red on the exterior. Incidentally, the shrimp and marinade could easily be blended several hours in advance (not overnight) and refrigerated until ready to toss under the broiler.

An excellent accompaniment for broiled scampi are curried sweet red peppers (bell peppers or "frying" peppers). This is a dish, too, that requires only a brief few minutes for cooking. While these two elements could easily suffice for a supper, the addition of rice would round out the meal rather nicely.

Crevettes "Scampi"
(Shrimp broiled in olive oil and seasonings)

2 pounds shrimp, the larger the better	⅛ teaspoon crushed red pepper flakes
½ cup olive oil	½ teaspoon dried crushed oregano
2 teaspoons finely chopped garlic	2 tablespoons fine fresh bread crumbs
2 tablespoons finely chopped parsley	Salt and freshly ground pepper to taste

1. Preheat the broiler to high.

2. Split the shrimp down the back side. Rinse and pat dry. Or peel them but leave the last tail segment intact. Rinse and drain well.

3. Add the remaining ingredients to the shrimp and toss to coat evenly and well.

4. Line a baking dish with foil and arrange the shrimp over it.

5. Place the shrimp under the broiler about three to four inches from the source of heat. Broil 5 to 6 minutes. It is not necessary to turn the shrimp as they cook. Baste the shrimp and serve hot with curried sweet peppers and rice.

Yield: Four servings.

Julienne de Poivrons au Kari
(*Curried sweet pepper strips*)

2 pounds sweet green or red peppers	**Salt and freshly ground pepper to taste**
4 tablespoons olive oil	**1 to 2 tablespoons curry powder.**

1. Cut the peppers in half. Scrape away and discard the seeds, white inner veins, and core. Place each pepper half, cut side down, on a flat surface and cut into half-inch crosswise strips (julienne). There should be about 8 cups.

2. Using a very large skillet, heat the oil and when it is hot but not quite smoking, add the pepper strips, salt, pepper, and curry powder.

3. Cook, stirring over high heat about 4 to 6 minutes, or until barely cooked. When ready, the pepper strips should be crisp-tender.

Yield: Four servings.

Riz au Four
(*Baked rice*)

3 tablespoons butter	**Salt and freshly ground pepper to taste**
⅓ cup minced onion	
1½ cups uncooked rice	**2 sprigs thyme or half a teaspoon dried thyme**
2¼ cups water	
2 sprigs parsley	**½ bay leaf**
	Tabasco sauce to taste.

1. Preheat the oven to 400 degrees.

2. Melt half the butter in a saucepan and add the onion. Cook, stirring, until wilted. Add the rice and stir to blend.

3. Add the water, stirring to make certain there are no lumps in the rice. Add the remaining ingredients. Cover with a close-fitting lid and when the water boils, place the pan in the oven.

4. Bake exactly 17 minutes. Remove the cover and discard the parsley, bay leaf, and thyme sprigs. Using a two-pronged fork, stir in the remaining butter. If the rice is not to be served immediately, keep covered in a warm place.

Yield: Four to six servings.

MOST PROFESSIONAL CHEFS THAT I KNOW ARE amused with the idea that the Creole cooking of Louisiana in general, and of New Orleans in particular, has a solid French foundation. While it is indisputable that the French influence is present in that highly specialized form of American cookery, it is, in some of its terminology and practices, anything but a carbon copy of the French.

That is by no means to disparage Creole cookery. Far from it. The gumbos, the fabulous assortment of oyster dishes such as Rockefeller and Bienville, and the trout Marguery as made in New Orleans are excellent. But they are regional and admirable creations. Consider one classic case. A true rémoulade sauce in French cookery is made with a mayonnaise base to which is added mustard, anchovy paste, capers, chopped cornichons, and herbs. The most popular rémoulade sauce in New Orleans is served on shrimp rémoulade. That version is made with an unthickened oil and vinegar base—a salad dressing really—to which is added chopped scallions, celery, parsley, Creole mustard, and paprika. And sometimes, anchovy paste. Perhaps it is nitpicking, but that, in basic French terminology, is more a ravigote than a rémoulade.

One of the best, tastiest, and most easily made of Creole dishes is shrimps Creole. This starts with a combination of chopped onion, green pepper, and celery (the base of a good many Creole dishes). Plus tomatoes. It is definitely not French although it could be vaguely related to the Midi or Provence in France where red, ripe tomatoes abound.

Shrimp Creole is an ideal dish for 60-minute cookery. After the vegetables have simmered briefly (they must retain their texture), the tomatoes are added and cooked for a short time. The shrimp are cooked separately, the two elements are combined, and that—with the addition of that traditional Southern seasoning, hot pepper sauce—is all there is to it. Serve with a platter of simply made boiled, buttered rice (in French kitchens we call that Riz Créole) and that is a very good balance.

Crevettes à la Créole
(Shrimps in Creole sauce)

1¼ pounds raw shrimp in the shell
4 tablespoons butter
2 cups finely chopped onion
2 teaspoons minced garlic
1 cup chopped celery
2 cups green pepper, cored, seeded and cut into 1-inch cubes
   Salt and freshly ground pepper to taste

3 cups fresh tomatoes cut into small cubes, or use an equal amount of canned imported tomatoes
4 tablespoons finely chopped parsley
1 bay leaf
   Tabasco sauce to taste.

1. Peel the shrimp and remove the intestinal tract down the back. Set the shrimp aside.

2. Heat half the butter in a saucepan and add the onion and garlic. Cook about 5 minutes without browning. Add the celery and green pepper. Add salt and pepper to taste.

3. Cook about 4 minutes, stirring often. Do not overcook. The vegetables should remain crisp.

4. Add the tomatoes, parsley, and bay leaf. Cover. At the boil cook about 10 minutes. Add Tabasco sauce to taste.

5. In a skillet heat the remaining butter and the shrimp. Sprinkle with salt and pepper. Stir. Cook only about 1 minute, or until the shrimp lose their red color.

6. Spoon the tomato mixture over the shrimp and stir. Bring to the boil. Serve piping hot with Creole rice.

Yield: Four servings.

Riz Créole
(*Boiled rice*)

4	cups water	1	cup long grain rice
	Salt and freshly ground pepper to taste	1	tablespoon butter
		1	teaspoon lemon juice.

1. Bring the water to a boil in a saucepan and add the salt and rice. When the water returns to the boil, let the rice boil vigorously in the water.

2. Let cook exactly 17 minutes. Drain in a colander and run hot water over it.

3. Add the butter, salt and pepper to taste. Sprinkle with lemon juice and toss until grains are coated.

Yield: Four servings.

N KITCHENS, AS ELSEWHERE, THE MOTTO IS "don't do as I do, do as I say." For years I have railed against any cooks who "pretended" that they were "cooking French," while dishing up platters of French dishes that were no more authentic than sushi or guacamole.

On the other hand, I was recently served a dish that the maker declared to be Indian, and while I have reasons to believe that it was more a flight of fancy than anything else, I was tempted to reproduce it. I have broadly labeled this recipe shrimp à l'indienne, and if the name offends any of my friends who are established Indian cooks, I apologize.

It is, on the other hand, a tasty dish made with, in addition to fresh shrimp, such spices as cardamom and cumin, hot chilies and coriander. It also contains sour cream, which I believe to be un-Indian.

A pot of saffron rice is recommended with this dish. Assemble all the ingredients for the main course. Then put the rice on to cook. It will not demand your attention again for seventeen to twenty minutes, or longer, so you can proceed to the shrimp dish with a certain leisure. The total cooking time for the dish (peeling the shrimp is the most time-consuming part of all) is less than ten minutes.

Crevettes à l'Indienne
(Shrimp in Indian sauce)

1½   pounds fresh shrimp, about 36 to 38
2   tablespoons butter
½   cup finely chopped onion
1   teaspoon chopped hot fresh green or red chilli or ¼ teaspoon dried red pepper
    Salt and freshly ground pepper to taste
¼   teaspoon ground cardamom or use an equal amount of curry powder

½   teaspoon ground cumin or use an equal amount of curry powder
    Juice of 1 lime
1   cup sour cream
½   cup plain yogurt
¼   cup chopped fresh coriander (cilantro) leaves, see note
    Saffron rice (see recipe).

1. Shell and devein the shrimp. Rinse well and pat dry. Set aside.

2. Heat the butter in a skillet and add the onion. Add the chili. Cook briefly and add the shrimp, salt and pepper to taste. Cook, stirring often, about 3 minutes.

3. Add the cardamom and cumin and stir. Add the lime juice, sour cream, and yogurt. Bring gently to the boil, stirring. Sprinkle with coriander and serve hot with saffron rice.

Yield: Four servings.

Note: Fresh coriander is available by the bunch in Chinese markets.

Riz au Safran
(*Saffron rice*)

---

1 tablespoon butter	**1 cup raw rice**
¼ cup finely chopped onion	**1½ cups water**
1 clove garlic, finely minced	**Salt to taste.**
½ teaspoon stem saffron, loosely packed	

1. Heat the butter in a saucepan and add the onion. Cook until wilted. Add the garlic and saffron and stir.

2. Add the rice. Stir well and add the water and salt. Bring to the boil. Cover and cook over low heat until rice is tender, about 17 to 20 minutes.

Yield: Four servings.

IT IS AN EASILY OBSERVED FACT IN THE WORLD OF food that most people have a special liking for foods that are "stuffed." It might be the roast turkey, a breast of veal, peppers, onions, zucchini, clams, mussels, lobsters, or oysters. After all, oysters Rockefeller are, in a sense, "stuffed" with a spinach filling.

The reasons are as numerous as they are obvious. A "filling," "stuffing," "dressing," or "farce," call it what you will, offers an appealing contrast both in flavors and textures. And almost anything within reason can go into a well-made filling, from ground or chopped leftover meats and vegetables to whole sausage. (One of the most interesting "stuffed" foods I've ever sampled was cooked by a Cuban acquaintance several years ago, a roast loin of pork stuffed with chorizos, a fleshy garlic sausage.)

The cooking time for stuffed foods, of course, can vary from what amounts to seconds to an hour and longer. If cooking time is a factor, raw shrimp would be an excellent food for a well-seasoned stuffing.

In the following recipe, the cleaned shrimp are "butterflied," which is to say, split part way down and flattened lightly. The stuffing consists of a few additional raw shrimp, chopped mushrooms, celery, garlic, and parsley. There is a small amount of fresh bread crumbs and egg to bind the filling together. A small amount of filling is heaped onto each flattened shrimp. The dish is dotted with butter and it is placed under the broiler until cooked, about five minutes. The dish must not cook for an extended time or the shrimp will dry out. One word of caution: You should should heat the shrimp in the baking dish on top of the stove before broiling. This will hasten the cooking time.

An excellent accompaniment for the shrimp are cherry tomatoes bordelaise, and these, too, of necessity, must be cooked in short order for more obvious reasons. If the tomatoes are overcooked their skins burst. They must be cooked in hot butter for a matter of moments. Their seasoning is chopped shallots and parsley, the traditional bordelaise flavors.

Crevettes Farcies
(Shrimp-stuffed shrimp)

22	to 32 medium to large shrimp, about 1¼ pounds		Salt and freshly ground pepper to taste
2	tablespoons butter	¾	cup plus 1 tablespoon fine, fresh bread crumbs
4	large mushrooms, slightly less than ¼ pound	¼	cup finely chopped parsley
⅔	cup finely chopped onion	1	egg, lightly beaten
⅔	cup finely chopped celery	3	tablespoons butter.
½	teaspoon finely minced garlic		

1 Preheat the broiler.

2. Peel and devein the shrimp or buy them already prepared. Set aside six-

teen large or twenty-four medium shrimp. Chop the remaining shrimp coarsely. There should be about ½ cup. Set aside.

3. Slice and finely chop the mushrooms. There should be about 1 cup. Set aside.

4. Heat the butter in a saucepan and add the onion, celery, and garlic. Cook until wilted and add the mushrooms, salt, and pepper. Stir. Cook about 3 minutes.

5. Remove the saucepan from the heat and add the chopped shrimp. Stir. Add ¾ cup of the bread crumbs, parsley, and egg. Stir to blend. Add salt and pepper to taste.

6. Butterfly the shrimp. That is to say, split them down the back almost but not all the way through. Open up the shrimp split side down on a flat surface.

7. Spoon equal portions of the stuffing on top of each shrimp as ''stuffing.''

8. Grease a baking dish large enough to hold the shrimp in one layer. Use 1 tablespoon of butter. Arrange the shrimp over the dish.

9. Sprinkle the shrimp with the tablespoon of bread crumbs and dot with 2 tablespoons of butter. Place the baking dish on top of the stove and bring the juices around the shrimp to the boil and heat thoroughly. (The butter will melt.)

10. Place the shrimp under the broiler about five inches from the source of heat. Cook about 5 minutes or until shrimp are heated through and are nicely browned.

Yield: Four servings.

Tomates Cerises Bordelaise
(Cherry tomatoes sautéed with shallots)

---

1 quart ripe but firm cherry tomatoes	2 tablespoons butter
Salt and freshly ground pepper to taste	1 tablespoon finely chopped shallots
	1 tablespoon finely chopped parsley.

1. Pick over the tomatoes and discard the stems. Rinse and drain the tomatoes.

2. Heat the butter in a large skillet and when it is quite hot but not brown add the tomatoes, salt, and pepper. Cook, shaking the skillet so that the tomatoes cook evenly.

3. Cook about 2 minutes. They should just be heated through. If they are overcooked they will collapse. Add the shallots and parsley and cook, shaking the skillet, about 15 seconds.

Yield: Four servings.

ONE OF THE FALSE CONCLUSIONS ASSUMED BY hundreds and thousands of amateur cooks is that the preparation time for any given recipe is in exact ratio to the number of ingredients it contains. It is an unfortunate conclusion and a pity, for you cannot equate the length of time to make a dish with what is known in the newspaper field as "column inches."

To choose an obvious example, many dishes in Indian cookery may call for as many as a dozen or more dried spices, most of which will come in jars with screw tops. Their use simply involves going to a pantry shelf, collecting the spices and measuring out the amounts required. It is an act that can be performed in minutes. In opposition to that, consider the French preparation known as a salade russe. Basically it involves a very few vegetables—carrots, turnips, and so on—but the dish is a bit tedious to make because it isn't the numbers of vegetables involved. It is what has to be done to them—the careful dicing, for example—that can require a great deal of time to arrive at a finished product.

It may come as a surprise to numerous readers to know that one version of the well-known Spanish dish called paella can easily be made within the confines of an hour. Basically it consists of cooking sausage and chicken pieces together before adding a few chopped vegetables, herbs and spices, rice, and liquids that include canned tomatoes. Seafood in the form of clams and shrimp is added and the dish is covered and simmered until it is ready for the table.

If you plot the timing and preparation carefully, it is a dish that can be made, start to finish, in about forty-five minutes. As the chicken and sausages cook, for example, there is ample time to chop the onions, green peppers, and so on for the second step. As these cook together, the seafood can be rinsed and peeled as a last addition to complete the dish.

A good paella is a meal unto itself but there is one salad that complements it admirably. This is a hastily made orange and black olive salad that is tossed together with an oil and vinegar dressing, with paprika and finely minced garlic.

Paella

2 tablespoons olive oil

4 sweet or hot Italian sausages

4 small chicken thighs (or use 2 thighs and 2 legs, separated to make 4 pieces) about 1 pound

1 green, unblemished sweet pepper, cored, seeded, and cut into 1-inch cubes

1 cup finely chopped onion

1 teaspoon finely minced garlic

1 hot dried red pepper, optional

½ teaspoon stem saffron

1 large bay leaf

1 sprig fresh thyme or half a teaspoon dried thyme

1 cup canned, undrained tomatoes

1 cup rice

¾ cup water
Salt and freshly ground pepper to taste

8 littleneck clams, the smaller the better

8 shrimp, peeled and deveined
Finely chopped parsley.

1. Heat the oil in a large skillet. Prick the sausages with a fork and add them. Cook, turning often, about 5 minutes.

2. Add the chicken pieces, skin side down, and continue cooking sausages and chicken until chicken skin is browned, about 5 minutes. Turn the pieces often and continue cooking about 10 minutes, or until sausages have cooked, a total of 20 minutes, and the chicken 15 minutes.

3. As the sausages and chicken cook, prepare the pepper, onion, and garlic. Add these to the skillet.

4. Add the saffron, bay leaf, and thyme. Stir.

5. Add the tomatoes, rice, water, salt, and pepper. Cover closely. Cook 15 minutes.

6. As the mixture cooks, rinse and drain the clams. Peel and devein the shrimp.

7. Add the clams and shrimp to the rice mixture. Cover again and let cook about 8 minutes longer. Serve sprinkled with chopped parsley.

Yield: Four servings.

Salade d'Oranges et Olives Noires
(Orange and black olive salad)

2 seedless navel oranges, about 1¼ pounds total weight
8 black olives, preferably imported
1 teaspoon paprika
½ teaspoon finely minced garlic
1 teaspoon red wine vinegar

3 tablespoons olive oil
   Salt and freshly ground pepper to taste
2 tablespoons finely chopped parsley.

1. Trim off the ends of the oranges. Peel oranges and cut them into quarter-inch slices. Put them in a mixing bowl.

2. Add the olives.

3. Blend the paprika, garlic, vinegar and oil, salt and pepper. Blend well and pour this over the oranges and olives. Blend well.

4. Sprinkle with parsley and serve.

Yield: Four servings.

Lamb

M
ORE AND MORE IN THIS DAY AND AGE, PEOPLE ARE learning that some of the simplest dishes have a grand and justified appeal.

Here is an outline in detail for two of the quickest and simplest methods for cooking lamb chops. One will be the chops cooked under the broiler flame. The other will be the chops pan broiled, which is to say, cooked in a skillet. I will all but ignore the use of a grill in cooking the chops.

Should you choose to cook lamb chops under the broiler of your home stove, the cooking time will depend primarily on two things. One consideration is how hot the source of heat is. That temperature will vary from one make of stove to the other, even when the heat is set at its highest setting. The second thing is how close the meat is placed to the source of heat. The primary choice is this: If you want the meat to be quite rare inside (bleu we say in French), you should put the meat quite close to the flame, turning once and browning well and quickly on both sides. In any event, the oven door should be left open at all times while broiling, or the meat will "steam."

Should you wish to pan broil your chops, the most important thing is the skillet. It should be heavy. A black iron skillet is ideal. Do not add any form of fat but heat the skillet until almost "smoking" or red hot. Add the chops and cook about three or four minutes to a side, longer if you want the meat well done. Turn the lamb chops and cook until they are nicely browned.

Côtes d'Agneau Grillées
(Broiled lamb chops)

---

8 lamb chops, about ½ pound each and about 1½ inches thick	Salt and freshly ground pepper to taste.

1. Preheat the broiler to high.

2. Sprinkle the chops with salt and pepper. Arrange the chops on a baking rack and place under the broiler about five or six inches from the source of heat. Leave the broiler door open. Broil about 5 minutes on one side and turn.

3. Continue broiling the second side. If you want to speed up cooking for a rarer interior, move the broiling pan closer to the source of heat, about three inches away. Cook about 3 minutes. If you want a medium or well-done interior, leave the broiler in its original position and broil about 5 to 10 minutes.

Yield: Four servings.

Côtes d'Agneau Poêlées
(Pan-broiled lamb chops)

---

8 lamb chops, each about ½ pound and 1½ inches thick Salt and freshly ground pepper to taste	4 tablespoons butter 1 teaspoon finely chopped garlic 2 tablespoons finely chopped parsley.

1. Sprinkle the chops with salt and pepper on all sides.

2. Use one or two heavy skillets such as a black iron skillet, large enough to hold the chops in one layer.

3. Heat the skillet until almost smoking. Do not add any oil or other fat. Add the chops and cook on one side about 4 minutes until well browned. The chops should be cooked at all times over moderately high heat. Turn the chops and pour off the fat from the skillet or skillets.

4. Continue cooking the chops on the second side about 3 minutes.

5. Turn the lamb chops on the sides to cook the rim of fat. It may be necessary to let them rest against the side of the skillet to keep them upright. Let cook about 2 minutes and return them to the second side and continue cooking about 1 minute.

6. Remove the chops to a warm platter and pour off the fat from the skillet. Add the butter, and when it is hot add the garlic. Cook briefly and pour over the chops. Serve sprinkled with chopped parsley.

Yield: Four servings.

Pommes de Terre à Cru
(Skillet-fried potatoes)

---

4 large Idaho potatoes, about 1½ pounds	Salt and freshly ground pepper to taste
¼ cup peanut, vegetable, or corn oil	1 clove garlic, finely minced
2 tablespoons butter	2 tablespoons finely chopped parsley.

1. Peel the potatoes and cut them into very thin slices, using a hand slicer. As they are sliced drop them into cold water to prevent discoloration. Or wait until the last moment before the potatoes are to be cooked to peel and slice them. There should be about 3 cups loosely packed sliced potatoes.

2. Heat the oil in a skillet, preferably one with rounded sides. Dry the potatoes with paper towels. When the oil is hot add the potatoes, tossing and shaking the skillet to prevent sticking. Cook about 15 minutes or until golden, turning them gently to prevent breaking the slices.

3. Drain the potatoes in a colander, pouring all the oil from the skillet. Add the butter to the skillet and when it is hot, add the potatoes, salt and pepper. Add the garlic and parsley and continue cooking, stirring and tossing gently about 3 minutes.

Yield: Four servings.

IF I WERE TO NAME THE ONE DISH THAT IS, WHERE quick-cooking is concerned, the most elegant and sophisticated, it would probably be the dish outlined here. It is a rack of lamb that is cooked under the broiler to the desired degree of doneness. It is a dish that would be equally suitable at a formal dinner or at a special dinner for two or four to celebrate an occasion.

There is no denying the fact that it is a preparation that is elevated not only where taste is the measure but price as well.

On the other hand, there are times when champagne can be the choice over a still wine, and the main course something a bit more special than the favorite family casserole.

At its most basic, a broiled rack of lamb consists of simply rubbing the meat—bones in, of course—with salt and pepper and oil. The meat is cooked under a broiler, turned to high heat, for approximately five minutes, fat side down. The rack is turned and cooked on the other side five minutes. Then the rack should be left to "rest" with the broiler off for an additional five minutes. Brush briefly with butter, and that's all there is to it. If you want to add embellishments, as indicated below, rub the meat with rosemary and, at the end, sprinkle with parsley.

There is one vastly important consideration in the preparation of this meat— most of the surface fat should be cut away, leaving only a light coating, before broiling.

Racks of lamb should be cooked until rare and served. Overcooking will seriously impair the flavor and texture. Serve, if desired, with rice and peas, which should be cooked before the lamb is put under the broiler.

Carré d'Agneau au Romarin
(*Rack of lamb with rosemary*)

---

2 racks of lamb, about 2 pounds each	1 tablespoon rosemary leaves
Salt and freshly ground pepper to taste	1 tablespoon olive oil
	1 tablespoon butter
	1 tablespoon chopped parsley.

1. Using a sharp chef's knife and the fingers, cut and pull away all but a thin layer of top fat.

2. Sprinkle the lamb all over with salt and pepper.

3. Crush the rosemary barely and rub it all over the lamb.

4. Sprinkle the lamb all over with the olive oil.

5. Pre-heat the broiler to high.

6. Place the lamb fat side down on a rack. Place under the broiler so that the ribs of lamb are about four inches from the source of heat. Cook 5 minutes.

7. Turn the lamb fat side up and return to the broiler once more, about

four inches from the source of heat. Broil 5 minutes. Turn the oven off and leave the door open. Let the meat stand 5 minutes before serving. Before serving, rub the lamb with the butter and sprinkle with chopped parsley.

Yield: Four to six servings.

Riz aux Pois
(Rice with peas)

4	tablespoons butter	1½	cups chicken broth
½	cup finely chopped onion	1	bay leaf
1	clove garlic, finely minced		Salt to taste
1	cup raw rice	1	cup fresh or frozen peas.

1. Heat half the butter in a saucepan and add the onion and garlic. Cook, stirring, until wilted. Add the rice and stir.

2. Add the broth, bay leaf, and salt to taste. Bring to the boil.

3. Cover and place the rice on a metal pad. Cook 17 minutes.

4. If the peas are fresh, cook them briefly until done. If frozen peas are used, heat in a skillet in 1 tablespoon of butter, stirring. Add the peas to the rice. Stir in the remaining 2 tablespoons of butter if fresh peas are used or the remaining 1 tablespoon butter if frozen peas are used.

Yield: Four servings.

A QUICKLY MADE MEAL AND A DINNER WITH STYLE are by no means mutually exclusive, and one of the most concrete expressions of that proposition is the following pair of recipes. The heart of this meal is one of America's choicest and most elegant cuts of meat—a tender, succulent rack of lamb.

The cost of a rack of lamb is, admittedly, somewhat elevated, but when this meal is thought of as a somewhat special dinner for four, the cost may not seem all that abhorrent.

When the lamb is purchased, it is best to have the butcher prepare it for cooking precisely as indicated in the recipe. Remember that fast cooking is essential to a proper rack of lamb. The total cooking time from the moment the lamb is placed under the broiler until it is taken from the oven should be from twelve to sixteen minutes. This should insure that the center of the meat ranges from pink to red. If the meat is overcooked, it will become grayish and not be so moist and succulent.

Grilled tomatoes go well with the lamb. Toss a salad at the last moment to be served with the main course or afterward. Serve pears and cheese at the conclusion of the meal.

Carré d'Agneau Persillé
(Parsleyed rack of lamb)

2 racks of lamb, about 2½ pounds combined weight	½ cup bread crumbs
	3 tablespoons chopped parsley
Salt and freshly ground pepper to taste	1 clove garlic, finely minced
	1 shallot, finely minced
4 tablespoons butter	1 teaspoon olive oil.

1. Have the butcher hack or saw off the chine bone (the flat, continuous bone at the top of the ribs), leaving the meat exposed.

2. Preheat the broiler to high. If the oven is heated separately, preheat it also to 500 degrees.

3. Using the fingers and a sharp knife, pull and slice off the top thick layer of fat from the racks of lamb. When ready, the loins and ribs should be almost clean of fat. Hack off the ends of the ribs, leaving about one-and-a-half inches of the ribs intact and extending from the loin meat.

4. Rub with butter a baking dish large enough to hold the racks of lamb in one layer and close together. Place the racks, meat side down, in the dish and dot the ribs with 2 tablespoons of butter.

5. Meanwhile, combine the bread crumbs, parsley, garlic, shallot and olive oil in a bowl.

6. Place the racks of lamb under the broiler and cook about 2 or 3 minutes. Turn and cook about 2 or 3 minutes.

7. Sprinkle the meaty side of the ribs with the bread crumb mixture. Melt

the remaining 2 tablespoons of butter and pour it over the ribs. Place in the oven and bake 8 to 10 minutes, depending on the degree of doneness desired.

Yield: Four to six servings.

Tomates Grillées à la Provençale
(*Grilled tomatoes with garlic and rosemary*)

---

2 red, ripe, firm, and unblemished tomatoes	**1½ teaspoons rosemary leaves**
3 cloves garlic, each cut into 4 or 6 slivers	**Salt and freshly ground pepper to taste**
	3 tablespoons olive oil.

1. Preheat the broiler to high.
2. Split the tomatoes in half and arrange them, cut side up, on a baking dish just large enough to hold the four halves compactly.
3. Stud the surface of each half with equal amounts of slivered garlic and rosemary leaves. Sprinkle with salt and pepper to taste. Spoon the olive oil over the tomatoes.
4. When ready to serve, place the tomatoes under the broiler and cook until the surfaces are blistered, bubbling and piping hot. Quickly remove and discard the garlic and rosemary and serve piping hot.

Yield: Four servings.

WHEN IT COMES TO WHAT MIGHT BE CALLED COOKing à la minute, the virtues of ground meat are immediately apparent. Chief among them is their cooking nature. Toss a quarter pound of first-quality ground beef on a hot grill or into a lightly oiled (or even unoiled) skillet, a touch of salt, a sprinkling of pepper and a dollop of butter and the results are almost foolproof.

Trouble is, a diet of ground beef can be cloying to the appetite, and fortunately there are numerous other ground meats to resort to, among them lamb and pork (ground chicken and fish can also be delicious).

Ground lamb patties are easily made and even more expeditious to cook. One thing to remember is that ground lamb should be cooked to the well-done stage—well-done, that is, but still moist inside—for most palates.

In the following recipes, the patties are flavored with dill and a touch of onion, plus bread crumbs to make them tender and one egg to bind them together. Dill is one of those herbs that are particularly complementary to lamb, thus it is also used in that quickly made light cream and mushroom sauce to accompany the patties once they are cooked. The total advance preparation of these patties can be reckoned in fifteen minutes or less and, if it seems more profitable, may be done several hours prior to cooking.

An ideal side dish for the meat are easily made broiled tomatoes, which can be assembled in a very brief while once the lamb patties have been shaped. If you wish a starch to accompany this meal, buttered fine noodles—plain or tossed with poppy seeds—are recommended.

Bitoks d'Agneau
(Broiled lamb patties)

1½ pounds ground lean lamb	Salt and freshly ground pepper
3 tablespoons plus 1 teaspoon	to taste
butter	¼ pound mushrooms, quartered or
⅓ cup finely chopped onion	sliced
½ cup fresh bread crumbs	1 tablespoon finely chopped
3 tablespoons plus 2 teaspoons	shallots
finely chopped dill or parsley	¼ cup dry white wine
1 egg, lightly beaten	½ cup heavy cream.

1. Place the lamb in a mixing bowl.

2. Heat 1 teaspoon of butter in a skillet and add the onion. Cook, stirring until wilted. Add this to the lamb.

3. Add the bread crumbs, 3 tablespoons chopped dill, one egg, salt and pepper to taste. Blend well and divide into eight portions. Shape each portion into a patty.

4. Heat 2 tablespoons of butter in a skillet and cook the lamb patties, 3 or 4 minutes to a side.

5. Remove the patties and wipe out the skillet. Add the remaining 1 tablespoon butter and the mushrooms. Cook until lightly browned. Add the shallots and wine. Cook until liquid evaporates almost entirely. Add the cream. Cook about 5 minutes and add the remaining dill. Serve the hot sauce poured over the patties.

Yield: Four servings.

Tomatoes Grillées
(Broiled tomatoes with garlic and marjoram)

4 small to medium red, ripe but firm tomatoes	4 teaspoons dried marjoram or oregano, crumbled
8 slivers garlic	8 teaspoons olive oil.
Salt and freshly ground pepper to taste	

1. Preheat the broiler to high.
2. Cut the tomatoes in half width-wise. Arrange them cut-side up in a baking dish. Insert one sliver of garlic in the center of each half.
3. Sprinkle with salt and pepper. Sprinkle with equal amounts of marjoram. Sprinkle each with 1 teaspoon of oil. Place under the broiler for 8 to 10 minutes, until bubbling and tips of garlic start to brown. Remove garlic and serve.

Yield: Four servings.

SOMEONE HAS ASKED IF WE LIKE LAMB DISHES, and the answer is an emphatic yes. Lamb is one of the best and most delicate of meats and, to our taste, more elegant than steak. Curiously, lamb—outside of chops, the saddle, and rack—generally requires a cooking period that would be in excess of an hour. One of the least expensive lamb dishes, on the other hand, is made with ground meat. It is a dish that I have prepared and served in luxury restaurants, and to the great pleasure of many customers.

Basically it is a lambburger, but that is not the sort of name one generally includes in dining places. Rather it is generally listed as bitoks d'agneau aux câpres. That, it seems, gives it status.

Bitoks is the Russian word for meatballs, and the dish in sum consists of the ground meat with seasonings, bread crumbs, a touch of onion and garlic, all shaped into spheres. The meatballs are browned and served with a dill and sour cream sauce. This sauce, with a few capers added, has nuances of flavor that go extremely well with the flavor of lamb, and the total preparation and cooking time is less than thirty minutes. Or perhaps forty-five if you are a little bit less than adept.

As with most meat dishes with a cream sauce (in this case sour cream), buttered noodles are the ideal accompaniment. To vary the noodles, add a light sprinkling of freshly grated nutmeg when they are tossed in the butter.

The name appended to the noodle dish here is "grenada." The reason is simple. The island of Grenada in the Caribbean is celebrated for its enormous annual production of nutmeg.

Bitoks d'Agneau aux Câpres
(Lamb patties with sour cream and capers)

1½ pounds ground lamb	Salt and freshly ground pepper
1 teaspoon peanut, vegetable or	to taste
corn oil	2 tablespoons butter
1 cup finely chopped onions	1 teaspoon paprika
1 small clove garlic, finely minced	¼ teaspoon dried thyme
½ cup fine bread crumbs	½ cup dry white wine
1 egg, lightly beaten	½ cup chicken broth
2 tablespoons finely chopped	2 cups sour cream
parsley	3 tablespoons drained capers.
4 tablespoons finely chopped dill	

1. Put the meat into a mixing bowl and set aside.

2. Heat the oil in a small skillet and add half the onion and the garlic. Cook until the onion is wilted. Let cool.

3. To the meat add the cooked onion mixture, bread crumbs, egg, parsley, 2 tablespoons chopped dill, salt and pepper to taste.

[**182**]

4. Shape the mixture into balls about two inches in diameter. There should be about 16 balls. Flatten slightly to make patties.

5. Heat 2 tablespoons butter in one or two skillets large enough to hold the patties. Add the patties to the skillet and cook about 5 minutes. Turn and cook the patties another 5 minutes or longer.

6. Transfer the patties to a warm platter and pour off the fat from the skillet. Add the remaining onion and cook, stirring, until wilted. Add the paprika and thyme and stir.

7. Add the wine, stirring. When it boils, add the broth and cook down to about ½ cup. Remove from the heat and stir in the sour cream. Add salt and pepper to taste. Return to the heat and heat gently without boiling. For a more refined sauce, put the mixture through a sieve.

8. Reheat, stirring, and add the capers.

9. Pour the sauce over the lamb patties and serve sprinkled with remaining dill. Serve with boiled noodles.

Yield: Four servings.

Nouilles Grenada
(*Noodles with nutmeg*)

½ **pound broad noodles**	**Freshly grated nutmeg to taste**
Salt to taste	**Freshly ground pepper to taste.**
3 **tablespoons butter**	

1. Cook the noodles in boiling salted water until tender.

2. Drain quickly and return them to the kettle. Add the remaining ingredients and salt to taste, tossing until the butter melts. Serve hot.

Yield: Four servings.

ONE OF THE QUESTIONS THAT SEEMS TO LOOM large in the home cook's mind is whether or not foods can be cooked with equal success under a broiler or on top of the stove, using a skillet. It is an understandable dilemma, for foods cooked under the broiler generate a good deal of smoke and odors in small facilities without proper ventilation.

Chops, as I have noted previously, are ideal for a meal to be cooked in less than an hour for obvious reasons. To my mind, pan-broiling in the home would be far preferable to cooking over or under a high heat for the reasons outlined above.

One of the pleasures of lamb chops is that they adapt well to so many seasonings, such as herbs and spices and sauces. They are excellent, of course, simply grilled and served with only melted butter. They can take on an added dimension when served with or on a provençale "garnish." This would be a quickly made, savory garnish with a base of tomatoes but including green and black olives, onion, garlic, and a bit of rosemary.

The lamb chops listed here weigh in the vicinity of one pound each. They require about forty-five minutes cooking if they are to be served medium rare. They must be cooked longer, of course, if you wish to serve them well done. Serve the chops and the provençale garnish, if desired, with rice cooked according to package directions.

The fact is that skillet cookery is sometimes far preferable for certain dishes that are usually broiled under direct heat. For example, foods that have a high fat content (such as chops that are rimmed with fat) or those that must be cooked for an extended period are best "pan-broiled." (Pan-broiled is a curious phrase, incidentally; in its most basic sense broiling involves cooking food under or over direct and intense heat such as hot coals or a flame.)

When fat is exposed to direct heat, it tends to flame up, which creates both smoke and odors. Foods that require long cooking also may burn under direct and intense heat.

The lamb chops in the recipe for the "hasty" meal outlined here are a case in point. It is a question of personal taste, but I prefer one thick lamp chop to a couple of chops with half the thickness.

Côtes d'Agneau à la Provençale
(Lamb chops with Provençale garnish)

4   thick lamb chops, about 1 pound each
Salt and freshly ground pepper to taste

1   tablespoon oil
1   teaspoon dried rosemary
Provençale garnish (see recipe)
Chopped parsley.

1. Sprinkle the chops with salt and pepper.
2. Heat the oil in a heavy skillet and add the chops. Cook until well

browned on one side, about 10 minutes. Turn and cook 7 or 8 minutes. Turn onto the side and cook to brown the fat well, about 10 minutes.

3. Turn the meat, meat side down, and cook 15 to 18 minutes until chops are nicely browned all over. Five minutes before chops are done, sprinkle on both sides with the rosemary. This produces a medium rare chop. Cook 15 minutes longer for well done meat.

4. Arrange the garnish over the bottom of a serving dish. Arrange the chops over and sprinkle with chopped parsley.

Yield: Four servings.

Garniture Provençale
(*Provençale garnish*)

2 tablespoons olive oil	Salt and freshly ground pepper to taste
2 tablespoons chopped onion	
1 teaspoon chopped garlic	1 teaspoon dried rosemary, chopped
1¼ pounds fresh tomatoes (about 3) cored, peeled, and cut into 1-inch cubes, about 2 to 3 cups	⅓ cup imported black olives, drained
	½ cup pitted green olives, drained.

1. Heat the oil in a skillet or casserole and add the onion and garlic. Cook briefly until wilted.

2. Add the tomatoes, salt, pepper, and rosemary.

3. Let cook about 5 to 10 minutes. Do not overcook. The tomatoes should not be mushy. Add the olives and heat through.

Yield: Four servings.

IT IS A COMMONPLACE TO OBSERVE THAT THE names of hundreds of recipes in French cookery (and in other cuisines as well) are based on places that exist geographically. Generally speaking, a name of one dish or another has to do with a specialty of that place—a region or town. To choose a few obvious examples, dishes périgourdine have truffles for which the region of Périgord is famous. Dishes provençale are made with the flavors of Provence—tomatoes, garlic, thyme, and so on. Dishes crécy are made with carrots, for carrots are famous around the small town of Crécy which is situated in the Seine-et-Marne region.

One of my favorite dishes made with lamb is listed as rouennaise, which requires a bit of explanation. Rouen is famous for its ducks. Lamb chops that bear that name are chops that have been cooked to a desired degree of doneness and served with a fine sauce made with a purée of poultry liver. In the beginning, the sauce was made with duck livers, but today it is often made with chicken livers.

This is a dish for special occasions and I offer a recipe here with one word of caution. This book is dedicated to food preparation that will require less than an hour. Generally speaking, I have tailored the recipe for a preparation time considerably less than sixty minutes. If you make lamb chops rouennaise, you should count on the full measure of time, but if you feel as enthusiastic about the dish as I do, in the end the time will be well spent.

The basis for the dish are rib lamb chops which have been trimmed of the chine bone at the top of the ribs. The lamb bones are then trimmed "French-style" (the fat is cut away to expose the clean rib bone), mostly for the sake of appearance. It is best to have your butcher do this to conserve time. The sauce is easy to prepare, although it takes time to chop the vegetables and simmer them in red wine and broth. The chicken livers (you could use duck livers if you are fortunate enough to obtain them) are puréed before adding to the sauce near the end. The chops themselves are cooked only about three or four minutes to the side. If the recipe is a bit time consuming, the accompaniments are simple and quickly made—grilled tomatoes and watercress.

Côtes d'Agneau Rouennaise
(*Lamb chops on liver toast*)

8 **"double" rib lamb chops, about 4 pounds**	½ **teaspoon dried thyme**
1 **tablespoon plus 1 teaspoon butter**	1 **cup dry red wine**
¼ **cup finely chopped onion**	¾ **cup beef broth**
½ **teaspoon finely minced garlic**	3 **or 4 chicken livers, about ¼ pound**
¼ **cup finely chopped celery**	1 **tablespoon coarsely chopped shallots**
¼ **cup finely diced carrot**	1 **teaspoon cognac**
½ **bay leaf**	½ **teaspoon arrowroot or cornstarch.**

1. If possible, have the butcher hack off and discard the flat chine bone at

the top of each rib. Using the fingers, pull away the fat from the outside of the chops. Scrape the bottom of the bone "French-style." Ideally, you should chop off one chop, leaving one intact. That, however, is simply for aesthetics. Ideally, you should have the chops made ready to cook by the butcher.

2. Heat 1 teaspoon of the butter in a saucepan and add the onion, garlic, celery, carrot, bay leaf, and thyme. Cook, stirring occasionally, until onion is wilted.

3. Add half the wine and broth and cook over moderately high heat about 15 minutes, or until cooked down to about 1 cup. Do not reduce it more than that. Put the sauce through a sieve, pressing to extract as much liquid as possible from the solids.

4. Put the livers on a flat surface and chop them finely. Put the livers in a sieve and press through with the back of a spoon or a plastic spatula. There should be about ⅓ cup. Set aside.

5. Sprinkle the chops with salt and pepper on both sides.

6. Heat the remaining tablespoon of butter in a skillet large enough to hold the chops in one layer. Add the chops and cook about 3 or 4 minutes on one side. Turn and cook about 3 or 4 minutes on the other side.

7. Transfer the chops to a serving dish and pour off the fat from the skillet. Add the shallots and cook briefly. Add the remaining ½ cup of red wine. Add the strained sauce and cook until reduced by half. As the sauce cooks, add any juices that may collect around the chops.

8. Turn off the heat from the sauce. Add the puréed livers, stirring with a whisk. Do not heat; the livers will cook from retained heat.

9. Ideally, you should put this sauce through a fine sieve, pressing and turning with a whisk to pass the livers through. This is not essential, however. Bring the sauce just to the boil.

10. Blend the cognac and arrowroot and stir it into the sauce. Spoon the sauce over the chops. Serve garnished with watercress and grilled tomatoes.

Yield: Four servings.

Tomatoes Grillées
(Broiled tomatoes)

---

2 red, ripe tomatoes	2 cloves garlic, peeled
Salt and freshly ground pepper to taste	1 tablespoon olive oil.

1. Preheat the broiler.

2. Cut the tomatoes in half and arrange them on a lightly oiled baking dish. Sprinkle with salt and pepper.

3. Cut the garlic into about 16 thin slivers. Stud the tomato halves with the slivers.

4. Place under the broiler and broil about 5 minutes or until garlic slivers start to burn. Discard the garlic and serve.

Yield: Four servings.

WHEN IT COMES TO "GOURMET" COOKERY, THERE is no chef in the world who would put a price on the ingredients. That is to say that a finely made omelet when eggs are at a peak of freshness can be just as seductive in flavor as a truffled pâté or nightingales' tongues (a legendary dish which I never hope to try).

The dishes printed in this book range from a humble sauerkraut to filet mignon; from hamburger creations to a richly endowed crabmeat in cream sauce.

Fine lamb is one of the great—and expensive—American delicacies. Lamb has limited qualities where cooking in less than sixty minutes is concerned. No choice where roast legs and saddles of lamb and stews are concerned.

Among the few dishes—variations on simply grilled or broiled chops—that require a brief period in preparation and cooking, is a dish—admittedly costly—called noisettes d'agneau à l'anglaise: boneless lamb chop English-style.

The name à l'anglaise is used in several ways in a French kitchen. At times it means foods cooked in water. In this case it implies a breaded dish sautéed in oil, and with hazelnut brown butter poured over when ready to serve.

The noisettes made from the choicest parts of loin lamb chops are fork-tender and eminently edible. The total cooking time for the noisettes or medallions is less than five minutes. It may be added that there is a final culinary conceit in the preparation of this dish. The butter is delicately scented with chopped tarragon, a flavor that marries admirably well with lamb.

The lamb itself could be accompanied by a simple platter of boiled parsley potatoes. An excellent salad for the meal would be cold string beans with a well-seasoned vinaigrette sauce.

Noisettes d'Agneau à l'Anglaise
(Breaded lamb medallions)

---

8 loin lamb chops, each about 6 ounces and about 1 inch thick
Salt and freshly ground pepper to taste
2 tablespoons flour
1 large egg, beaten
1 tablespoon water

1½ cups bread crumbs
3 tablespoons peanut, vegetable, or corn oil
¼ cup butter
1 tablespoon chopped fresh tarragon or 1 teaspoon dried.

1. Hack off, or have the butcher hack off, the top chine bone and cut away the rib bone of each chop. Trim away all but a light layer of fat from around the chop. Using a flat mallet, lightly flatten each chop. When flattened, the meat should be about half an inch thick.

2. Sprinkle the medallions on both sides with salt and pepper. Dredge lightly in flour and shake off excess. Beat the egg with the water. Dip the medallions in the egg mixture to coat well. Place in the crumbs and dredge to coat

thoroughly on both sides. Pat lightly with the side of a heavy metal knife to help the crumbs adhere.

3. Heat the oil in a heavy skillet large enough to hold the medallions in one layer. Add the medallions and cook about 1½ minutes, or until golden brown, on one side. Continue cooking until golden brown on the other side, about 2 minutes. Remove to a warm serving dish.

4. Heat the butter in a skillet until it is foamy and turns a hazelnut brown. Do not let it burn. Remove from the heat and add the tarragon. Stir quickly and pour the sauce over the medallions.

Yield: Four servings.

Haricots Verts Vinaigrette
(String beans with vinaigrette sauce)

¾ **pound string beans**   ½ **cup vinaigrette sauce.**

1. Trim or snap off the ends of the beans. Otherwise, leave the beans whole. Drop them into boiling water and cook until crisp-tender, about 5 minutes. Do not overcook.

2. Drain and run the beans briefly under cold running water. Drain again while beans are still warm.

3. Pour sauce over beans.

Yield: Four to six servings.

Sauce Vinaigrette
(Vinaigrette sauce)

1 **teaspoon imported mustard each as Dijon or Düsseldorf**
1 **tablespoon finely chopped shallots**
½ **teaspoon finely minced garlic**
2 **tablespoons finely chopped parsley**

1 **tablespoon red wine vinegar**
¼ **cup peanut or olive oil**
Salt and freshly ground pepper to taste.

1. Put the mustard, shallots, garlic, parsley, and vinegar in a mixing bowl.

2. Gradually add the oil while stirring with a wire whisk. Add the salt a little at a time. Add pepper. Stir until well blended.

Yield: About half a cup.

INDIAN COOKERY, FOR THE MOST PART, IS ONE OF the most intricate—as well as most versatile—of foreign cuisines. Over the years I have dined at numerous Indian tables, both professionally and socially. And while I have never tried to master that country's cooking in depth (the curry that I prepare is almost a study in French adaptation), I do enjoy preparing skewered kebabs with a basic assortment of "traditional" spices—turmeric (which gives curry powder its yellow color), coriander, and cumin. And happily, I almost invariably have at my disposal fresh ginger and (invariably) fresh garlic.

I am also keen on a kind of "chutney" taught me by an Indian friend, a chilled cucumber and yogurt relish that is simple and quick to prepare, a dish that makes a happy foil for the "spiciness" of the kebabs.

The preparation of the kebabs and their arrangement on skewers requires but a nick in time, and this is another of those dishes that may be done at the last moment, or perhaps the evening before. Some people aver that it is preferable to prepare the meat in its marinade the evening before, but it isn't essential. The cooking time for the kebabs is about ten minutes when cooked under a home broiler.

The classic accompaniment for such a dish is plain rice, which could be cooked in fifteen to twenty minutes. The best way to set about such a meal is, in my mind, to prepare the meat in its seasonings. Put the rice on to boil and prepare the cucumber relish. Skewer the meats and place them under the preheated broiler.

Brochettes d'Agneau à l'Indienne
(Lamb kebabs)

24	cubes of lean lamb, about 1¾ pounds, preferably meat from the leg	½	teaspoon ground coriander
		½	teaspoon ground cumin
		⅛	teaspoon ground hot red pepper (cayenne)
1	teaspoon finely chopped garlic		Salt and freshly ground pepper to taste
2	teaspoons finely chopped ginger		
2	tablespoons lemon juice	1	tablespoon grated onion.
¼	cup peanut, vegetable, or corn oil		
½	teaspoon ground turmeric		

1. It will expedite the preparation if you have the butcher cube the lamb.
2. Add the lamb to a bowl and add the remaining ingredients.
3. Preheat the broiler to high.
4. When ready to cook, arrange equal amounts of the meat on four skewers.
5. Place the skewered lamb about four or five inches from the source of heat. Cook, turning so as to cook the meat evenly, about 10 minutes. Serve with rice and a yogurt and cucumber sauce.

Yield: Four servings.

Sauce de Concombres à l'Indienne
(Cucumber with yogurt sauce)

1 cucumber, about ¾ pound	Salt to taste
¾ teaspoon whole cumin seeds	1 teaspoon peanut, vegetable, or
2 teaspoons chopped, seeded, hot	corn oil
fresh green chiles, optional	½ teaspoon finely chopped garlic.
1 cup yogurt	

1. Use the coarse blade of a grater. Grate the cucumber coarsely and put it in a bowl. Set aside.
2. Put the cumin seeds in a small saucepan and cook until "toasted." Do not burn. When they start to crackle, remove from the heat, shaking the skillet.
3. Combine the yogurt with the cucumbers, cumin seeds, chiles, salt, oil, and garlic. Blend well and chill.

Yield: About two cups.

Veal
and Calves' Liver

LTHOUGH THE BEST CUTS OF VEAL MOST AS-
suredly rest in the luxury category where meats are concerned,
they are difficult to ignore when it is a question of cooking
gourmet-style within an hour's time. This recipe then is for those times when
you wish to stretch the budget a bit for a hurried but special occasion.

First of all, if you're going to deal with veal in the kitchen, don't skimp. Buy
the best chops and of an adequate size. Half a pound per person is about right.

Select veal from a butcher who can offer you veal of a pinkish white color.
Run like fury if he offers you reddish meat; it's baby beef and certainly not
worth an elevated price.

Veal cooks quickly for the simple reason that once browned on both sides it
is only necessary for the meat to be cooked piping hot to the center. Ten minutes on one side and a brief period in the skillet on the other is sufficient. If the
chops are overcooked, they become dry and less palatable. The juicier the meat
the better.

For the menu here—veal chops teamed with cauliflower that has been broken
into "flowerets" before cooking—the cooking time for both the meat and the
vegetable is the same. Assemble all the ingredients, including a peeled, hard-
cooked egg. Then start preparation of the meal with the vegetable.

Sprinkle the meat with salt and pepper and have it ready. Start cooking the
cauliflower, and as it simmers cook the veal. As they cook, chop the egg for
garnish. Both dishes can be finished in seconds.

Côtes de Veau Du Barry
(Veal chops with cauliflower)

---

4 veal chops, about ½ pound each	3 tablespoons vinegar
Salt and freshly ground pepper to	½ cup chicken broth
taste	Cauliflower with parsley
4 tablespoons butter	(see recipe).

1. Sprinkle the chops on all sides with salt and pepper.

2. Heat 3 tablespoons of the butter in a heavy skillet, and when it is quite
hot add the chops. Cook about 10 minutes or until golden brown on one side.
Turn the chops.

3. Cook the chops until golden brown on the second side. Remove to a
warm dish. Add the vinegar to the skillet and stir with a wooden spoon or rubber spatula to dissolve the brown particles that cling to the bottom and sides of
the skillet. Cook until it is almost evaporated.

4. Add the chicken broth and cook briefly until the sauce is slightly syrupy.
Swirl in the remaining butter. Pour the sauce over the chops and serve immediately with the cauliflower.

Yield: Four servings.

Chou-fleur Persillé
(Cauliflower with sieved egg and parsley)

1 small head, about 1¾ pounds, cauliflower	**1** hard-cooked egg, peeled and put through a fine sieve
4 cups water	**5** tablespoons butter
Salt	Freshly ground pepper to taste
¼ cup milk	**2** tablespoons finely chopped parsley.

1. Trim away and discard the core of the cauliflower. Break the vegetable into "flowerets." Add the pieces to a saucepan and add the water, salt and milk. Bring to the boil and simmer 10 minutes or until tender. Do not overcook or the vegetable will become mushy. Drain. At this point the vegetable may be set aside and the final preparation done later.

2. Prepare the egg and set it aside.

3. When ready to cook, heat 1 tablespoon of butter in a skillet and add the cauliflower pieces. Toss and stir briefly until the pieces start to take on color. Transfer to a serving dish.

4. Heat the remaining butter and add the sieved egg, salt and pepper to taste. Pour this over the cauliflower and sprinkle with chopped parsley. Serve immediately.

Yield: Four servings.

THERE IS A SMALL MAGAZINE, EDITED AND PUB-
lished in Manhattan, that is little known to the world at large,
but is admired and respected by many chefs in the United
States. It is the official publication of the Vatel Club, to which most of the
finest French chefs in this country belong, and the editors declare that it is "the
only culinary review in the French language published in North America."

I was much amused, in a recent issue, to read about the origins of one of the
best and most quickly made veal dishes in the French repertory. The dish is
called côtes de veau Foyot or veal chops in the style of Foyot. The magazine
outlines the history of the Café Foyot, in its heyday one of the greatest restaurants in Paris. It was still in existence during the siege of Paris in 1870, until, I
believe, shortly after World War I.

The dish is made as follows: You take a fine, pink-textured veal chop and
cook it on both sides in butter. It takes only two minutes to a side, if the skillet
is heavy enough and the heat is high enough.

You combine fresh bread crumbs with grated Parmesan cheese and a portion
of butter at room temperature. This mixture is "workable." That is to say, it is
firm enough to be shaped by hand. You shape the mixture in four flat portions,
just large enough to cover each chop, arrange the chops in the skillet containing
chopped shallots, and pour in a touch of dry white wine. Then you bake it ten
minutes uncovered and then loosely covered with foil, for about thirty minutes
in all.

That's all there is to it. The dish is, to me, a classic example of how great
French cooking need not take hours and days of preparation to be brought to
simple perfection. Côtes de veau Foyot is a dish suitable for a gathering of your
most discriminating friends. It is worthy of a good wine, too, perhaps a fine
Burgundy of good vintage. An easily made and excellent accompaniment for
the dish would be noodles with a quickly, simply, and freshly made tomato
sauce.

Côtes de Veau Foyot
(Veal chops with Parmesan cheese in white wine)

---

4   veal chops, about ¾ pound each
Salt and freshly ground pepper to
taste
6   tablespoons butter at room
temperature
½   cup fresh bread crumbs

½   cup freshly grated Parmesan
cheese
2   tablespoons finely chopped
shallots
¼   cup dry white wine.

   1. Preheat the oven to 400 degrees.
   2. Sprinkle the chops on both sides with salt and pepper.
   3. Heat 2 tablespoons of butter in a heavy skillet and add the chops. Cook
over high heat until golden brown on one side, about 2 minutes. Turn the chops

and cook 2 minutes longer or until golden brown on the other side. Transfer the chops to a platter and keep warm.

4. Meanwhile, blend the bread crumbs, cheese, and remaining 4 tablespoons butter with the hands, until thoroughly worked together and blended. Divide the mixture into four portions of equal size.

5. Sprinkle the shallots over the bottom of the skillet in which the chops cooked. Return the chops to the skillet.

6. Work the bread crumb mixture into flat sheets to fit the top of each chop. Place on the tops of the chops.

7. Pour the wine around the chops.

8. Place, uncovered, in the oven and bake about 10 minutes until tops are appetizingly brown. Place a layer of foil on top, letting it rest loosely over the veal. Return to the oven and continue baking about 20 minutes.

9. When ready to serve, do not spoon the sauce over the veal. Spoon it around the veal.

Yield: Four servings.

Nouilles à la Sauce Tomate
(Noodles with fresh tomato sauce)

2	tablespoons butter	1	bay leaf
¼	cup finely chopped onion		Salt and freshly ground pepper to
1	small clove garlic, finely minced		taste
1	14-ounce can imported tomatoes with tomato paste	½	pound noodles of medium width.

1. Heat half the butter in a saucepan and add the onion and garlic. Cook, stirring briefly, and add the tomatoes. Add the bay leaf, salt, and pepper and cover.

2. Let simmer about 10 minutes. Remove the bay leaf. Swirl in the remaining butter.

3. Cook the noodles to the desired degree of doneness. Drain well and serve hot with the sauce.

Yield: Four servings.

BELGIAN ENDIVE IS, TO MY TASTE, ONE OF THE FINest of cooked vegetables when braised. It does require an extended cooking time, time in which the other ingredients for a meal can be assembled, chopped, heated, and so on.

There is an eception to that lengthy cooking time for the vegetable (which also, uncooked, makes a fine addition to a salad bowl). If the endive is shredded, the cooking time is greatly reduced.

One of the meats that is enormously complemented when served or cooked in tandem with endive is a nice cut of pink, tender veal. When placed in combination with braised endive, which has an uncommon, subtle flavor that is at once slightly bitter and slightly sweet, the veal should not be overpowering. The simpler the better.

One of the simplest ways of cooking veal (other than grilling it, of course) is a simple sauté, topping it off with a sauce consisting of nothing more than a few tablespoons of chopped shallots, a dash of white wine, and a little veal or chicken broth to thin and increase the quantity of the juice.

Incidentally, the sauce for the veal calls for swirling in butter as a last step before serving. I have often been asked why this is done. It is for the simple reason that butter, in effect, tends to thicken if it is swirled in. Care must be taken, however, not to boil the sauce after the butter is added or it will separate.

Both the veal and endive in these recipes are cooked quickly and may be put on the stove to cook simultaneously. There will be ample time for preparing a mixed green salad as an accompaniment.

Côtes de Veau aux Endives
(*Veal chops with braised endives*)

4 loin veal chops, ½ pound each
   Salt and freshly ground pepper
4 tablespoons butter
2 tablespoons chopped shallots

¼ cup dry white wine
½ cup fresh or canned chicken broth
   Braised endives (see recipe).

1. Sprinkle the chops on both sides with salt and pepper.
2. Heat 3 tablespoons of butter in a heavy skillet large enough to hold the chops in one layer. Add the chops and cook on one side about 5 minutes o. until golden brown.
3. Turn the chops and cook on the other side about 6 minutes or until cooked through. Do not overcook or the veal will be dry.
4. Remove the chops to a serving platter and cover with foil to keep warm.
5. Add the shallots and cook briefly, stirring. Add the wine and cook down to half the quantity. Add the broth and cook down quickly until reduced to about half the original quanity. Swirl in the remaining butter.
6. Spoon the sauce over the chops and serve with braised endives.

Yield: 4 servings.

Endives Braisées
(Braised endives)

1¼ pounds fresh Belgian endives
2 tablespoons butter
Juice of half a lemon or lime

Salt and freshly ground pepper
to taste
¼ teaspoon sugar.

1. Trim off the ends of each endive. Place the endives on a flat surface and cut on the diagonal into very thin strips. There should be about 6 cups of shredded endives.

2. Heat the butter in a heavy skillet and add the endives. Add the lemon juice, salt, pepper, and sugar.

3. Cook, stirring often, about 3 minutes or until wilted. Cover and cook about 8 minutes. Uncover and continue cooking, stirring often, about 3 or 4 minutes or until lightly browned.

Yield: Four servings.

Salade Panachée
(Mixed green salad)

1 bunch watercress
1 head Boston lettuce
1 red, ripe tomato, cored and cut into eighths
6 radishes, trimmed and thinly sliced
2 tablespoons tarragon vinegar

1 clove garlic finely minced
1 tablespoon imported mustard, such as Dijon or Düsseldorf
6 tablespoons olive oil
Salt and freshly ground pepper to taste.

1. Trim off the tough stems of the watercress. Core the Boston lettuce and separate the leaves. Rinse the greens and shake off excess moisture. Put the greens in a mixing bowl and add the tomato and radishes.

2. Blend the vinegar and minced garlic and mustard in a mixing bowl. Stir with a whisk, gradually adding the oil. Add salt and pepper to taste.

3. Toss the greens with the dressing.

Yield: Four servings.

ONE OF THE BEST, TASTIEST, AND FASTEST GROUND meat dishes in the French repertory is known as veal cutlets Pojarski. Like bitoks, it is a kind of hamburger. The story of the origin of the name is well known. There was a tavern in a Russian town called Torjok, and the proprietor of the inn was named Pojarski. Legend has it that he created one or more of the ground beef dishes that bear his name, and these he served to passengers who passed his way in their carriages.

There are numerous basic ingredients other than veal that may be used in making Pojarski. It can be made, for example, with ground chicken and salmon.

To prepare veal Pojarski, the meat is twice ground (or it may be ground in a food processor). The meat is mixed with bread crumbs and cream and seasoned lightly with nutmeg, salt, and pepper. This is divided into equal portions and each portion shaped into "cutlets," that is to say, in the shape of chops such as pork or lamb chops. The cutlets are cooked in butter and served with a bit of noisette butter poured over.

Fresh peas have been used as an accompaniment for the veal Pojarski, the peas combined with cooked potatoes.

To go about it, cook the potatoes in their jackets, and peel them when cool enough to handle. As the potatoes cook, prepare the peas, Meanwhile, blend the veal with the other ingredients. Blend the potatoes with the peas.

Côtes de Veau "Pojarski"
(Ground veal cutlets with bread crumbs and cream)

1½ pounds lean veal, ground twice	Salt and freshly ground pepper
1 to 1¼ cups fine, fresh bread	to taste
crumbs	¾ cup heavy cream
¼ teaspoon grated nutmeg	4 tablespoons butter
Few drops of Tabasco	Lemon wedges, optional.

1. The veal may be ground by the butcher or it may be ground in a food processor. Place the veal in a mixing bowl and add ½ cup of crumbs, nutmeg, Tabasco, salt, and pepper. Beat vigorously with a wooden spoon or blend in the food processor.

2. Gradually beat in the cream. Eggs are not required in this recipe.

3. Divide the mixture into four portions and shape into ovals. Roll the ovals lightly in the remaining crumbs. Flatten the ovals to make "chops" about half an inch thick. Actually, the "chops" should be shaped by hand to resemble pork chops.

4. Heat half the butter in a skillet and add the chops. Brown about 5 minutes on the other side or until cooked.

5. Transfer the patties to a warm serving dish. Heat the remaining butter in

another skillet until it is hazelnut brown. Pour over the patties and serve hot. If desired, serve with lemon wedges.

Yield: Four servings.

Pommes de Terre et Pois au Printemps
(Potatoes and peas in cream sauce)

8   new, red, "waxy" potatoes,
    about 1 pound
    Salt
¾   cup freshly shelled green peas,
    about ¾ pound in the shell
1   tablespoon butter
1   very small white onion, peeled and
    thinly sliced

1   large leaf Boston lettuce, finely
    shredded
    Freshly ground pepper to taste
¼   teaspoon sugar
¼   cup heavy cream
¼   cup milk.

1. Place the potatoes in a saucepan and add water to cover and salt to taste. Bring to the boil and cook about 20 minutes. Drain.

2. In another saucepan, combine the peas, butter, onion, shredded lettuce, salt and pepper to taste, and sugar. Cover closely and simmer about 5 to 10 minutes, depending on the age of the peas. Cook until tender.

3. Meanwhile, peel and cut the potatoes into quarter-inch-thick slices. Add the potatoes to the peas. Add the cream and milk, salt and pepper to taste. Cook down about 5 minutes. Serve hot.

Yield: Four servings.

ONE OF THE BEST, MOST EASILY MADE, AND LEAST costly of fine dishes is the one known in France as escalopes de veau viennoise. Escalopes de veau are simply scaloppine of veal. Viennoise means in the style of Vienna, and the dish is the French version of wiener schnitzel.

It is a dish that offers a good lesson in one of the basics of cookery, which is to say the technique of breading. The meat—a quarter of a pound per person is sufficient—is first pounded lightly and then, in classic fashion, dipped first in flour, then in beaten egg and finally in bread crumbs. The breaded scallops are cooked in oil until golden brown on both sides and served with a garnish, and, more often than not, with beurre noisette, or butter that is heated until it takes on the color of hazelnuts.

The garnishes for escalopes de veau viennoise are anchovies, capers, sieved and/or chopped hard-cooked egg, and parsley. The preparation time for the dish is approximately fifteen minutes; the cooking time less than ten. A good accompaniment for the breaded veal are cooked potatoes, sliced and browned in a skillet. Logically, the potatoes should be put on to simmer and, as they cook, the veal should be made ready.

The main course should be followed by a salad; watercress and Belgian endive are an excellent combination. The dessert—purchased, perhaps—should be as simple as fresh fruit or a fruit compote.

Escalopes de Veau Viennoise
(Breaded veal with lemon and caper garnish)

4	veal scaloppine, about ¼ pound each	¼	cup finely chopped parsely
	Salt and freshly ground pepper	4	thin slices lemon, seeded
2	eggs, lightly beaten	4	flat fillets of anchovies
3	tablespoons water	¼	cup drained capers
	Flour for dredging	¼	to ½ cup peanut, vegetable, or corn oil
1	cup fresh bread crumbs	6	tablespoons butter.
1	hard-cooked egg		

1. Place the scaloppine, one at a time, between sheets of plastic wrap and pound them with a flat mallet or the bottom of a heavy skillet until quite thin.

2. Sprinkle the meat on all sides with salt and pepper.

3. Beat the eggs with the water and season with salt and pepper. Add this mixture to a large flat plate.

4. Have ready two other large flat plates, one containing the flour, the other containing the bread crumbs.

5. Coat the slices on both sides with flour. Dip the slices, one at a time, in egg until well coated, and then in bread crumbs until uniformly coated. As the

slices are prepared set them aside. Tap each slice lightly with a flat spatula to help the crumbs adhere.

6. Before cooking the meat, prepare the garnishes.

7. Slice the egg in half. Chop the white and put the yolk through a fine sieve. Set them aside in separate batches. Have the chopped parsley ready.

8. Arrange the lemon slices on a plate. Shape each anchovy fillet into a round band and arrange one band on each lemon slice. Fill each anchovy band with capers.

9. Heat ¼ cup of oil in one large skillet or use two skillets, if necessary, and add more oil. Cook the meat until nicely browned on one side. Turn and cook on the other side until browned.

10. Arrange the slices on each of four hot plates. Heat the butter in a skillet, swirling it around until it foams up and becomes hazelnut brown. Do not burn the butter. When the foam subsides, pour equal portions of butter over each meat slice.

11. Garnish each slice with a slice of anchovy-topped lemon. Garnish the ends of each slice with neat spoonfuls of chopped egg white, chopped yolk, more capers and chopped parsley.

Yield: Four servings.

Pommes de Terre Sautées
(*Skillet potatoes*)

---

4 medium-size potatoes, about 1¼ pounds Salt to taste	3 tablespoons peanut, vegetable, or corn oil 1 tablespoon butter.

1. Place the unpeeled potatoes in a saucepan and add cold water to cover. Add salt to taste and bring to the boil. Simmer 15 to 20 minutes until tender. Do not overcook. The potatoes must remain firm. This may be done a day in advance.

2. Peel the potatoes and cut them into slices one-quarter inch thick or slightly thicker.

3. Heat the oil and butter in a heavy skillet and add the potato slices. Add salt and pepper. Cook, shaking and tossing the skillet to redistribute the potatoes. Cook until the potatoes form a crisp outside crust and are nicely browned. Serve hot.

Yield: Four servings.

A GOOD, EASILY-MADE REDUCTION OF TOMATOES— an essence of tomatoes to use another phrase—can be one of the greatest boons to rapid cooking. The reduction can be added to soups and sauces, and turned into a fine spaghetti sauce simply by heating it in oil with garlic, oregano, and chopped parsley. The essence will also keep well if tightly stored in the refrigerator, particularly if a light layer of oil is spooned over the top to help preserve it. It can also be frozen.

One example of its use is demonstrated here in a scaloppine dish made with the sauce plus scaloppine and mozzarella cheese. It is simply a rolled version of veal parmigiana but a trifle more fancy, perhaps.

Veal scaloppine, of course, is almost by its nature a meat that should never require prolonged cooking. The longer it cooks the drier it becomes, whether it is a quick sauté as in veal scaloppine marsala, veal francese or veal piccata.

In the dish outlined below, the veal is wrapped around fingers of mozzarella cheese, cigarette fashion. These rolls are browned quickly in hot oil and a rapid-fire tomato sauce is prepared in the same skillet with garlic and wine. The scaloppine rolls, the sauce, parsley, and Parmesan cheese are layered and baked until piping hot.

This is the kind of dish that would be compatible with almost any form of pasta and one interesting form, available in Italian markets, is called bavette. Serve with a crusty loaf of bread and a good dry Italian red wine such as Valpolicella or Bardolino.

Unless otherwise indicated, it is recommended that this menu include the usual salad with cheese as a second course and, if desired, a final course of fresh fruit or a purchased or previously made dessert.

Escalopine de Veau au Mozzarella Parmigiana
(*Scaloppine and Mozzarella Parmigiana*)

1 2-pound, 3-ounce can imported tomatoes, about 4 cups	¼ pound whole-milk mozzarella cheese
8 slices scaloppine of veal, about 1¼ pounds	2 tablespoons olive oil
Salt and freshly ground pepper to taste	2 cloves garlic, finely minced
	¼ cup dry white wine
½ teaspoon finely chopped rosemary	3 tablespoons finely chopped parsley
	¼ cup grated Parmesan cheese.

1. Place the tomatoes in a heavy saucepan and bring to the boil. Let cook until thickened and reduced to 3 cups.

2. Pound the meat lightly with a flat mallet without breaking the fibers. Place the slices on a flat surface and sprinkle with salt, pepper, and rosemary. Cut the mozzarella into eight thin "fingers" of equal size. Arrange one finger in the center of each veal slice. Fold over the edges, then roll, envelope fashion, to enclose the cheese. Tie each roll neatly with string in two places.

3. Preheat the oven to 400 degrees.

4. Heat the roll in a heavy skillet and brown the rolls quickly and evenly over high heat, about 4 minutes. Transfer the rolls to a baking dish. Remove the string.

5. To the skillet add the garlic and cook briefly. Add the wine and stir to dissolve the brown particles that cling to the bottom and sides of the pan. Add the cooked-down tomatoes, salt and pepper. Cook 5 minutes and add the parsley.

6. Pour the sauce over the meat rolls and sprinkle with Parmesan cheese. Bake 10 to 15 minutes until piping hot. Serve with cooked buttered imported Italian noodles such as bavette.

Yield: Four servings.

A N ACQUAINTANCE FROM SWITZERLAND, A PROFES-
sional chef, passed through town and advised me that while
veal zurichoise made only with veal, was acceptable—and is
often prepared that way even in Swiss kitchens—the real, the true, the original
veal zurichoise is made with three principal ingredients, namely, veal, pork,
and fresh mushrooms. It is certainly a fine combination of flavors and textures
and I would never dispute a Swiss native.

There are several things to be noted in preparing this recipe. First, the meats
and mushrooms must be cut into very fine or thin strips. Two, they must be or
should be cooked over very high heat and you should have a sieve ready to
drain them as they cook (the drippings from the meat will be returned to the
final cream sauce). Three, the ingredients should be cooked in a large skillet to
hasten the cooking time.

It is best in this recipe, as in almost all recipes, to have all the ingredients
prepared or laid out and ready to go into the skillet before starting to cook. This
is a great time-saver.

The recommended seasonings for this dish include fresh chives, parsley, and
tarragon, all of which can be bought fresh when in season. If they are not available, however, a sprinkling of chopped fresh parsley—which is available all
year long—would suffice.

One traditional accompaniment for this dish (another is skillet or rosti potatoes) are buttered noodles. Before cooking the meat, have water on to boil to
receive the noodles at the last minuute.

Veau Zurichoise
(Veal with pork and mushrooms)

½ pound veal, cut into very thin
strips
½ pound lean pork, cut into very
thin strips
3 cups sliced mushrooms, cut into
very thin strips
3 tablespoons peanut, vegetable, or
corn oil
Salt and freshly ground pepper to
taste

2 tablespoons butter
2 tablespoons chopped shallots
½ cup dry white wine
½ cup chicken broth
2 cups sour cream
1 tablespoon finely chopped chives
1 tablespoon finely chopped parsley
1 teaspoon finely chopped tarragon.

1. Prepare the veal, pork and mushrooms and set them aside in separate
batches.

2. Heat 2 tablespoons of oil in a large skillet and add the pork. Cook briefly,
stirring and shaking the skillet, about 45 seconds. Add the veal and cook, stirring and shaking the skillet, until the veal loses its pink color.

3. Drain in a sieve but catch the drippings for later use.

4. To the skillet add 1 more tablespoon of oil and cook the mushrooms, stirring and shaking the skillet, until they give up their liquid. Cook until liquid evaporates. Add the mushrooms to the meat. Add salt and pepper to taste.

5. Heat the butter in the skillet and add the shallots. Cook until wilted and add the wine. Cook until almost completely reduced and add the broth plus the drippings from the meat. Cook down by about one-third and add the sour cream. Stir without boiling. Add the meat, salt, pepper, chives, parsley, and tarragon. Heat until piping hot, but do not boil or the cream will curdle. Serve hot with noodles.

Yield: Four servings.

Nouilles au Beurre
(Buttered noodles)

½ **pound broad noodles**   2 **tablespoons butter.**
    Salt to taste

1. Drop the noodles into boiling salted water to cover and stir until water returns to the boil. Cook until noodles are tender, 7 minutes or longer.

2. Drain and return the noodles to the pot. Add the butter and toss well until coated.

Yield: Four servings.

WHEN IT IS A QUESTION OF SPEED-COOKING, THAT IS to say in less than an hour, the advantages of boneless cuts of meat are obvious. And of all those boneless cuts, there are few with more flavor than veal. Veal, on the other hand, requires a bit more knowledge of meat cookery than does, let us say, beef, lamb, or pork. Although beef and lamb may be cooked rare or well-done or some point in between, according to taste, the cooking time is fairly easy to manipulate. Pork, of course, must be cooked to a fairly well-done state because of the nature of the meat (and there is sometimes something to be said, even, for pork that has been long cooked until it is fork tender).

Undercooked veal is a trifle unappetizing. Overcooked veal has a tendency to be dry and chewy. But veal that is cooked to the exact point of doneness, cooked so that the center is moist yet no longer pink, is one of the choicest morsels that any cook could bring to the table.

Choice veal for the most part doesn't require a great deal of embellishing to be good, although the meat does adapt well—because of its basically neutral nature—to a variety of herbs and spices including rosemary or sage (very Italian) or tarragon (very French). It is excellent Hungarian-style (or my idea of what that style is) with a touch of paprika and a smattering of sour cream. The total cooking time for an individual veal steak (preferably taken from the leg of the animal) is approximately ten minutes. The final sauce demands not more than another ten minutes or so.

Like almost any dish made with a sour cream sauce, this veal goes extremely well with noodles, and can be given an added fillip with a bit of caraway seed. The preparation and cooking time for broccoli, another good side dish, and noodles is scarcely more than fifteen minutes, if that. And with the proper coordination and organization, all the dishes may be prepared simultaneously.

Steak de Veau Hongroise
(Sautéed veal steak with paprika)

4 boneless veal steaks, preferably taken from the leg, about 1½ pounds total weight	⅓ cup finely chopped onions
	1 teaspoon garlic
	⅓ pound sliced or quartered mushrooms, about 3 cups
Salt to taste	
Freshly ground pepper to taste	1 tablespoon paprika
2 tablespoons flour	½ cup dry white wine
3 tablespoons butter	½ cup sour cream.

1. Sprinkle the meat on both sides with salt and pepper. Dredge on both sides in flour.

2. Heat the butter in a heavy skillet and cook the meat on one side until golden brown, about 5 minutes. Turn and cook on the other side about 5 minutes.

3. Remove the meat and keep it warm.

4. To the skillet add the onions and garlic. Cook until onion is wilted. Add the mushrooms and paprika and cook until mushrooms are wilted, about 5 minutes. Sprinkle with salt and pepper. Add white wine and cook until it is almost evaporated. Add salt and pepper to taste.

5. Stir in sour cream and heat without boiling. Return the meat to the skillet. Turn it in the skillet and serve with the sauce spooned over. Serve with buttered noodles.

Yield: Four servings.

I HAVE OFTEN REFLECTED ON THE DIFFERENCES, as I see and remember them, between home kitchens, those of my childhood and those in this country.

I was brought up in a rural community in Burgundy, and we literally lived off the land. Our home garden was not vast, but it was copiously planted and carefully tended. There was one small quarter given over to sweet green herbs and that was my grandmother's pride. She grew an abundance of parsley and chives, tarragon and chervil. Those were the basics, not only of her herb plot but also of her kitchen.

It was years later, as an apprentice in a Paris restaurant, that I learned that these were the most traditional herbs of the classic French kitchen. These four herbs are what are known as "les fines herbes," and they are the requirements for a few thousand dishes, the best known of which is in an omelette aux fines herbes.

I have discovered, happily, that more and more Americans are making use of these herbs, except for chervil, which, for some reason, has never been very popular here. More often than not, it can be easily dispensed with.

One of the best uses for les fines herbes is with a sauté of liver, which demands a quick treatment if it is to be served with maximum flavor and texture. Long-cooked liver (and minutes in this case can matter) is dry, tasteless, and dull.

The preparation of foie de veau aux fines herbes is simplicity itself. The liver is lightly floured and seasoned and cooked hastily on both sides in oil. The slices are removed, the skillet wiped clean and butter added. Shallots are cooked quickly, and a dash of vinegar is added. The hot sauce is poured over and all of it is sprinkled with the herbs. Grilled tomatoes and steamed potatoes are classic accompaniments for the dish.

Foie de Veau aux Fines Herbes
(Calves' liver sautéed with herbs)

---

8 thin slices calves' liver, about 1½ pounds
   Salt and freshly ground pepper to taste
¼ cup flour
2 tablespoons peanut, vegetable, or corn oil
6 tablespoons butter

2 tablespoons finely chopped shallots
1 tablespoon red wine vinegar
2 tablespoons finely chopped parsley
2 tablespoons finely chopped chives
1 teaspoon finely chopped fresh tarragon.

1. Place the liver slices on a flat surface and sprinkle on both sides with salt and pepper. Dredge on both sides in flour and shake off excess.

2. Heat the oil in a large skillet and cook as many pieces of liver at one time as will fit comfortably in the skillet. Cook about 1 minute or longer until nicely

browned. The cooking time will vary depending on the thickness of the slices. Turn and cook about 1 minute or longer to the desired degree of doneness.

3. Remove the slices to a warm platter and continue adding slices in one layer. As the slices cook, remove them and add more. Continue until all the slices are cooked. Transfer the liver to the platter and keep warm.

4. Pour off any fat that is left in the pan. Wipe out the pan with a clean cloth or paper toweling. Add the butter and cook over high heat until the butter is hazelnut brown. Add the shallots, stirring, and cook about 5 seconds. Add the vinegar and pour the hot butter over the liver. Sprinkle with parsley, chives, and tarragon.

Yield: Four servings.

Tomates Grillées
(Grilled tomatoes)

2 large red, ripe tomatoes
1 tablespoon plus 4 teaspoons peanut, vegetable, or corn oil

1 large clove garlic, cut into slivers
Salt and freshly ground pepper to taste.

1. Preheat the broiler.
2. Core the tomatoes and slice them in half.
3. Grease a baking dish large enough to hold the tomato halves with 1 tablespoon oil. Arrange the halves over it, cut side up. Insert slivers of garlic inside the cut side of the tomatoes.
4. Sprinkle each half with salt and pepper. Sprinkle about 1 teaspoon oil over each half and place them under the broiler. Broil about 5 minutes. Quickly remove the garlic slivers and serve.

Yield: Four servings.

Pommes Vapeur
(Steamed potatoes)

8 small, red "new" potatoes, about ¾ pound

Salt to taste.

1. Peel the potatoes and put them in a saucepan. Add water to cover and salt to taste.
2. Bring to the boil and simmer about 12 minutes or until potatoes are tender. Drain and serve. These potatoes are frequently served without butter or other garnish.

Yield: Four servings.

HISTORIANS CONTEND, OF COURSE, THAT ITALY was actually the cradle of French cooking (I have yet to find a French chef, including myself, willing to admit to the truth of that claim) and that it all began with the arrival of Catherine de Médicis, who came to France to wed Henry II in the sixteenth century. To be sure, there are certain dishes in French cooking that are dead ringers for those produced in Italian kitchens and vice versa. One of the most conspicuous of these is the dish known in France as foie de veau lyonnaise, or calves' liver and onions, and in Italy as fegato alla veneziana. The former is "in the style of Lyon," the latter, "in the style of Venice."

The two dishes are remarkably similar in their traditional preparations. The liver in both is cooked with a considerable amount of onions and both have just a trace of vinegar added to the skillet before serving.

Origins aside, calves' liver lyonnaise is a tasty, excellent dish, easily prepared and quickly cooked. Ideal for cooking in less than an hour.

The most difficult part of preparing such a meal, if indeed it could be called complicated, is in cutting the liver and onions to the required size. The liver should be cut into very thin strips, the onions sliced wafer thin.

The onions take far more time to cook than the liver; as a matter of fact, they should cook until they become slightly more than golden, almost caramel colored. This long cooking (and they must be stirred often to prevent sticking) brings out the natural sugars or sweetness of the onions. Thus, prepare and start to cook the onions. As they cook, prepare the remaining ingredients.

The liver should not take more than five minutes for the entire batch to cook.

As the onions cook the potatoes should also be put on to boil. Potatoes with parsley are the traditional accompaniment for calves' liver lyonnaise.

Foie de Veau Lyonnaise
(Calves' liver and onions)

2 large onions, about 1½ pounds total weight	Salt and freshly ground pepper to taste
4 tablespoons peanut, vegetable, or corn oil	1 pound calves' liver
1 bay leaf	2 tablespoons butter
	2 tablespoons vinegar
	Chopped parsley for garnish.

1. Peel the onions and quarter them. Slice them thinly. There should be about 5 cups.

2. Heat 2 tablespoons of the oil in a skillet and add the onions, bay leaf, salt, and pepper. Cook, stirring as necessary, until onions are golden brown, about 20 minutes. Set aside.

3. Meanwhile, cut the liver into thin strips about half an inch wide or slightly less. Sprinkle with salt and pepper.

4. Heat the remaining oil in a skillet and when it is hot and almost smoking, add half the liver, stirring rapidly and turning the pieces as necessary so that they brown evenly. Cook about 2 minutes in all and drain in a sieve. Return the oil to the skillet and when hot add the remaining liver. Cook the same way and drain.

5. To the skillet add the butter. Add the liver and toss. Add the onions and blend well. Add the vinegar and blend. Serve piping hot, garnished with chopped parsley. Serve with boiled potatoes.

Yield: Four servings.

Pommes Miettes
(Sautéed potato cubes)

1½ pounds potatoes, peeled	⅓ cup peanut, vegetable, or corn
Salt and freshly ground pepper	oil
to taste	2 tablespoons butter.

1. Cut the potatoes into half-inch slices. Cut the slices into half-inch strips. Cut the strips into half-inch cubes. As the cubes are formed, drop them into cold water to prevent discoloration.

2. Drain the potatoes and add them to a saucepan. Add water to cover and salt to taste. Bring to the boil and let simmer about 2 minutes. Drain.

3. Heat the oil in a skillet, preferably one with rounded sides. Add the potatoes. Add salt and pepper to taste. Cook, shaking the skillet and stirring occasionally, so that the potatoes cook evenly. When stirring, stir gently so that the pieces do not break. Cook about 10 minutes or until the potato cubes are nicely browned.

4. Drain the potatoes into a colander. Return them to the skillet and add the butter. Toss the potatoes in the butter, cooking over high heat about 5 minutes. Serve.

Yield: Four servings.

THERE ARE NUMEROUS FOODS THAT BY THEIR very nature demand hasty cooking. A case in point is calves' liver—if, that is, you prefer thin cuts of liver, as I do. Properly done, the liver should cook no more than two to three minutes to a side. If the liver is overcooked, it becomes, to my taste, dry and therefore unpalatable.

Thus liver falls into that category of meals where the time-consuming elements are the dishes destined to accompany it.

The ideal accompaniment for calves' liver is a purée of potatoes and such other vegetables as complement it in flavor, color, and texture.

A sauté of zucchini and tomatoes provençale is highly compatible with sautéed liver. The dish is called provençale in its use of oil, garlic, and the tomatoes. It takes about seven minutes to cook, once the ingredients are ready for the skillet.

To save time in preparing the menu here, put the potatoes up to boil first (the cooking, including the final preparation, is approximately half an hour). As the potatoes cook, prepare and cook the zucchini dish. Finally sauté the liver quickly.

The liver, by the way, takes a thin, delicate pan sauce, made by addition of a little vinegar and a touch of butter to the skillet the moment the liver is cooked and removed.

Serve with the usual salad and cheese and a light, purchased dessert, such as a fruit sherbet.

Foie de Veau au Vinaigre
(Calves' liver with vinegar)

4 slices calves' liver, about 1 pound total weight
Salt and freshly ground pepper to taste
Flour for dredging

2 tablespoons oil
3 tablespoons plus 2 teaspoons butter
1 tablespoon red wine vinegar
1 tablespoon finely chopped parsley.

1. Sprinkle the liver with salt and pepper. Dredge it on both sides in flour to coat thoroughly. Shake off excess flour.

2. Heat the oil and 2 tablespoons of butter in a large, heavy skillet, and when the mixture is very hot and starting to brown, add the liver slices. Cook about 1 minute over high heat or until nicely browned. Turn the liver and cook about 1 minute—or longer, if desired.

3. Remove the liver and pour off the fat from the skillet. Add the remaining butter and cook over high heat, stirring until it is hazelnut brown. Quickly add the wine vinegar and let it boil up. Pour this mixture over the liver. Sprinkle with chopped parsley and serve.

Yield: Four servings.

Purée de Pommes
(*Puréed potatoes*)

1½   pounds potatoes
    Salt to taste
¾   cup milk

3   tablespoons butter at room
    temperature
⅛   teaspoon freshly grated nutmeg
    or to taste.

1. Peel the potatoes and quarter or cut them into two-inch cubes.

2. Place the potatoes in a saucepan, and add cold water to cover and salt to taste. Bring to a boil and simmer 20 minutes or until potatoes are tender.

3. Drain the potatoes and put them through a food mill or potato ricer. Return them to the saucepan.

4. Meanwhile bring the milk to a boil.

5. While the milk is being heated, use a wooden spoon and add the butter to the potatoes while beating. Add salt and nutmeg to taste and beat in the hot milk.

Yield: Four servings.

Courgettes et Tomates Cerises à la Provençale
(*Zucchini and cherry tomatoes with garlic*)

2   firm, unblemished zucchini,
    about ¾ pound total weight
3   tablespoons olive oil

Salt and freshly ground pepper to
taste
2   large cloves garlic, unpeeled
16   cherry tomatoes.

1. Trim the ends from the zucchini. Quarter the zucchini lengthwise. Cut each quarter into half-inch lengths. There should be about 3½ cups.

2. Heat the oil, and when it is hot, add the zucchini. Sprinkle with salt and pepper to taste. Add the garlic and cook, shaking the skillet and stirring until zucchini starts to brown, about 5 minutes.

3. Add the tomatoes and continue to cook, stirring gently so the tomatoes cook evenly without breaks in the skin. Cook about 2 minutes, just until the tomatoes are heated. Do not overcook, or the tomatoes will break. Remove and discard the garlic and serve hot.

Yield: Four servings.

THE VIRTUES OF VEAL SCALOPPINE AS THE BASIS for hasty dishes have been elaborated on at considerable length. One of the most interesting aspects of veal is the remarkable manner in which it is complemented by other foods and flavors. Almost any sweet herb or spice goes agreeably well with veal, whether it be a sweetly perfumed herb like basil or tarragon or something as pungent and assertive as curry powder.

Veal is, admittedly, one of the most expensive of meats as well as one of the choicest in its versatility. There is another virtue in the fact that scaloppine can be "stretched" by combining it with other complementary foods, such as mushrooms, ham, and cheese. And, in fact, the four ingredients go well together in one dish, as demonstrated in the quickly cooked one outlined here.

This dish has Italian origins, and ideally it is made with prosciutto although plain boiled ham could be used. Similarly, the traditional cheese for this dish is Fontina, although Gruyère or Swiss also work well.

Because the dish involves fresh mushrooms in a cream sauce, buttered noodles make an admirable accompaniment—plain buttered noodles or buttered noodles with seeds such as caraway, as indicated below.

Once the ingredients for this dish are assembled, the final preparation is child's play.

Almost any well-made tossed green salad would go well with this meal. A bowl of arugula blended, perhaps, with pieces of crisp romaine and tossed with oil and vinegar would be excellent. A bottle of dry red Italian wine or chilled dry white wine would make a good accompaniment. For dessert try chilled, ripe, unblemished pears and cheese.

Escalopes de Veau à la Crème
(Veal with mushrooms in cream)

1½ pounds veal cut into eight thin slices	Salt and freshly ground pepper to taste
3 tablespoons butter	2 tablespoons dry white wine
1 tablespoon finely chopped shallots	1 cup heavy cream
½ pound mushrooms, thinly sliced, about 3 cups	8 thin slices prosciutto or boiled ham
	8 thin slices Fontina, Gruyère, or Swiss cheese.

1. Pound the veal lightly with a flat mallet to make it thinner. Set aside.

2. Melt 2 tablespoons of butter in a saucepan and add the shallots. Cook briefly and add the mushrooms, salt and pepper to taste. Sprinkle with wine and cook about 10 seconds. Add the cream. Cook down over high heat until cream has a saucelike consistency, about 3 minutes. Set aside.

3. Heat the remaining 1 tablespoon butter in a heavy skillet and add the

veal. Cook to brown lightly on one side, about 2 minutes. Turn and cook to brown on the other side, about 2 minutes.

4. Transfer the veal to a platter.

5. Cover each slice of veal with a slice of prosciutto. It should be trimmed to fit the veal neatly or fold the slice over.

6. Spoon equal portions of creamed mushrooms on the ham. Arrange one piece of cheese on each serving. Run briefly under the broiler just until the cheese melts. Serve immediately.

Yield: Four servings.

Nouilles au Carvi
(*Buttered noodles with caraway seeds*)

½ **pound broad noodles**
    Salt to taste

2 **tablespoons butter**
½ **teaspoon caraway seeds.**

1. Drop the noodles into boiling salted water to cover and stir until water returns to the boil. Cook until noodles are tender, 7 minutes or longer.

2. Drain and return the noodles to the pot. Add the butter and caraway seeds and toss well until coated.

Yield: Four servings.

I F EVER THERE WAS A DISH TAILOR-MADE FOR quick cooking—and pure enjoyment—it is of the sort known in French as an émincé, a word for which there is no exact English equivalent. An émincé consists of any sort of meat cut into shreds and cooked quickly with liquids and seasonings added to make a sauce. Next to an omelet, perhaps, there are few dishes to be cooked in such a hurry.

There is no accounting of why an émincé of veal is so characteristically Swiss, although, like watches and yodeling, it is. It is the sort of dish that would, of necessity, be included in any comprehensive Swiss cookbook.

A traditional accompaniment for the dish are rosti potatoes, and a recipe for each is given here. Untypically, the side dish, the potatoes, requires a touch more effort than the main course.

A meal of émincé of veal and rosti potatoes plus a salad, followed by a cheese with new apples, would be sufficient for a meal unto itself. If you insist on a dessert, however, an apple tart or pie—purchased to conserve time—would be ideal.

By all means, start this menu with the potatoes, and as they cook occupy yourself with the meat and accompaniments.

Émincé de Veau à la Crème
(Veal in cream sauce)

1 pound thin veal slices, preferably taken from the leg	Salt and freshly ground pepper to taste
¼ pound thinly sliced prosciutto or boiled ham	1 tablespoon finely chopped shallots
2 cups thinly sliced mushrooms	½ cup dry white wine
2 tablespoons butter	1½ cups heavy cream.

1. Cut the veal into the thinnest possible (julienne) strips. Set aside.

2. Stack the prosciutto slices and cut them into the thinnest possible strips. Set aside.

3. Prepare the mushrooms and set aside.

4. Heat the butter in a skillet and when it is hot without browning, add the veal, stirring rapidly. Sprinkle with salt and pepper and cook about 45 seconds over very high heat, stirring. Add the prosciutto, cook about 10 seconds and, using a slotted spoon, remove the meats. Set aside.

5. To the skillet add the mushrooms and cook until wilted. Add the shallots, cook about 30 seconds, stirring, and add the wine. Cook until almost completely reduced and add the cream. Cook about 5 minutes over high heat. Add the meats and any liquid they give up. Cook briefly until piping hot. Sprinkle with salt and pepper and serve immediately with rosti potatoes.

Yield: Four servings.

Galette de Pommes de Terre
(*Rosti potatoes*)

5 or 6 Maine potatoes, about 1½ pounds
Salt to taste
¼ cup oil

7 tablespoons butter, approximately
Freshly ground pepper to taste.

1. Place the potatoes in a kettle and add cold water to cover and salt to taste. Bring to the boil and simmer about 15 minutes. Do not fully cook.

2. Drain the potatoes and let them cool.

3. Peel the potatoes and grate them using the coarse blade, or slice the potatoes thinly and cut into julienne strips.

4. Meanwhile, cure a black iron skillet by heating ¼ cup oil to the smoking point. Let stand half an hour or so. Pour out the oil and wipe out the skillet with paper towels.

5. Heat 2 tablespoons of butter in the skillet and add the potatoes in one thick layer. Sprinkle with salt and pepper. Cook, pressing down with the flat side of a spatula. When golden brown on one side, after about 10 minutes, carefully but quickly invert a plate over the potatoes and turn the ''pancake'' into the plate. Slip the pancake, uncooked side down, back into the skillet. Add another 2 tablespoons of butter, letting it melt around the pancake. If necessary, add more butter. Cook, pressing down occasionally, until golden brown on the other side. Serve sliced in wedges.

Yield: Four servings.

THERE ARE A DOZEN OR SO QUESTIONS THAT SEEM inevitable in casual conversation in any chef's life. Things like, "What's your favorite food?" "Do you ever eat junk food?" and "Do you have to watch your weight?"

A fourth recurrent query is whether or not the chef can recreate a particular dish after a single sampling. A dish, that is, heretofore not encountered. The answer to that one is an almost unqualified yes. Provided it is a dish within the Western tradition. It stands to reason that cooks and chefs of the Middle East and Far East—in places like India and Thailand and Korea—indulge in spices and seasonings that are generally unknown to French and American kitchens.

One of the trickiest foods, one that required more than a little amount of time to figure out, came about while having dinner at a small Italian restaurant in Boston a few years back. The dish in question was a boneless chicken filled with an incredibly light "custard" that seemed to melt in the mouth.

How, one wondered, could an uncooked custard mixture, a blend of eggs and cream and seasonings, be inserted inside the cavity of a bird without having the custard seep out the enclosure. We even tried sewing up the cavity with very tight stitches using a trussing needle and thread. To no avail. A short while later, by accident, I was faced with a batch of leftover scrambled eggs, untouched by a house guest. Suddenly it dawned on me that if this were used as a filling, it might—just possibly—come out smooth and custard-like. I tried it and it worked.

Since then I've discovered that scrambled eggs make a fine filling for many things, including the hastily made dish that follows, rollatine of veal, the kind that is sometimes called in French "veal birds." The egg filling is easily made and seasoned with a touch of cream and herbs. The preparation of the dish is quick and simplicity itself. Because the veal is cut in the form of scaloppine, it cooks quickly. The dish is accompanied in an ideal sense with a very simple and good quick fresh tomato sauce.

Rollatine de Veau
(Rollatine of veal with egg filling)

---

8   pieces veal scaloppine, about ¾ pound
    Salt and freshly ground pepper to taste
2   large eggs
2   tablespoons heavy cream

1   tablespoon finely chopped herbs such as tarragon, chives, parsley, or a combination of two or more
1   tablespoon butter
    Flour for dredging
2   tablespoons butter
    Fresh tomato sauce (see recipe).

1. Place the veal slices between slices of plastic wrap and pound lightly. Do not make holes in the meat. Sprinkle with salt and pepper.

2. Break the eggs into a mixing bowl and add the cream, herbs, salt and pepper to taste. Beat lightly to blend.

3. Heat 1 tablespoon butter in a saucepan and add the egg mixture. Cook, stirring gently from the bottom using a rubber or plastic spatula. Cook to the soft-cooked but not too-runny stage. Remove from the heat. Let cool briefly.

4. Spoon equal portions—about 1 tablespoon per slice—of scrambled eggs in the center of each slice. Roll the veal slices to enclose the egg in the center. Tie the rolls with string, or skewer them with toothpicks. Tying with string is a bit more tedious but it is preferable.

5. Sprinkle the rolls with salt and pepper and dredge on all sides in flour. Shake off excess.

6. Heat 2 tablespoons butter in a small skillet and add the veal rolls. Cook about 5 or 6 minutes.

7. If you are to serve a fresh tomato sauce (see recipe), do not wipe the skillet out. Use it to make the sauce. Serve the rollatine with the sauce spooned over. Serve with ziti, penne, or rigattoni tossed with melted butter and grated Parmesan.

Yield: Four servings.

Coulis de Tomates
(*Fresh tomato sauce*)

---

2 cups tomatoes, cored and cut into 1-inch cubes
2 tablespoons butter
¼ cup finely chopped onion
½ teaspoon finely minced garlic

⅓ cup dry white wine
3 fresh basil leaves or 1 teaspoon dried basil
Salt and freshly ground pepper to taste.

1. Prepare the tomatoes and set aside.

2. If you are to serve this dish with the rollatine of veal (see recipe), you will not have to use additional butter. Use the same skillet with drippings. Otherwise, add the butter to a skillet.

3. Add the onion and garlic and cook briefly. Add the wine and cook to reduce about half. Add the tomatoes, basil, salt and pepper to taste. Cook about 5 minutes.

4. Pour the mixture into the container of a food processor and blend to a purée. Reheat and serve.

Yield: About two-and-one-half cups.

F I HAD TO NAME ONE SINGLE ULTIMATE CUT OF meat that would produce the finest quickly cooked dishes of which any cook is capable, it would probably be scaloppine of veal. Veal scaloppine (sometimes called cutlets) have all the qualities to be desired for a hastily produced and excellent main course.

First of all, quick cooking is essential with scaloppine. If they cook too long, they tend to dry out or to lose their moist inner goodness. Second, the nature of the veal is such that it marries well with a multitude of flavors. It is the perfect foil for such bland foods as mushrooms in cream sauce (veal with morals à la crème is one of the sublime dishes of the world). It is complemented by tomato sauce in almost any form. It takes well to spicy things like mustard and is oddly complemented by fish and seafood—consider vitello tonnato with tuna and anchovies, and veal à la Oskar with crayfish, shrimp, or crabmeat.

One of the finest and most basic of scaloppine dishes is scaloppine of veal with *fines herbes*. As pointed out on numerous occasions, the traditional *fines herbes* in French kitchens are parsley, tarragon, chervil, and chives. Chervil is not all that common in America and may be omitted. The preparation of the dish consists in cooking veal scaloppine—thin slices that have or should be pounded lightly with a flat mallet—in very hot butter. The cooking takes only about forty-five seconds to a side. Only an omelet can cook that quickly to such advantage. And omelets can be boring. Veal, properly cooked, is never boring. The herbs are added along with a bit more butter and the dish is ready to serve.

It is a dish so simple that more attention may be paid to an accompanying vegetable dish. An excellent accompaniment for this would be a savory Italianate ratatouille, this one baked with mozzarella cheese. A bit tangy and good. Prepare the vegetable dish before turning your attention to the veal.

Escalopes de Veau aux Fines Herbes
(*Scaloppine of veal with herbs*)

16 thin scaloppine of veal, about 1¼ pounds	**1** tablespoon finely chopped parsley
Salt and freshly ground pepper to taste	**2** teaspoons finely chopped tarragon
6 tablespoons butter	**2** teaspoons finely chopped chives.

1. Place the meat on a flat surface and pound lightly. Sprinkle on both sides with salt and pepper to taste.

2. Heat 4 tablespoons of butter in one or two large skillets, and when it is very hot add the meat. This may be done in one skillet in two steps. Add the pieces of veal and cook briefly, about 45 seconds on each side. As the pieces brown, transfer them to a warm platter.

3. Add the remaining butter to the skillet and add the parsley, tarragon, and chives. Pour the sauce over and serve hot.

Yield: Four servings.

Légumes à la Napolitaine
(A baked mélange of vegetables with mozzarella)

---

3 tablespoons olive oil	1 bay leaf
¾ cup finely chopped onions	Salt and freshly ground pepper
1 tablespoon finely minced garlic	to taste
3 cups peeled eggplant cut into 1-inch cubes	1½ cups tomatoes, cored and cut into 1-inch cubes
2 cups trimmed, unpeeled zucchini cut into 1-inch cubes	4 slices mozzarella cheese, each slice about ¼ inch thick
2 sprigs fresh thyme or one teaspoon dried thyme	2 tablespoons grated Parmesan cheese.

1. Preheat the oven to 400 degrees.

2. Heat the oil in a large heavy skillet and cook the onion and garlic until onion is wilted.

3. Add the eggplant and zucchini and stir. Cook about 1 minute and add the thyme, bay leaf, salt and pepper to taste. Cook, stirring as necessary to prevent sticking, about 5 minutes.

4. Add the tomatoes and cook about 5 minutes longer, shaking the skillet to prevent sticking.

5. Spoon the mixture into a baking dish and cover with slices of mozzarella cheese. Sprinkle with Parmesan cheese. Place on a baking sheet to catch any drippings. Bake 10 minutes.

Yield: Four servings.

Beef

IN ANY BROAD CONCEPT OF 60-MINUTE COOKERY, gourmet-style, it would be impossible to ignore some of the more expensive cuts of meat, for many of these most emphatically play an important role in what might be called the resources of the hasty cook.

Filet mignon does, of course, fit into this category. But one thing is apparent to me in shopping at the meat counter of a supermarket in my hometown. There are times when this cut of beef can be quite reasonably priced, particularly when on special sale, as it often seems to be. There is a second, if obvious, thought, too. In any filet, be it red meat, chicken, or fish, there is no waste.

Classically, a filet mignon with a Madeira wine sauce is made with what is known as demi-glace, or a glace de viande. A demi-glace is a rich-bodied base, standard in professional kitchens, which requires many hours of simmering before straining. It congeals on cooling and can simply be introduced at the end of the preparation of a dish and does not require flour. A glace de viande is a demi-glace that has been reduced several hours longer and is rather firm in texture, like caramel candy. This serves a similar purpose, but only a dab of it stirred into a thin liquid will give body to the sauce without flour.

In that such sauces are rarely to be found in home kitchens, it is necessary to use some form of thickener to make a sauce such as sauce madère, a sauce bordelaise, and so on.

The filet mignon with sauce madère outlined here requires about fifteen minutes cooking time, and the sauce is thickened using one teaspoon of flour for four servings. A combination of quickly sautéed vegetables is suggested as an accompaniment and the total cooking time for these is less than ten minutes. Thus, to prepare this meal in less than an hour it is best to prepare the basic ingredients for the beef, the sauce, and the vegetables, and then start to cook.

Filet Mignon Sauce Madère
(Filet mignon in Madeira wine sauce)

4	filet mignon, about ½ pound each	¼	cup Madeira wine
	Salt and freshly ground pepper to taste	¾	cup fresh or canned beef broth
		3	teaspoons butter
2	tablespoons olive oil	1	teaspoon flour
2	tablespoons finely chopped shallots	2	teaspoons chopped parsley.

1. Sprinkle the meat on both sides with salt and pepper. Heat the oil in a skillet and when very hot, add the meat. Cook over high heat about 5 minutes. Cook longer if you want medium or well-done meat.

2. Turn the meat and continue cooking over high heat about 5 minutes. Or cook longer if you want medium or well-done meat. Remove the meat to a warm platter and keep warm. Pour off the fat from the skillet. Add the shallots.

3. Add the wine and cook over high heat about 30 seconds. Add the broth and bring to a full rolling boil, stirring to dissolve the brown particles that cling to the bottom and sides of the skillet. Add a little salt and pepper to taste.

4. Cook until reduced by half.

5. Meanwhile, blend 2 teaspoons of butter and flour in a small mixing bowl. Stir it into the simmering sauce and cook briefly.

6. Swirl in the remaining teaspoon butter. Strain the sauce over the meat and dot the center of each filet with a dab of parsley. Serve immediately.

Yield: Four servings.

Sauté de Légumes Fermière
(Sauté of fresh vegetables)

½	pound carrots		Salt and freshly ground pepper to
⅓	pound white turnips		taste
½	pound fresh mushrooms	2	tablespoons finely chopped
3	tablespoons butter		shallots
			Chopped parsley.

1. Trim the carrots and cut into very thin slices. There should be about 1½ cups.

2. Trim the turnips and cut into very thin slices. There should be about 1½ cups.

3. Rinse and drain the mushrooms. Dry well. Slice thinly. There should be about 3 cups.

4. Heat the butter in a skillet and add the carrots and turnips. Sprinkle with salt and pepper. Cook, tossing and stirring, over high heat, about 3 minutes.

5. Add the mushrooms and cook, tossing and stirring, about 2 minutes.

6. Add the shallots and toss. Cook briefly. Serve sprinkled with parsley.

Yield: Four servings.

HE ULTIMATE MAIN COURSE IN THE WORLD OF
hasty cooking is doubtlessly a slice of beef. If the meat is of
first quality, it is culinary sacrilege to cook it for an extended
period. There is an interesting misconception in the public mind about a filet
mignon, which is generally considered the most luxurious cut of the animal.
Actually, it is not the most expensive steak on the market, and, furthermore, it
is all meat, no waste. The cost of a shell steak comes to considerably more.

Cost aside, the simplest adornment for a filet of beef is, of course, melted
butter with, perhaps, a sprinkling of parsley. There are times, however, when
you might wish a sauce a bit more innovative, and one of the best is an easily
made sauce bordelaise meaning, of course, a sauce in the style of Bordeaux
and made with a red wine of the region. But any good, dry red wine will do, be
it from Bordeaux, Burgundy, or California.

This sauce, in a professional kitchen, is made with a tediously prepared and
long-simmered sauce known as an espagnole or demi-glace. Such a sauce is
unreasonable except for the most dedicated amateur cooks; a substitute is essential. The solution—shocking though it will appear to purists—is tinned brown
beef gravy. That's right, out of a can. Try it cooked with shallots and a reduction of dry red wine. You may be pleasantly surprised.

I prepared this dish recently and served it with braised Belgian endive, which
require a far longer cooking time than the meat. The two dishes complement
each other, but any other green vegetable such as broccoli or zucchini would
also be suitablee with the beef.

Should you decide to prepare the endive with the beef, by all means put it on
about 30 to 45 minutes before the dinner hour. The cooking period will depend
on the size of the endive. As they cook there is more than ample time to
prepare the meat and any other accompaniments you plan to serve before or
after the meat.

Filet Mignon Bordelaise
(Filet mignon in a Bordeaux wine sauce)

1¼ pounds filet mignon, cut into 4
slices, each approximately 1 inch
thick
Salt and freshly ground pepper
to taste
1 tablespoon peanut, vegetable, or
corn oil

2 tablespoons butter
1 tablespoon finely chopped
shallots
½ cup dry red wine
½ cup brown sauce or canned
brown beef gravy.

1. Sprinkle the meat with salt and pepper to taste. Heat the oil in a heavy
skillet, large enough to hold the slices in one layer. Brown the meat on both
sides, about 1 to 2 minutes to a side. Or cook longer if you prefer meat well
done.

2. Transfer the meat to a warm serving platter. Pour off the fat from the skillet. Add 1 tablespoon of butter and when it is hot, add the shallots. Cook briefly, stirring, and add the wine. Cook until almost reduced by half. Add the brown sauce and cook about 2 minutes. Put through a fine strainer into a small saucepan. Add salt and pepper to taste. Swirl in the remaining tablespoon of butter. Serve piping hot spooned over the meat. Serve with braised endive, if desired.

Yield: Four servings.

Endives Braisées
(*Braised endives*)

4	heads of Belgian endive	½	teaspoon sugar
2	teaspoons butter		Juice of half a lemon
	Salt and freshly ground pepper to taste	½	cup water.

1. Trim around the stem ends of the endive to cut away any browned rims.
2. Place the endive in one layer, snugly, in a saucepan with a tight-fitting cover. Add the remaining ingredients and cover closely. Bring to the boil and cook about 30 to 45 minutes or until tender and the liquid has evaporated. Towards the end of the cooking time, uncover and brown lightly on both sides, turning once.

Yield: Four servings.

THERE IS A DISH THAT ENJOYED AN OVER-
whelming popularity back in the days when I first came
to New York. To tell the truth, I never dined on the
dish in its place of origin, but numerous customers who came to the Pavillon
while I was chef there would request it.

It was called steak Diane and it was the specialty of the house—twenty years
ago and more—at the old Drake Hotel. The person most closely associated with
steak Diane was known in dining circles throughout the city as Nino of the
Drake. His full name was Beniamino Schiavon, born in Padua, Italy; he died
eleven years ago.

One of the key points in the preparation of the dish is the quick cooking of
the steak itself. The total cooking time on both sides is about two minutes. This
recipe calls for chives, but if chives are out of season, chopped shallots can
serve the purpose, or even, for that matter, chopped scallions.

Almost any very tender cut of meat will do for this dish. The maître d'hôtel
for whom the dish was celebrated generally used boneless sirloin, which was
pounded to about one-quarter inch thick. Filet mignon also works well. The
pounding of the meat with a mallet is important, for it breaks down the fibers
and hastens cooking.

Because of the haste with which the steak is cooked, an accompanying vegetable dish may be a bit more time-consomung and elaborate.

Steak Diane
(*Steak in chive sauce*)

---

4 filet mignon steaks, about 6 ounces each, or use 4 boneless sirloin steaks Salt and freshly ground pepper to taste 2 tablespoons olive oil 3 tablespoons butter 3 tablespoons chopped chives or shallots	2 tablespoons cognac 3 tablespoons chopped parsley 1 teaspoon imported mustard ½ teaspoon Worcestershire sauce 2 teaspoons fresh or canned meat broth, preferably beef, although chicken can be used.

1. Place the slices of filet mignon or the sirloin steaks on a flat surface and
pound with a flat mallet to about ¼-inch thickness.

2. Sprinkle the meat on both sides with salt and pepper.

3. Heat 2 tablespoons of oil and 2 tablespoons of butter in a large skillet and
when very hot, add two of the steaks. Cook about 1½ minutes on one side and
turn. Cook 30 seconds on the other side. Do not cook much longer or they will
be overcooked and dry. Transfer the steaks to a hot serving dish.

4. Add the other steaks to the skillet and cook them identically in the fat that
remains in the pan. Transfer the steaks to the serving dish.

5. Remove skillet from the heat and add the chives. Return skillet to the stove and cook about 10 seconds. Add the cognac and stir. Add parsley, mustard and Worcestershire sauce. Add the broth and stir. Swirl in remaining tablespoon of butter. Sprinkle the steaks with pepper and pour the sauce over them. Serve at once.

Yield: Four servings.

Mélange des Légumes
(Mixed buttered vegetables)

3 Idaho potatoes, about 1½ pounds	3 tablespoons butter
½ pound green beans	1 clove garlic, barely crushed
Salt to taste	Freshly ground pepper to taste.

1. Peel the potatoes and cut them into half-inch slices. Stack the slices and cut them into half-inch strips. Cut the strips into half-inch cubes. Drop the cubes into cold water. Set aside.

2. Trim off the ends of the green beans and cut the beans into one-inch lengths. Set aside.

3. Drain the potatoes and put them in a casserole or saucepan. Cover with water and salt to taste. Bring to the boil.

4. In another saucepan, bring enough water to the boil to cover the beans when added. Add the beans and salt to taste. Bring to the boil.

5. Cook the potatoes about 3 minutes and drain.

6. As the beans continue to cook, heat the butter in a large skillet and add the potatoes. Add the crushed garlic clove and toss over high heat. Stir as necessary. When the potatoes start to brown, reduce the heat to moderate. Add salt and pepper to taste. Continue cooking, tossing and stirring, about 8 minutes.

7. When the beans have cooked for a total of 8 minutes, drain them.

8. Add the beans to the potatoes, toss and stir to blend. Cook 2 or 3 minutes to blend flavors. Remove the garlic clove and serve.

Yield: Four servings.

I HAVE NOTED THAT THERE IS A GREAT DEAL OF mystique in the public mind about the complexity of widely ordered dishes in French restaurants. There are numerous dishes, excellent creations, which, made at home or in a professional kitchen, do not demand long-simmered sauces, a complicated series of steps, and legerdemain on the part of a chef.

There is steak au poivre, for example, which delights many American palates. It has a lot going for it—the piquant flavor of freshly crushed peppercorns and a light sauce made of butter, shallots, white wine, and cream. The steak should be of first quality, and a boneless shell steak is my choice. The peppercorns should—must—be freshly cracked and although a flat, heavy, metal mallet works well for this, you can improvise by using the bottom of a clean, heavy saucepan.

There are endless combinations of foods that go well with steak au poivre, two of which are outlined here.

One of these is Vichy carrots. To prepare them, the carrots are cut into thin rounds and cooked briefly with butter and only a couple of tablespoons of water. They are ready for the table in about five minutes total cooking time. The other is duchesse potatoes, which take longer but may also be prepared in advance if they are brushed with melted butter to keep a crust from forming.

Because of the quick-cooking nature of the carrots and steaks, it would be best to approach them by first preparing all the ingredients that go into them. Set them aside until ready to cook.

Start the cooking process with the potatoes. Before cooking the steak, start the carrots.

Follow the main course with salad and cheese, if you wish, and a simple purchased dessert.

Steaks au Poivre
(Steaks with crushed peppercorns)

---

4 boneless shell steaks, about 10 ounces each	5 teaspoons butter
Salt to taste	2 tablespoons finely chopped shallots
1 tablespoon peppercorns	½ cup dry white wine
3 tablespoons peanut, vegetable, or corn oil	½ cup heavy cream.

1. Sprinkle the steaks with salt.

2. Using a mallet or the bottom of a heavy saucepan, crush the peppercorns but not too finely. Sprinkle the steaks with equal amounts of pepper on both sides. Press down with the hands to help the peppercorns adhere to the meat.

3. Heat the oil in a heavy skillet and when it is hot and almost smoking, add

the steaks. Cook about 3 minutes and turn. Cook about 2 minutes or longer, if you wish your steaks well-done, and remove to a warm platter.

4. Pour the fat from the skillet and add 2 teaspoons of butter. Add the shallots and cook, stirring, until wilted. Add the wine and cook, stirring with a wooden spoon, until wine has almost totally reduced. Add the cream and cook over high heat about 1 minute. Swirl in the remaining butter and pour the sauce over the steaks.

Yield: Four servings.

Pommes de Terre Duchesse
(Mashed potatoes with eggs)

---

6 **medium potatoes**	¼ **teaspoon freshly grated nutmeg**
Boiling salted water	2 **whole eggs**
3 **tablespoons butter**	2 **egg yolks**
Salt and freshly ground pepper to	
taste	

1. Peel the potatoes and boil in salted water to cover until soft but still firm.
2. Put through a food mill and then beat with a wooden spoon until smooth.
3. Add the butter, salt, pepper, nutmeg and eggs, which have been lightly beaten with the egg yolks. Whip until fluffy.

Yield: Four servings.

Carottes Vichy
(Steamed carrots)

---

5 **to 6 carrots, about ¾ pound**	¼ **teaspoon sugar**
3 **tablespoons butter**	2 **tablespoons water.**
Salt to taste	

1. Trim off and discard the ends of the carrots. Scrape the carrots. Cut the carrots into rounds about one-eighth inch thick.
2. Place the butter in a heavy saucepan and add the carrots, salt, sugar, and water. Cover closely and cook over high flame about 5 minutes. Serve hot.

Yield: Four servings.

THERE WAS A TIME NOT MANY YEARS AGO WHEN mustard was generally regarded in this country as a condiment for hot dogs, for assorted sausages, salamis, and ham sandwiches. More and more it has crossed my notice that mustard is being used to a far vaster extent these days as an ingredient to give a piquancy to sauces—and not only the likes of mayonnaise and hollandaise—but a variety of hot sauces as well.

It is also true that mustard flavors have increased in France under the banner of la nouvelle cuisine—a dab of mustard in cream sauces for mussels, for veal, and for chicken. One of the best "new" dishes I have sampled in some time was that of Jean Troisgros, who visited East Hampton recently. The dish consisted of thin slices of veal smeared wih mustard, sprinkled with mustard seed, and cooked quickly on both sides. That dish can be served with a variety of sauces including one of fresh tomatoes.

Mustard also gives a fine and welcome lift to a tasty and well-textured steak and the preparation of such a dish literally takes minutes. Perhaps the best cut of meat for the dish is sirloin steak—and I recommend that you cut away the bone (it is then called in this country New York sirloin) which not only facilitates cooking, but adds, perhaps, a touch of elegance.

Basically, the dish consists of cooking the steaks four or five minutes to a side in very little, very hot oil. The steaks are transferred to a hot serving dish and the oil poured off. Chopped shallots, cognac, and heavy cream are added in quick succession and, at the very last, a tablespoon or more imported mustard is added to the sauce. Once mustard is added to a hot cream sauce, the sauce should not be allowed to boil. If cooked, the flavor of the sauce is altered and not favorably.

Many dishes would go well with this steak—pan-fried potatoes, rice, or simply a vegetable. I recommend here a combination of vegetables cooked briefly in very little water and butter. The vegetable preparation, in fact, should be done first—it requires considerably more time than the steak itself.

Steak à la Moutarde
(*Steak with mustard cream sauce*)

4 sirloin steaks, about ¾ to 1 pound each	2 tablespoons finely chopped shallots
Salt and freshly ground pepper to taste	¼ cup cognac
2 tablespoons peanut, vegetable, or corn oil	1½ cups heavy cream
2 tablespoons butter	1 tablespoon prepared imported mustard such as Dijon or Düsseldorf.

1. Carefully trim around the bones of the steak. This will facilitate and hasten cooking. The trimmed steaks are known as New York sirloin. Sprinkle the steaks on both sides with salt and pepper.

2. Heat the oil in a large, very heavy skillet. A heavy copper or black iron skillet would be good for this. When the oil is hot and almost smoking, add the steaks. Cook about 4 or 5 minutes and turn. Continue cooking 4 or 5 minutes or to the desired degree of doneness.

3. Remove the steaks to a serving platter and keep warm. Pour off the fat from the pan. Add the butter, and when melted add the shallots. Add the cognac and ignite it.

4. Add the cream and bring to the boil. Cook over high heat, stirring often, about 5 minutes. Remove from the heat and stir in the mustard. Do not boil. Add salt and pepper to taste. Add any drippings that may have accumulated around the steaks. Strain the sauce over the steaks. Serve with rice or assorted vegetables.

Yield: Four servings.

Mélange des Légumes
(*Blended vegetables*)

1	or two carrots, trimmed, scraped, and quartered	1 rib celery
1	medium-size zucchini	2 tablespoons butter
1	to 3 small turnips	2 tablespoons finely chopped onion
⅓	pound fresh string beans	2 tablespoons water.

1. Cut the quartered carrots into batons about one inch long. There should be about 1 cup.

2. Trim off the ends of the zucchini. Cut the zucchini into pieces the same size as the carrots. There should be about 1 cup.

3. Peel the turnips and cut into pieces the same size as the carrots and zucchini.

4. Trim off the ends of the beans. Cut them into one-inch lengths. There should be about 1 cup.

5. Cut the celery rib into one-inch lengths. Cut each length into half-inch strips. There should be about ½ cup.

6. In a very heavy saucepan heat the butter and add the onion and celery. Cook briefly and add the carrots, string beans, turnips, and zucchini. Add salt and pepper to taste.

7. Add the water and cover closely. If the saucepan is heavy enough and the cover fits snugly, this should be sufficient water. Take care the saucepan does not become dry or the vegetables will burn.

8. Cook over gentle to moderate heat, stirring and shaking the saucepan to redistribute the vegetables so that they cook evenly, about 8 minutes.

Yield: Four servings.

THERE MAY BE MANY CHEMISTS WHO ARE EX-cellent cooks. Among the few chemists I have met, however, their enthusiasms have been far more directed to test tubes and molecular structures than to food processors and pots and pans. In turn, I know very few cooks or chefs who could explain in any kind of depth the scientific reason why egg yolks will thicken when beaten with oil or butter, to produce a mayonnaise or a béarnaise sauce. But, in a sense, a well-used experimental kitchen is, in its own way, a sort of laboratory.

I would be hard put to explain why one of the best and easiest dishes, made with shell steaks or other tender cuts of beef, can be produced using both vinegar and cream. A good cook or chef, without a chemist's training, learns through empirical means what will and will not curdle sauces, what will cause an emulsion and so on.

Today, influenced by la nouvelle cuisine, there are scores of fine dishes that rely on vinegar as a flavoring. Not straight, mind you, but in a highly reduced state. Two of the most successful of the "new" dishes are salmon slices with a mild vinegar sauce and goose or duck livers in a similar sauce.

The recipe printed here for steaks in a cream sauce, lightly seasoned with a trace of reduced vinegar, is simplicity itself and delectable. The steak is seared and cooked briefly in a hot skillet with butter. It is removed, and vinegar is added to the skillet and greatly reduced. Cream, salt, and pepper are added, and this mixture, too, is reduced almost by half. When the steaks are returned to the sauce and turned in it, finely chopped shallots are added and the steaks are ready for serving.

Mushrooms bordelaise make a perfect accompaniment for this dish: fresh mushrooms—whole, cut in half, or sliced—are cooked in hot oil until brown and crisp. They are drained and finished with the classic bordelaise garniture—bread crumbs, shallots, and parsley.

Steaks au Vinaigre
(Steaks with vinegar sauce)

1½ pounds boneless, tender steak, fat removed, such as shell steak or filet mignon	2 tablespoons butter
	¼ cup red wine vinegar
	1 cup heavy cream
2 teaspoons paprika	2 tablespoons finely minced
Salt and freshly ground pepper to taste	shallots.

1. If shell steaks are used, leave them whole. If filets, have them cut into eight pieces. Sprinkle the steaks on both sides with paprika, salt and pepper.

2. Heat the butter in a skillet and when it is very hot and almost brown, add the steaks in one layer. Cook about 2 minutes on one side and turn. Cook about 2 minutes until golden on the other side. Remove and keep warm.

3. Pour off the fat from the skillet. Add the vinegar, stirring to dissolve the brown particles that cling to the bottom and sides of the skillet.

4. Cook until the vinegar is almost evaporated and add the cream. Cook, stirring, over high heat until reduced almost by half. Add any juices that have accumulated around the meat. Add salt and pepper to taste.

5. Return the steaks to the skillet and turn in the sauce.

6. To the sauce add the shallots. Heat briefly, without cooking. Serve.

Yield: Four servings.

Champignons Bordelaise
(Mushrooms with a bordelaise garnish)

¾ **pound fresh mushrooms**	1 **tablespoon fresh bread crumbs**
¼ **cup peanut, vegetable, or corn oil**	1 **tablespoon finely chopped shallots**
Salt and freshly ground pepper to	1 **tablespoon finely chopped**
taste	**parsley.**
1 **tablespoon butter**	

1. Rinse the mushrooms in cold water and drain well.

2. If the mushrooms are large, slice them or cut them in half. If small, leave them whole or cut in half.

3. In a very heavy skillet, heat the oil.

4. When the oil is hot and almost smoking, add the mushrooms, salt and pepper to taste. Cook over very high heat, shaking the skillet and stirring so that the mushrooms cook evenly, until they are quite brown and crisp. They should be almost mahogany colored.

5. Pour the mushrooms and cooking oil into a sieve to drain.

6. To the skillet add the butter. When melted, add the mushrooms. Sprinkle quickly with bread crumbs, shallots, and parsley. Toss and serve.

Yield: Four servings.

HERE ARE, GENERALLY SPEAKING, TWO STAN-
dard and accepted methods of broiling foods in or on a
home stove. The most obvious is the use of a kitchen broiler.
This method of cookery can be exceedingly complicated for amateur cooks because of the variables involved—the intensity of the heat, the distance of the
food from the source of heat and so on.

The other method, and frankly I prefer it, is what is known as "pan-
broiling." Purists may point out that this is not broiling at all but skillet cookery, but the results are admirable and the name simply implies that any foods
destined to be broiled can also be cooked in a skillet or pan.

There is much less guesswork in pan-broiling. The meat, or whatever, must
be seared over high heat so that the juices within are sealed. The meat then
continues to cook at a leisurely pace to the desired degree of doneness. This
works particularly well with thick cuts of meat and is eminently suited to porterhouse steaks. For what it's worth by the way, I find that a prime porterhouse
steak costs less than sirloin with bone in or club steaks.

A marchand de vin sauce is excellent for this and other steaks. Its preparation, if you will resort to half a cup of canned brown beef gravy, is simplicity
itself. When the steak is done, it is removed and the skillet wiped out. A bit of
butter and shallots are added, then a half cup of dry red wine is added and
reduced. The "brown sauce" is swirled in and heated with another touch of
butter and the sauce is ready to serve.

In restaurants, of course, they use a classic brown sauce rather than the
canned gravy, but the latter is an acceptable substitute—as long as it is im-
proved upon.

It is recommended that this menu include the usual salad with cheese as a
second course and, if desired, a final course of fresh fruit or a purchased or
previously made dessert.

Porterhouse Marchand de Vin
(*Porterhouse with red wine sauce*)

1 3-pound porterhouse steak, about
   2½ inches thick
   Salt and freshly ground pepper to
   taste
2 tablespoons peanut, vegetable, or
   corn oil

3 tablespoons butter
1 tablespoon finely chopped shallots
½ cup dry red wine
½ cup brown sauce or canned
   brown beef gravy.

1. Select a very heavy skillet for this. A heavy, traditional black iron skillet
is excellent. Sprinkle the steak all over with salt and pepper. Use a fairly generous amount of black pepper. Pat it with the fingers to make seasonings adhere.

2. Heat the oil in the skillet and when quite hot, add the steak. The primary

goal is to sear the steak well on both sides over moderately high heat. Cook the steak on the first side about 5 to 7 minutes until it is quite dark without burning.

3. Turn the steak and cook about 10 minutes on the second side until it is quite dark without burning. Remember that these cooking times are more or less arbitrary, but they were the times used when this recipe was tested.

4. After the steak has been seared on both sides (5 minutes on one side, 10 on the other), reduce the heat only slightly and turn it again. Cook about 10 minutes longer and turn again. Continue cooking, turning as necessary. The total recommended cooking time for the steak, start to finish, is about 45 minutes.

5. Remove the steak and cover loosely with aluminum foil. It is best for the steak to "rest" after cooking so that the interior juices are redistributed.

6. The moment the steak is removed from the skillet, pour off the fat from the skillet. Wipe lightly with absorbent paper toweling. Immediately add 1 tablespoon of the butter to the skillet and stir to dissolve the browned particles that cling to the bottom of the skillet. Add the shallots and cook briefly. Add the wine and reduce about 30 seconds. Add the brown sauce and reduce to two-thirds. When boiling, remove from heat and swirl in the remaining butter.

7. To serve, spoon a few tablespoons of the pan sauce onto each of four hot plates. Slice the steak and place the slices on the sauce.

Yield: Four servings.

Pommes de Terre Maître d'Hôtel
(Potatoes in cream sauce)

---

4 **Idaho potatoes, about 1¾ pounds**	**Pinch of cayenne pepper**
Salt to taste	½ **cup finely chopped scallions**
1 **cup heavy cream**	**Freshly ground pepper to taste.**
⅓ **teaspoon freshly grated nutmeg**	

1. Peel the potatoes and drop them into cold water.

2. Drain and cut them lengthwise into quarters. Cut each quarter into one-inch lengths.

3. Add the pieces to a small skillet and add water to cover. Add salt to taste and bring to the boil. Simmer about 5 minutes. Drain.

4. Add the cream, nutmeg, salt, cayenne, and onions. Add salt and pepper to taste. Bring to the boil and cover. Cook about 4 minutes or until almost tender.

5. Uncover and cook about 1 minute longer or until the potatoes are tender and the cream sauce is lightly thickened.

Yield: Four servings.

As in any other métier, if the kitchen is your domain (both professionally and as a hobby), food associations occur as naturally as thought. We were wondering about the possible origins of the dish known as London broil, which English sources assure us is of American inspiration, and then the speculation began. Perhaps there was a restaurant called London in some town or city; perhaps it was an English chef or cook who first threw a flank steak on the grill and served it with mushroom sauce.

In any event, it was generally agreed that a London broil made with a flank steak of impeccable quality, seared and broiled quickly on both sides, and served with a conscientiously made mushroom sauce can, without qualification, be a memorable dish. And both the steak and the sauce are child's play to prepare.

The sauce, of course, is just as important as the steak, and when I recently made the dish, I decided on the mushroom sauce known in French as a sauce chasseur. It is not one of those thick, mucilaginous sauces made throughout the United States with canned mushrooms. This one is made with fresh butter, shallots, tomatoes, fresh mushrooms, and a dry white wine. It also uses beef broth. In the interest of texture, a touch of arrowroot or cornstarch is added to the sauce.

There is one important thing to remember. After the flank steak is grilled or broiled (the total broiling time is ten minutes or less), it should be left to stand briefly to redistribute the inner juices. The steak should always be sliced on the bias or diagonally, in the interest of texture. The procedure; Heat the broiler or grill, prepare the meat and the green vegetable, green beans with lemon and parsley, simultaneously.

Bavette de Boeuf Sauce Chasseur
(*London broil with sauce chasseur*)

1 2-pound flank steak	3 tablespoons butter
2 tablespoons peanut, vegetable, or corn oil	3 tablespoons finely chopped parsley
Salt and freshly ground pepper to taste	Sauce chasseur (see recipe).

1. Preheat a broiler rack with the broiler set on high. Or use a charcoal grill, although the warm-up takes a while.

2. Rub the flank steak on both sides with oil and sprinkle with salt and pepper. Use a generous amount of pepper.

3. Place the meat on the broiler rack or on the hot grill and let it cook about four or five inches from the source of heat. Broil about 3 to 5 minutes and turn the meat. Broil on the other side 3 to 5 minutes. Cooking time will depend on the desired degree of doneness.

4. Transfer the steak to a hot platter and dot with butter. Let the steak stand in a warm place about 5 minutes to redistribute the internal juices of the meat.

5. Juices will accumulate as the steak stands. Add these to the sauce chasseur. Sprinkle the meat with chopped parsley and carve it on the diagonal. Serve with the sauce.

Yield: Four servings.

Sauce Chasseur
(*Hunter's sauce*)

⅓ pound mushrooms, sliced, about
   2 cups
½ cup peeled, chopped fresh or
   canned tomatoes
1 tablespoon butter
1 tablespoon finely chopped shallots
   Salt and freshly ground pepper to
   taste

⅓ cup dry white wine
½ cup fresh or canned beef broth
½ teaspoon chopped fresh tarragon
   or half the amount dried
1 teaspoon arrowroot or cornstarch
2 teaspoons water.

1. Set the mushrooms and tomatoes aside in separate bowls.
2. Melt the butter in a saucepan and add the mushrooms, shallots, salt and pepper to taste. Cook about 10 minutes.
3. Add the wine and simmer briefly over high heat. Add the tomatoes and beef broth and tarragon. Cook about 5 minutes, stirring occasionally.
4. Blend the arrowroot and water. Stir into the sauce. Cook briefly and serve.

Yield: One-and-a-half to two cups.

Haricots Verts au Citron
(*String beans with lemon*)

---

1 pound green beans, trimmed and
   cut into 2-inch cubes
   Salt to taste
2 tablespoons butter at room
   temperature

   Juice of half a lemon
2 tablespoons finely chopped parsley
   Freshly ground pepper to taste.

1. Rinse the beans and drain them. Put them into a saucepan with water to cover and salt to taste.
2. Bring to the boil and simmer 10 minutes or until tender. The beans must remain a trifle firm or al dente.
3. Drain the beans and return them to a hot saucepan. Add the butter and sprinkle with lemon juice, parsley, and pepper. Toss. Serve hot.

Yield: Four servings.

THE IDEA HAS BEEN EXPLORED THAT THE COMMON hamburger might have had Russian origins. The Russian name usually given for ground meat patties that are cooked and served with or without sauce, is bitok and sometimes bitock or bitoke. Many people have tried to associate the name with a distortion in pronunciation of the words "beef steak."

Bitoks are absolutely ideal for quick-cookery. Although the raw meat is frequently blended with chopped onion before cooking, I personally dislike this technique. You get a more refined product if the meat is handled as little as possible without kneading. Simply press the unseasoned meat between the palms to make it adhere neatly as it is shaped into rounds like hamburgers.

I've never admired that old saying in French kitchens that goes, "C'est la sauce qui fait la poisson," or, "It is the sauce that makes the fish." In my own mind it smacks of the necessity of using a sauce to disguise the flavor of a fish that is none too fresh.

On the other hand, a well-made sauce can be an admirable addition to foods like plain, unadorned hamburgers, or, if you wish, bitoks. The sauce may be a simply made one of butter, chopped parsley, lemon juice, and a touch of Tabasco or perhaps Worcestershire. But a slightly more complicated sauce involving sour cream and, if you wish, a splash of cognac, is a nice complement.

Fresh asparagus makes a fine accompaniment for this dish. So does plain rice cooked according to your favorite recipe.

The obvious way to go about such a meal is to prepare the rice and start it cooking. Scrape the asparagus and have them ready to cook. Shape the meat into patties and have all the ingredients measured and at hand. Use your own judgment as to when to start cooking the bitoks. Put the asparagus on to simmer and cook the meat and vegetable simultaneously.

Bitoks à la Russe
(*Hamburgers with sour cream*)

1½ pounds ground sirloin	1 tablespoon finely chopped
Salt and freshly ground pepper	shallots
to taste	2 tablespoons cognac
2 tablespoons plus 1 teaspoon	1 cup sour cream.
butter	

1. Shape the meat into four compact patties. Do not knead the meat when working with it. Simply divide it into four portions and shape it, pressing between the hands, into four patties. Sprinkle the patties with salt and pepper.

2. Heat 1 tablespoon of butter and when hot, add the meat. Cook about 3 minutes to a side or longer if you prefer your meat well done. Remove the patties to a warm platter. Pour off the fat from the skillet.

3. To the skillet, add 1 teaspoon of butter and the chopped shallot. Cook

briefly and add the cognac. Cook briefly and add the sour cream, salt and pepper to taste. Heat thoroughly. Strain through a fine sieve into a saucepan. Reheat and swirl in the remaining tablespoon of butter. Serve with the bitoks.

Yield: Four servings.

Asperges au Beurre
(*Buttered asparagus*)

12 to 16 fresh asparagus spears
Salt to taste

2 tablespoons butter, melted.

1. Cut off the ends of the asparagus, about one inch from the bottom. Place the asparagus in a skillet and add water to cover and salt to taste. Bring to the boil and simmer until barely tender, about 2 to 5 minutes, depending on the size of the spears.

2. Drain quickly and add the melted butter. Serve hot.

Yield: Four servings.

T HERE IS AN INTERESTING IF CURIOUS NOTION THAT French chefs live on the likes of foie gras and sturgeon, cocks' combs and caviar. That they turn up their nose at the thought of such down-to-earth fare as American hot dogs and corn on the cob and barbecued spareribs. Nothing could be further from the truth. I, personally, have a great liking for liverwurst sandwiches, pastrami on rye, and a well-made hamburger. On occasion, however, when I serve typically American—and un-French—foods in my home, there may be a temptation at times to give these dishes a French touch.

Take hamburgers. Now there's nothing wrong with the standard burger-on-a-bun, tomato ketchup and sliced onion included. But a hamburger cooked to resemble a steak au poivre can be an elegant and tasty dish that nobody could criticize. It isn't a question of putting on airs; it's a question of taste.

Hamburgers au poivre, if one wishes to call them that, are easy to make. You simply dip them on both sides with crushed peppercorns; cook them for a reasonable time on both sides and finally, add a judicious amount of butter, shallots, red wine, and cognac. A bit of beef broth and parsley and the dish is done. The entire preparation and cooking time should require considerably less than half an hour.

This preparation goes very well, I discovered recently, with another American invention, potatoes O'Brien, a dish I learned to make soon after my arrival in this country, nearly forty years ago.

Don't ask me who O'Brien was. No one ever bothered to say. But the combination of cubed potatoes plus sweet peppers and pimentos, properly cooked, has a lot going for it by way of flavor. There are those who say that potatoes O'Brien should be made with cream, but that's another recipe.

If you should make this combination of dishes—to be prepared and cooked in less than an hour—get all the ingredients ready, peeled and chopped and cubed as necessary, before starting to cook. The two can then be cooked—within reason—simultaneously.

Steak Haché au Poivre
(Hamburgers with peppercorn sauce)

1½ pounds ground chuck	¼ cup dry red wine
Salt to taste	1 tablespoon cognac
1½ to 2 tablespoons crushed peppercorns	¼ cup fresh or canned beef broth
2 tablespoons butter	2 tablespoons finely chopped parsley.
1 tablespoon finely chopped shallots	

1. Shape the meat into four patties of equal size. Sprinkle with salt and sprinkle all over with crushed peppercorns. Press down on the meat to help the peppercorns adhere.

2. Heat a heavy iron skillet and do not add fat of any kind. When the skillet is quite hot (if oil were used, it would almost smoke) add the patties. Cook about 5 minutes on one side.

3. Using a spatula or pancake turner, quickly scoop up the patties and turn them over. Cook about 5 minutes longer (if you want them well-done, cook about 10 minutes longer).

4. Remove the patties to a warm platter and, to the skillet, add 1 tablespoon of the butter and the shallots. Cook, stirring with a wooden spoon, until shallots are wilted. Add the wine and cook about 1 minute. Add the cognac and let reduce to about half. Add the broth and cook until reduced to about 3 tablespoons. Swirl in the remaining butter. Return the patties to the skillet, turning once off the heat. Serve garnished with chopped parsley.

Yield: Four servings.

Pommes de Terres ''O'Brien''
(*Potatoes with peppers and pimentos*)

6	to 8 potatoes, about 1½ pounds		Freshly ground pepper to taste
	Salt to taste	1	cup cubed sweet green pepper
3	tablespoons peanut, vegetable,	1	tablespoon butter
	or corn oil	⅓	cup cubed pimento.
⅓	cup finely chopped onion		

1. Peel the potatoes and cut them into half-inch cubes. There should be about 3 cups. As they are cubed drop them into cold water.

2. Drain the potatoes and add them to a saucepan or small skillet. Add water to cover and salt to taste. Bring to the boil and simmer about 1 or 2 minutes. Drain well.

3. Heat the oil in a skillet and add the potatoes. Cook, stirring and shaking the skillet as necessary, until potatoes become golden, about 8 to 10 minutes.

4. Add the onion, salt and pepper and cook briefly. Add the green pepper and cook, stirring gently, about 3 minutes.

5. Add the butter and cook about 2 minutes. Add the pimento and stir gently. Cook until heated through.

Yield: Four servings.

SOME INVENTIONS IN FOOD THAT ARE ABSOLUTELY delectable seem to have come from some bizarre and adventurous brain. An ingredient may seem odd, perhaps daring. There is a Swedish recipe for roast lamb with coffee (including the cream) and a Southern creation known as "red eye gravy," a sauce made by adding hot coffee to the skillet in which a slice of country ham cooked. Eggs or fish au beurre noir, which is to say with a burnt butter sauce, would not seem likely if it were not an actual and traditional blend of foods. Asafoetida, the resinous substance that is foul-smelling to some nostrils, has an honorable place (used in small quantities) in Indian kitchens, particularly those that deal in vegetarian cooking.

To those who are unfamiliar with foods cooked à la Holstein or chopped steak with eggs "à cheval," the combination of ingredients must seem strange indeed—fried eggs, anchovy fillets, capers, and brown butter sauce. It sounds like a fantasy but it isn't.

The name à cheval, the equivalent of saying "on horseback," and steak haché with eggs à cheval, simply means that the eggs are placed on top of grilled chopped meat, horseback-style. It is an extremely easy dish to cook and it is certainly quick to prepare. You simply cook a ground beef patty as you would a hamburger; fry an egg and place it on top; garnish it with criss-crossed or otherwise placed flat anchovy fillets, and add an ample amount of capers that have been cooked in beurre noisette or brown butter.

When I served this dish recently in my home, one of the guests ate his portion with considerable gusto and made an interesting speculation. Isn't it possible that the person who invented steak tartare (supposedly on the West Coast of the United States) got his idea for the dish while dining on ground meat with eggs à cheval? This dish, incidentally, is so easy to prepare and so hastily cooked that there is more than ample time to prepare an accompaniment. A sauté of potatoes would be extremely compatible with the dish.

Steak Haché avec Oeufs à Cheval
(*Hamburger with egg and anchovy*)

1½ pounds ground sirloin	4 eggs
Salt and freshly ground pepper to taste	6 to 12 flat anchovy fillets
4 teaspoons plus 4 tablespoons butter	2 tablespoons drained capers
	1 tablespoon finely chopped parsley.

1. Divide the meat into four equal portions. Shape them first into balls and flatten into patties like broad hamburgers, about four inches across and half an inch thick. Sprinkle the meat on both sides with salt and pepper.

2. The hamburger may be cooked on a hot grill such as a barbecue grill, under a hot broiler, or in a very hot skillet without additional fat. Turn once

while cooking and cook to the desired degree of doneness. Cook 2 to 5 minutes on each side according to taste. Transfer the patties to each of four plates.

3. Heat 1 teaspoon of butter at a time in one or more small skillets and add one egg to each skillet. Cook them without turning until the white is firm and the yolk remains soft and runny. Sprinkle with salt and pepper. And slip each, yolk side up, onto each patty.

4. Use the anchovy fillets either split in half lengthwise or whole. Arrange the halved or whole fillets around the yolks in a triangular fashion.

5. Heat the 4 tablespoons butter until it is foamy and add the capers and parsley. When the foaming starts to subside and the butter begins to brown, pour equal amounts of the sauce over each serving and serve hot.

Yield: Four servings.

Pommes Sautées au Beurre
(*Sautéed potatoes*)

---

12 to 14 "new" potatoes, red-skinned	3 tablespoons peanut, vegetable, or corn oil
Water to cover	3 tablespoons butter
Salt and freshly ground pepper to taste	1 teaspoon finely chopped garlic
	3 tablespoons finely chopped parsley.

1. Wash the potatoes and place them in a saucepan. Add water to cover and salt to taste. Bring to the boil and simmer until tender, about 30 minutes. Drain. When cool enough to handle, peel and slice the potatoes. There should be about 6 cups.

2. Heat the oil and 2 tablespoons of butter in a skillet. Add the potatoes and salt and pepper to taste. Cook, tossing and stirring but avoid breaking up the potato slices. Cook about 10 minutes and when crusty brown, add the remaining butter. Add the garlic and parsley. Toss and stir to blend. Serve.

Yield: Six to eight servings.

DURING A RECENT DISCUSSION ABOUT BEEF STRO-
ganoff—one of the long-time, classic dishes in quick cookery—I had to admit I had never heard of the dish's origin.
Someone recalled one of the rare books on Russian food to have been
printed in this country, *The Best of Russian Cookery,* by Princess Alexandra
Kropotkin (Charles Scribner's Sons, 1964).

According to that source, the dish was named for a member of Russian nobility, Count Paul Stroganoff. He was a member of the Court of Czar Alex-
ander II and a member of the St. Petersburg Imperial Academy of Arts. The
count was known as a fin bec during the latter part of the 18th century, but at
what particular time beef Stroganoff was created and named for him is not
divulged in the princess's notes.

There are many variations of beef Stroganoff. Some use sliced onions, others
chopped. Some include mustard, others paprika. Some add a touch of tomato
purée, others don't. Only beef and sour cream seem to be the invariable ingredients.

Quite honestly, I can't recall the origin of my version of the dish. In any
event, it is one that I prepared hundreds, if not thousands, of times while I was
chef at La Pavillon. It has one touch that I have never seen elsewhere and that
is cornichons, or small, imported sour pickles. The pickles are cut into fine
julienne strips and added at the end of the cooking time.

Perhaps the most ordinary accompaniment for beef Stroganoff is rice. An al-
ternative is noodles. I happen to enjoy it with sautéed potatoes, but it is a question of personal taste. Take your choice.

The beef Stroganoff cooks in less than ten minutes. Should you decide on
potatoes, get them started, then proceed to the ingredients for the beef.

Beef Stroganoff

1 pound fillet of beef cut into julienne strips	**⅓ cup finely chopped onion**
1 tablespoon sweet or hot paprika	**½ cup dry white wine**
Salt and freshly ground pepper to taste	**1 cup sour cream**
2 tablespoons butter	**½ cup cornichons (sour pickles) cut into thin strips.**

1. Sprinkle the meat with paprika, salt, and pepper and blend well.

2. Heat the butter in a very hot skillet and add the meat, stirring to separate
the pieces so that they cook evenly, about 2 or 3 minutes. Remove the meat
with a slotted spoon.

3. Add the onion to the skillet and cook, stirring, about 1 minute. Add the
wine and cook down to reduce by about half. Lower the heat and add the sour
cream, stirring. Do not allow the sauce to boil or the sour cream will curdle.

4. Return the meat to the skillet and stir to blend. Add the sour pickles and blend. Serve with noodles, rice or sautéed potatoes.

Yield: Four servings.

Pommes Lyonnaise
(Potatoes sautéed with onions)

1½	pounds small potatoes	¼	cup peanut oil
	Salt and freshly ground pepper	½	cup thinly sliced onions
	to taste	1	tablespoon butter.

1. Do not peel the potatoes. Place them in a kettle with water to cover and salt to taste.
2. Cook until tender, about 20 minutes. Drain and let cool. When cool enough to handle, peel them.
3. Cut the potatoes into quarter-inch thick slices or slightly larger.
4. Heat the oil in a skillet and when it is quite hot, add the potatoes. Cook, shaking the skillet and stirring gently. Turn the potatoes with a spatula. Take care to keep the slices whole. Cook about 6 to 8 minutes.
5. Add the sliced onion and salt and pepper. Continue cooking, turning the potatoes gently until nicely browned on all sides, about 5 minutes. Dot with 1 tablespoon of butter and heat through.

Yield: Four servings.

IF YOU WERE TO PLAY A GAME OF WORD ASSOCIA-tions with cooks and chefs who are much involved in food, the name Provence would conjure up in the cook's mind tomatoes and garlic, and assorted herbs; Greece would summon thoughts of lamb, tomatoes, and feta cheese; China would bring to mind images of garlic and ginger, soy sauce, and fermented black beans. Similarly, the name Hungary or dishes labelled hongroise, as they are called in French, brings up thoughts of paprika, onions, sweet peppers, and cream, either sweet or sour.

A good many dishes bearing the name hongroise are ideally suited to hasty cooking, foods that can be made ready for the table in less than sixty minutes. The basic procedure for the preparation of these dishes is as follows: Butter or oil is heated in a skillet and onions and sweet peppers are added. These are cooked quickly. In another skillet a bit more butter is heated, small pieces of beef coated lightly with paprika are added, and this too is quickly cooked. If the meat is overcooked it will become dry. The two elements are combined, tossed together, and cream is added as a final ingredient. The cream is cooked until it thickens slightly, only four to five minutes. Then the dish is ready.

A simple platter of buttered noodles would be infinitely appropriate as an accompaniment. But if you want to be just a touch more creative, you might consider a hastily made skillet of sautéed potatoes.

Sauté de Boeuf Hongroise
(Beef strips with paprika cream sauce)

1¼ pounds lean, tender, boneless beef, preferably from shell steak	1 cup finely minced onions
Salt and freshly ground pepper to taste	2 cups thinly sliced sweet green or red peppers, preferably a combination of both
2 teaspoons paprika	½ cup dry white wine
2 tablespoons butter	1 cup heavy cream.

1. Cut the meat into strips about half an inch thick and two inches long. Sprinkle with salt and pepper and paprika. Blend well with the fingers to coat meat.

2. Heat half the butter in a heavy skillet and add the onions and green peppers. Sprinkle with salt and pepper. Cook, stirring, about 5 minutes.

3. Meanwhile, heat the remaining butter in a skillet and add the beef pieces, stirring and turning over high heat about 2 minutes. Remove the pieces of meat and set aside. Do not wash or wipe out the skillet.

4. Add the green pepper mixture to the skillet in which the meat cooked. Add the wine and cook about 1 minute, stirring.

5. Add the cream. Bring to the boil and cook over high heat about 4 or 5 minutes. Add meat and drippings and serve.

Yield: Four servings.

Pommes Sautées
(Sautéed potatoes)

5	new, thin-skinned, red or white potatoes, about 1¼ pounds Salt and freshly ground pepper to taste
⅓	cup peanut, vegetable, or corn oil

1	tablespoon butter
1	small clove garlic, finely minced
2	tablespoons finely chopped parsley.

1. Put the potatoes in a saucepan or kettle and add water to cover and salt to taste. Simmer about 20 minutes, or until tender.

2. Drain the potatoes and when cool enough to handle, peel them. Cut each potato into quarter-inch thick slices.

3. Heat the oil in a well-cured, black iron skillet, preferably with curved sides. Add the potatoes. Add salt and pepper to taste.

4. Cook, stirring and tossing gently, about 5 to 8 minutes or until nicely crisped and brown. Try not to break up the potato slices as they cook.

5. Drain the oil from the potatoes. Add the butter and let melt. Sprinkle with garlic and parsley. Stir and toss gently and serve.

Yield: Four servings.

A S ANYONE CONVERSANT WITH CHINESE COOKING can testify, there is one broad and far-reaching category of food preparation known in English as the "stir-fry" technique. This involves adding small pieces or thin slices of food to a wok containing oil and cooking over very high heat and as hurriedly as possible before serving.

I mention this because a vast majority of the beef dishes used in stir-fry cookery are made with flank steak cut on the bias into very thin strips. There is, of course, a very good reason for this. It is the quality of flank steak—its tenderness and juiciness—that adapts itself admirably to quick cooking. It is no exaggeration to say that where French cooking is concerned, flank steak could be used in any hasty cooking that calls for thinly sliced (and far more expensive) filet mignon or club steak.

One such recipe is beef à la Deutsch, which is a quick sauté (one could say that a quick sauté is to a French chef what stir-frying is to a Chinese) of beef with mushrooms, green peppers, shallots, and cream. I have no earthly idea why this dish is known as à la Deutsch or German-style. It is an excellent bit of cookery, and for all I know it was created by a good German chef. In any event, the name is a convenient coinage to express a basic style of preparing one particular dish.

Because the dish embraces both meat and vegetables, and because it is lightly sauced (the sauce is lightly laced with sherry wine), buttered noodles are a hastily made and ideal accompaniment. The noodles may be served simply tossed with butter. Or you may add a few poppy or caraway seeds. Crushed or chopped green peppercorns, which have become somewhat vogueish within recent years, may also be used as a neat and flavorful addition. By all means, however, use the peppercorns packed in a plain nonacid brine rather than those that are freeze-dried or packed in vinegar

---

Boeuf à la Deutsch
(A quick sauté of beef)

1½ pounds flank steak
    Salt and freshly ground pepper
    to taste
 3 tablespoons peanut, vegetable, or corn oil
 1 tablespoon butter
 1 cup diced green peppers
¼ pound mushrooms, thinly sliced, about 2 cups

2 tablespoons finely chopped shallots
¼ cup plus 2 teaspoons dry sherry wine
½ cup fresh or canned beef broth
¾ cup heavy cream
1 tablespoon arrowroot.

1. Put the flank steak on a flat surface. Trim it of all surface fat. Cut the beef lengthwise into strips two inches wide. Cut the strips crosswise into half-inch lengths. Sprinkle with salt and pepper and toss.

2. Use a large, heavy skillet. Heat the oil, and when it is very hot and almost smoking add half the meat. Cook, shaking the skillet and stirring to redistribute the pieces, about 1 or 2 minutes. Spoon the meat from the skillet. Quickly add the remaining meat and cook, shaking the skillet and stirring about 1 or 2 minutes.

3. Transfer the meat to the first batch.

4. To the skillet add the butter. When butter is melted, add the green pepper and mushrooms. Cook until mushrooms wilt. Add the chopped shallots and cook, stirring, about 1 minute.

5. Add ¼ cup of the sherry. At the boil add the beef broth. Cook about 1 minute and add the cream.

6. Blend the arrowroot with the 2 teaspoons sherry. Blend. Stir this into the sauce. Cook, stirring, and add the meat. Stir to coat and heat through. Add salt and pepper to taste and serve piping hot.

Yield: Four to six servings.

Nouilles au Beurre de Poivre Vert
(*Noodles with green peppercorn butter*)

½ pound thin or medium noodles
Salt to taste

1 teaspoon green peppercorns packed in liquid
3 tablespoons butter.

1. Cook the noodles in boiling salted water to cover to the desired degree of doneness.

2. Chop the peppercorns and add them to a skillet large enough for tossing the noodles when added.

3. Add the butter to the peppercorns and blend.

4. Drain the noodles and add them to the peppercorn butter. Toss.

Yield: Four servings.

I N THE WORLD OF FOOD, THE NATIONAL VARIATIONS on one theme or another are fascinating. The most basic along this line are the ravioli of Italy, the won ton of China, and the pelmeny of Siberia, each a variation on a filled dumpling.

Similarly there are the various stuffed, rolled meats that exist in almost every Western kitchen. They are called paupiettes or roulades in French, rouladen in German, and rollatine in Italian. More interestingly, they are often referred to as "birds" in various languages. In this country we speak of veal or beef birds; in France, they are called—in addition to other things—oiseaux sans têtes, or birds without heads; and in Italy, they are referred to—in addition to other things—as uccelletti di campagne or "birds" country-style. Whatever they are called, this is one more proof of the universal popularity of "stuffed" dishes.

The fillings for "birds" vary widely from a basic bread-crumbs-with-herbs to ground meat. One of the most interesting fillings is a sort of scrambled egg filling.

Meat rolls such as the paupiettes (or beef birds) outlined here are relatively easy to prepare, and the cooking time will depend to a great extent on the cut of beef used. The differences in cooking time will vary widely and, if you want to conserve time, I recommend that you use a very tender cut of meat in making the dish. In any event, it is best—whatever cut you use—to make the slices even thinner by pounding them with a flat mallet before filling and rolling. Take care, however, not to pound them so that the meat is torn.

Paupiettes de Boeuf
(Beef rolls with egg filling)

---

8 thin slices tender beef, about 1¾ pounds	½ cup finely chopped celery
4 eggs	½ teaspoon finely minced garlic
⅓ cup heavy cream	⅔ cup coarsely chopped carrot
Salt and freshly ground pepper to taste	1 bay leaf
	½ teaspoon dried thyme
2 tablespoons finely chopped parsley	½ cup plus 1 tablespoon dry white wine
⅛ teaspoon freshly grated nutmeg	1 tablespoon arrowroot or cornstarch
3 tablespoons butter	Finely chopped parsley for garnish.
½ cup finely chopped onion	

1. The important thing is that the beef be taken from a very tender cut. Shell steak is ideal. Or use large slices of fillet. Do not use chuck. The slices should be thin. Place each slice of meat between sheets of plastic wrap and pound until even thinner with a flat mallet.

2. Break the eggs into a mixing bowl and add the cream, salt, pepper, parsley, and nutmeg. Beat with a wire whisk until well blended.

3. Heat 1 tablespoon of the butter in a skillet and add the egg mixture. Cook

over low heat, stirring slowly with a rubber or plastic spatula, letting the spatula gently scrape and clear the bottom and sides of the pan so that the eggs cook evenly.

4. When the eggs are set, as in scrambled eggs, remove from the heat. Spoon the eggs into a plate.

5. On a flat surface, sprinkle the beef slices with salt and pepper.

6. Place equal portions of the egg mixture into the center of each slice of beef. Roll the slices to enclose the egg filling. Tie each beef roll in two or three places with string to keep the filling intact.

7. Heat the butter in a large, heavy skillet, and when it is quite hot add the beef rolls. Cook until nicely browned on' one side and turn to the other side. Cook until browned. Continue turning the rolls in the skillet so that they brown evenly all over, about 5 minutes.

8. Add the onions and celery and garlic. Cook briefly and add the carrots and wine. Add the broth and bring to the boil. Cover and cook about 15 to 20 minutes. Very tender beef will cook in the shorter length of time.

9. Remove the beef rolls and remove the strings. Keep the rolls covered. Remove and discard random pieces of egg filling that may have gone into the sauce. Blend the arrowroot or cornstarch with the wine and stir it into the simmering sauce. Return the beef rolls to the sauce and turn them in it. Serve hot, sprinkled with finely chopped parsley.

Yield: Four servings.

Pommes Purées au Gratin
(Mashed potatoes baked with cheese)

---

4 large potatoes, about 1½ pounds	2 tablespoons butter
Salt to taste	2 tablespoons finely grated
1 cup milk	Parmesan cheese.

1. Preheat the broiler.

2. Peel the potatoes and rinse well. Cut the potatoes lengthwise in half. Cut each half into four pieces. There should be about 4 cups.

3. Put the potatoes in a saucepan with water to cover. Add salt to taste and bring to the boil. Cook about 12 to 15 minutes or until potatoes are tender. Drain. Put through a food mill or food ricer into a saucepan.

4. Meanwhile, heat the milk in a saucepan.

5. Add the butter to the potatoes and stir with a wooden spoon until melted. Add the hot milk gradually, stirring with the spoon. Add salt to taste.

6. Spoon the potatoes into a heat-proof serving dish. An oval dish measuring 1½ x 6½ x 9½-inches is suitable. Smooth the top with a spatula.

7. Sprinkle with Parmesan and place under the broiler until nicely browned.

Yield: Four servings.

Pork and Ham

T O COOK WITH HASTE AND PRECISION IMPLIES cooking efficiently. And to cook efficiently implies familiarization with the basic techniques of cookery. One of the most useful formulas is the one used for breading foods, which we speak of in French kitchens as à l'anglaise (English-style) or foods panés or panées (breaded).

The breading technique is simple. There are three steps. First, the food is dipped or dredged in flour. Any excess flour should be shaken off to leave a light coating.

Second, the food is dipped in raw egg that has been beaten, more often than not with salt, pepper, and a little water. Third, the food is dipped in crumbs, coating the food all over. When the food is removed from the crumbs, it is best to tap it lightly with the flat side of a heavy knife to help the crumbs adhere.

Finally, the food is cooked in heated butter or oil or a combination of both. When it is golden brown on one side, the food is turned and browned on the other. If you are dealing with food that cooks rapidly—such as fish—by the time the food is browned on both sides it is generally ready to serve. Some foods require much longer cooking and that would include pork chops. On the other hand, the chops recommended in this recipe are not only thin, they are pounded lightly to hasten cooking. Total time is about ten minutes.

Ideally, all the ingredients for this meal should be made ready before you start to cook. The accompanying dish proposed for the pork chops is a purée of carrots and potatoes. After the carrots and potatoes are put on to cook (total time about twenty minutes), start breading and cooking the chops. The vegetables, incidentally, can—within reason—be reheated to advantage.

Côtes de Porc Panées
(*Breaded pork chops*)

8 thin (about ½-inch thick) loin pork chops, about 1¼ pounds Salt and freshly ground pepper to taste	**1** egg, lightly beaten
	2 tablespoons water
	2 cups bread crumbs
1 cup flour	**⅓** cup peanut, vegetable, or corn oil
	1 tablespoon butter.

1. Sprinkle the chops with salt and pepper. Place between two sheets of plastic wrap and pound lightly with a flat mallet.

2. Dip the chops lightly in flour.

3. Beat the egg lightly with water, salt and pepper to taste. Dip the chops in this, smearing it over with the fingers so that it adheres.

4. Dip the chops in the bread crumbs so that they are coated all over. Pat lightly with the flat side of a heavy knife to help the crumbs ahere.

5. Heat the oil and butter in a large, heavy skillet and cook the chops until golden brown on one side, about 3 to 4 minutes. Turn and cook on the other

side about 3 or 4 minutes. It may be necessary to do this in two steps if all the chops will not fit in the skillet.

Yield: Four servings.

Purée de Legumes
(Puréed carrots and potatoes)

4	carrots, about ¾ pound	**Freshly ground pepper to taste**	
3	potatoes, about 1¼ pounds	**¼**	**teaspoon freshly grated nutmeg**
	Salt to taste	**½**	**cup hot milk.**
2	tablespoons butter		

1. Trim off the ends of the carrots and scrape them with a swivel-bladed vegetable scraper. Cut them into one-inch lengths. There should be about 2 cups.

2. Peel the potatoes and cut them into eighths. Place the carrots and potatoes in a saucepan and add cold water to cover and salt to taste. Bring to the boil and simmer about 20 minutes or until vegetables are tender. Do not overcook or they will be watery and mushy.

3. Put the vegetables through a food mill, potato ricer, or process in a food processor. Return them to a clean saucepan.

4. Add salt, butter, pepper, and nutmeg and blend. Place over heat and add the hot milk, beating rapidly with a wooden spoon. Serve immediately.

Yield: Four servings.

UCH HAS BEEN MADE OF VARIOUS MANIFESTA-tions involved in the nouvelle cuisine of French cookery. One of the dishes that has captured the public fancy is poulet au vinaigre, actually a sauté of chicken with a trace of vinegar and, generally, tomato among the ingredients.

The use of vinegar as an important ingredient in serious cookery is not a new invention. The mildly acid taste of the liquid has long been part of the sauces used with certain foods, principally pork and such sauces as Robert and charcuterie.

Vinegar, as a matter of fact, complements foods that have somewhat high fat contents, including pork chops.

There is here a version of sautéed pork chops with Robert sauce. The components include not only vinegar but a touch of tomato, dry white wine, and a dab of mustard for added piquancy.

Pork chops are best cooked either in a short span of time, to prevent them from drying out, or over a long period of time, to make them more tender.

In the dish here, the pork chops should be cooked rapidly, preferably five to six minutes to a side. The thickness of the chops is a factor: The thinner the chops, the faster they will be in and out of the skillet.

The total cooking time for this dish is approximately twenty minutes. To my mind an ideal side dish for such chops is puréed potatoes, which should be cooked during the same period as the chops. They may be finished with butter and milk at the last moment.

Côtes de Porc Sautées
(Sautéed pork chops)

8 pork chops, each about ½-inch thick	6 tablespoons plus 1 teaspoon dry white wine
Salt and freshly ground pepper to taste	2 tablespoons red wine vinegar
2 tablespoons peanut, vegetable, or corn oil	1 cup chicken broth
½ cup finely chopped onion	1 tablespoon tomato paste
	1 teaspoon cornstarch
	1 tablespoon mustard such as Dijon or Düsseldorf.

1. Sprinkle the chops with salt and pepper.

2. Heat the oil in a heavy skillet in which the chops will fit in one layer. Add the chops and cook about 5 minutes or until well browned on one side.

3. Turn the chops on the other side 5 to 6 minutes. The chops must be cooked rapidly over very high heat or they will toughen. Total cooking time should be from about 10 to 12 minutes.

4. Remove the chops to a warm serving platter and pour off most of the fat from the skillet. Add the onions and cook briefly, stirring. Add 6 tablespoons of

the wine and the vinegar and stir with a wire whisk to dissolve the brown particles that cling to the bottom and sides of the pan.

5. Add the chicken broth and tomato paste and stir to blend. Cook about 5 minutes. Blend the cornstarch and remaining 1 teaspoon wine and stir it into the sauce.

6. Spoon and scrape the sauce into a saucepan and add the mustard. Add any juices that have accumulated around the chops, salt and a generous amount of black pepper. Heat the sauce without boiling and serve with the chops. Serve with puréed potatoes.

Yield: Four servings.

Purée de Pommes
(Puréed potatoes)

1½	pounds potatoes	3	tablespoons butter at room
	Salt to taste		temperature
¾	cup milk	⅛	teaspoon freshly grated nutmeg
			or to taste.

1. Peel the potatoes and quarter or cut them into two-inch cubes.

2. Place the potatoes in a saucepan and add cold water to cover and salt to taste. Bring to the boil and simmer 20 minutes or until potatoes are tender.

3. Drain the potatoes and put them through a food mill or potato ricer. Return them to the saucepan.

4. Meanwhile bring the milk to the boil.

5. While the milk is being heated, use a wooden spoon and add the butter to the potatoes while beating. Add salt and nutmeg to taste and beat in the hot milk.

Yield: Four servings.

OMEWHERE, YEARS AGO, I READ AN ESSAY ON pork that quoted Auguste Escoffier: "However deservedly pork may be praised, it could never have been included among the preparations of first-class cookery (except subsidiarily) had it not been for the culinary value of ham." I have never known the source of that quote but it fascinates me that he spoke of ham exclusively and not of the entire range of charcuterie. I consider the sausages and salamis, the pork-based pâtés and terrines of my homeland to be among the great contributions to civilization.

It is true that pork is generally regarded as something to feast on more in the home than at grand banquets. And yet, there is a great deal to be said for the infinite preparations of the meat.

A loin of pork, studded discreetly with garlic and seasoned with thyme and roasted to a golden brown, is a great creation—particularly if it is served with a mound of mashed potatoes. But, of course, that requires a lengthy time to cook.

A tender loin chop of pork makes for fine dining on a winter's day and, although pork must be cooked longer than most meats, a savory platter of chops can be cooked in much less than sixty minutes.

The recipe here—pork chops sautéed with apples—is not tedious to prepare and it is certainly tempting fare with its light sauce made of white wine and a little chicken broth.

As a vegetable accompaniment, Brussels sprouts are excellent. Like pork, sprouts may not achieve poetic heights, but in season they can be delectable. Both the pork and the sprouts require about the same cooking time.

Filets de Porc aux Pommes
(Loin pork chops with apples)

---

4 loin pork chops, each about 1-inch thick, about 2½ pounds
Salt and freshly ground pepper to taste
1 tablespoon peanut, vegetable, or corn oil

2 apples, peeled, cored, and quartered
1 clove garlic, unpeeled
¼ cup dry white wine
⅓ cup chicken broth.

1. Sprinkle the chops with salt and pepper.

2. Heat the oil in a heavy skillet large enough to hold both chops and quartered apples—when they are added—in one layer.

3. Add the chops and garlic to the skillet and brown well on one side, about 5 minutes. Turn and brown on the other side, about 10 minutes.

4. Push the chops aside and add the apples in one layer. Continue cooking 15 minutes, turning the apples so that they brown and cook evenly.

5. Remove the chops and apples to a serving dish. Pour off the fat from the skillet. Add the wine, stirring to dissolve the brown particles that cling to the

bottom and sides of the pan. Add the broth and simmer down to a saucelike consistency. Discard the garlic. Pour the sauce over the chops and apples and serve.

Yield: Four servings.

Choux de Bruxelles
(*Brussels sprouts*)

---

1 pint [10 to 12 ounces] Brussels sprouts	**2 tablespoons butter**
	¼ cup finely chopped onion.
Salt to taste	

1. Trim off the ends of the sprouts and make a small gash in the bottom of each. Add to a saucepan with water to cover and salt to taste.
2. Bring to the boil and simmer to the desired degree of doneness, 10 minutes or longer. Drain.
3. Heat the butter in the saucepan. Add the onion and cook until wilted. Add the sprouts and cover. Cook 5 minutes, shaking the pan on occasion.

Yield: Four servings.

FOR MOST FRENCH CHEFS, HUNGARY'S GREATEST contribution to the culinary arts is the use of paprika, an ingredient used in most of the world's kitchens to provide a hasty dash of color to a finished dish or to a piece of broiled fish.

Essentially, however, paprika has a distinct flavor related to that of sweet peppers, and the flavor spectrum ranges from sweet to mild to hot. If you want to explore the various natures of these peppers, you can go to any well-stocked spice shop and purchase samples of these paprikas.

Paprika-flavored dishes—often dubbed paprikash—can embrace a lot of territory. The spice can complement a lot of foods, chief among which may be veal, chicken, and pork, both the obvious cuts and the less well-known parts called the innards.

Pieces of pork are excellent basics for the paprika flavor and although tenderloin is preferable, the loin (cut from chops) will serve very nicely. In the recipe outlined here, the pork pieces are flattened lightly with a mallet (always an aid in preparing certain foods for hasty cookery) to speed the cooking process.

After the pieces are cooked, chopped onion, paprika, and sour cream are used in making the sauce.

An excellent accompaniment for this dish, since it takes a few minutes longer to prepare than the pork, is a ragout of potatoes, a "country stew" with the delicate but obvious flavor of coarsely chopped onions and a touch of garlic. One basic flavor for this ragout is also that of smoked bacon.

The total cooking time for the potato dish is approximately half an hour. Prepare this first and then proceed to the pork, providing ample time for preparing the latter.

Côtelettes de Porc "Paprika"
(Pork cutlets with paprika in sour cream)

---

8 slices boneless loin or tenderloin of pork, about 1¼ pounds
Salt and freshly ground pepper to taste
1 teaspoon sweet or mild paprika
2 tablespoons butter
¼ cup finely chopped onion

½ cup dry white wine
½ cup fresh or canned chicken broth
½ to ¾ cup sour cream
Finely chopped parsley for garnish.

1. Place the meat on a flat surface and pound with a mallet to flatten without breaking the meat.

2. Sprinkle the meat on both sides with salt and pepper to taste.

3. Hold a small sieve over the meat and add the paprika. Tap on the sieve, moving it over the pieces so that they are evenly coated with paprika.

4. Heat the butter in a skillet large enough to hold the meat in one layer.

Cook over high heat to brown on one side, about 3 minutes. Turn and brown on the other side, about 3 to 4 minutes.

5. Transfer the pieces to a platter. Pour off the fat from the skillet. To the skillet add the onion. Cook, stirring briefly, until wilted. Add the wine and stir to dissolve the brown particles that cling to the bottom and sides of the skillet. Add the chicken broth and simmer about 5 minutes.

6. Remove the sauce from the heat and stir in the sour cream. The sauce may be spooned over the meat now, but it is preferable to put it through a fine sieve and reheat it briefly before using. After the sauce is spooned over the meat, sprinkle with the parsley and serve.

Yield: Four servings.

Ragoût de Pommes
(*Potato ragoût*)

6 new, light-skinned potatoes, about 1¼ pounds	1½ cups fresh or canned chicken broth
6 to 8 slices bacon	1 bay leaf
1 cup coarsely chopped onions	Salt and freshly ground pepper to taste.
½ teaspoon finely chopped garlic	
1 tablespoon tomato paste	

1. Peel the potatoes and cut them into one-inch cubes. Cover with cold water until ready to use.

2. Cut the bacon into crosswise quarter-inch strips.

3. Put the bacon in a saucepan and cook until rendered of fat. When the bacon is crisp, pour off all the fat but leave the bacon in the saucepan.

4. Add the onions and cook briefly, stirring, about 1 minute. Drain the potatoes and add them. Add the garlic and tomato paste. Cook, stirring, until pieces are coated.

5. Add the chicken broth, bay leaf, salt and pepper to taste.

6. Cover and bring to the boil. Simmer 20 minutes or until potatoes are tender.

Yield: Four servings.

I F THE MAIN DISH OF THE MEAL IS TO BE PORK chops, there are two ways to cook them—fast and slow. If they are to be braised—that is, browned and cooked slowly— the time element is not critical.

The pork chops here—they are called hongroise because they contain paprika and, to a French mind, paprika is associated with Hungary—fall into the "cooked quickly" category. The total cooking time is about twenty-five minutes for the chops, five minutes more for the sauce. Thus the chops should be cooked about half an hour before they are to be served. If they stand, they are more than apt to become tough and chewy.

The accompaniments for the chops include baked acorn squash, which requires forty-five minutes of cooking and should, therefore, be placed in the oven early. And then there's a sauté of Brussels sprouts. The cooking time for this varies—about twenty-five minutes—but the sprouts can be cooked, drained, and set aside and then sautéed quickly in butter before serving.

A Boston lettuce salad, with cheese, followed by sweetened orange sections, would be appropriate.

Côtes de Porc Hongroise
(Pork chops with paprika in cream sauce)

4 loin pork chops, about two pounds	¾ cup finely chopped onion
Salt and freshly ground pepper to taste	½ cup dry white wine
1 teaspoon paprika	½ cup heavy cream
2 teaspoons peanut, vegetable, or corn oil	1 tablespoon imported prepared mustard such as Dijon or Düsseldorf.

1. Sprinkle the chops on both sides with salt, pepper, and the paprika.

2. Heat the oil in a heavy skillet and add the chops. Cook about 10 minutes, or until nicely browned on one side. Turn and cook 15 minutes longer. Pour off the fat.

3. Sprinkle the onion between the chops and cook briefly. Remove the chops to a warm platter. Add the wine to the skillet and cook, stirring, until the liquid is almost totally reduced. Add the cream and cook over high heat about 5 minutes. Remove from the heat and stir in the mustard. Serve the chops with the sauce spooned over.

Yield: Four servings.

Courges au Four
(*Baked acorn squash*)

2 acorn squash
2 tablespoons butter
2 tablespoons brown sugar

Salt and freshly ground pepper to taste.

1. Preheat the oven to 400 degrees.
2. Split the squash in half. Using a spoon, scrape out and discard the seeds and fibers from the cavity. Cutt off and discard a thin slice from the bottom of each squash half, so the squash will rest flat during baking.
3. Rub the cavity of each squash half with one-quarter of the butter, and sprinkle the cavities with equal amounts of brown sugar. Sprinkle with salt and pepper. Place on a baking dish and bake 40 to 45 minutes or until the flesh is tender.

Yield: Four servings.

Choux de Bruxelles Sautés au Beurre
(*Sautéed Brussels sprouts*)

1 pint, about ¾ pound Brussels
   sprouts

Salt and freshly ground pepper to taste
1 tablespoon butter.

1. Pull off and discard any tough outer leaves from the Brussels sprouts.
2. Trim the bottoms neatly. Cut a cross in the bottom of each.
3. Put the sprouts in enough boiling salted water to cover them. Let the water return to a boil, and simmer the vegetable about 20 to 25 minutes or until tender.
4. Heat the butter in a heavy skillet and add the sprouts. Sprinkle with salt and pepper to taste and cook quickly, shaking the skillet until the sprouts are golden brown all over. Serve.

Yield: Four servings.

SOME OF THE BEST AND MOST QUICKLY MADE dishes of the Italian kitchen, particularly those kitchens that specialize in cooking in the style of Naples, are those with pizzaiola. These sauces have a tomato base, which has been reduced considerably, and olive oil and a touch of garlic. Plus one indispensable ingredient, oregano. Beef quickly cooked—grilled, pan-fried—adapts itself well to a pizzaiola sauce, but I prefer pork chops. The recipe here includes a variation on the basic sauce—the use of mushrooms and green peppers. On the day the recipe was tested, both ingredients happened to be lying in the refrigerator with no other immediate destination.

Now an agreeable accompaniment for pork chops pizzaiola would be a simple dish of buttered noodles, but the refrigerator that day also yielded a spare eggplant. There was time to cook this, too, and yet remain well within the scope of an hour in the kitchen, so another simple but appetizing recipe happened—slices of eggplant brushed with a blend of butter and Parmesan cheese, salt, and pepper, and baked until tender. This dish goes well with the tomato sauce in which the pork chops are served and remains within the scope of Neapolitan cookery.

The total cooking time for the pork chops is approximately fifteen minutes, which offers ample time to prepare both the noodles and, if desired, the eggplant. If I were to choose wine for this meal, it would be along the lines of a Valpolicella or a Bardolino. A salad made with crisp leaves of romaine lettuce and a nice, ripe slice of Gorgonzola cheese, which is available in abundance in the best shops, would be nice accompaniments.

Côtes de Porc "Pizzaiola"
(Pork chops in tomato sauce with oregano)

2 cups imported canned tomatoes	1½ cups thinly sliced fresh mushrooms
Salt and freshly ground pepper to taste	1½ cups green pepper cut into one-inch pieces
4 loin pork chops, about ½ pound each	½ cup dry white wine
2 tablespoons olive oil	1 teaspoon oregano.
2 teaspoons chopped garlic	

1. Put the tomatoes in a saucepan and bring to the boil. Cook, stirring occasionally, until reduced to about 1½ cups. Add salt and pepper to taste.

2. Sprinkle the chops with salt and pepper.

3. Heat the oil in a skillet and brown the chops on all sides, about 5 minutes to a side. Add the garlic, mushrooms and green peppers. Cover closely and cook about 5 minutes. Add the wine, tomatoes, and oregano and salt and pepper to taste.

4. Cover closely and cook about 35 to 40 minutes. Serve with buttered noodles sprinkled with Parmesan cheese.

Yield: Four servings.

Aubergines au Four "Parmigiana"
(*Baked eggplant parmigiana*)

1 1½- to 2-pound eggplant
4 to 5 tablespoons butter at room temperature
3 tablespoons grated Parmesan cheese

Salt and freshly ground pepper to taste
Chopped parsley for garnish.

1. Preheat the oven to 400 degrees.

2. Peel the eggplant and trim off the ends. Cut the eggplant into six to eight slices, each about half an inch thick.

3. Blend the butter and cheese and spread the eggplant slices on both sides with the mixture. Sprinkle with salt and pepper.

4. Arrange the slices on a baking sheet in one layer. Bake 15 to 20 minutes or until eggplant is tender throughout. Serve sprinkled with chopped parsley.

Yield: Four servings.

URING A BRIEF VISIT TO BELGIUM WE CHANCED TO
stop in a little-known restaurant outside Brussels. It was a
small place and generally undistinguished, but we were
tempted by one dish that the owner, a gentleman from Liège, told us was his
own creation and a specialty of the house. I don't recall his name, but the dish I
remember well. Perhaps all the more so because it is reminiscent of a dish I've
eaten in France called pork chops avesnoise.

Basically it consists of pork chops that have been browned on both sides and
cooked until done. They are then smeared with a mixture of cheese, mustard,
egg yolk, and cream and glazed under a broiler until done. Very simple. Very
quick. And very, very good. My version of this dish I call liègeoise—in the
style of Liège.

The chef from Liège had embellished on these ingredients a bit and added
garlic, chives, and a touch of white wine, which gives the dish a bit more character. The total cooking time for that dish is scarcely half an hour, and the
preparation time negligible.

More and more one can find small baby carrots of good flavor in plastic
bags, and those need only to be scraped before cooking. Carrots go well with
the pork dish, particularly if they have the added fillip of fresh mint.

To prepare these dishes in less than an hour, it is best to assemble and
prepare all the ingredients for the chops. As the chops are browned on both
sides there is ample time to scrape the carrots and get the ingredients for that
dish ready.

Côtes de Porc Liègeoise
(Pork chops glazed with cheese)

4 loin pork chops, about 1½ pounds	1 tablespoon imported mustard
Salt and freshly ground pepper to	such as Dijon or Düsseldorf
taste	1 tablespoon heavy cream
1 tablespoon peanut, vegetable, or	½ teaspoon finely chopped garlic
corn oil	1 tablespoon finely chopped chives
¼ pound grated Gruyère or Swiss	1 egg yolk
cheese, about 1 cup	2 tablespoons dry white wine
	2 tablespoons water.

1. Sprinkle the chops with salt and pepper.

2. Heat the oil in a heavy skillet and add the chops. Cook until nicely
browned on one side, about 10 minutes. Turn and continue cooking until
browned and cooked through.

3. Preheat the broiler.

4. As the chops cook, blend the cheese, mustard, cream, garlic, chives, and
egg yolk. When the chops are cooked, smear one side with equal portions of
the cheese mixture, smoothing it over.

5. Run the chops under the broiler until the topping is browned and nicely glazed.

6. Meanwhile, pour off the fat from the skillet in which the chops cooked. Add the wine to the skillet, stirring, and add the water. Bring to the boil. Stir to dissolve the brown particles that cling to the bottom and sides of the skillet. Pour the hot sauce over the chops and serve.

Yield: Four servings.

Carottes à la Menthe
(*Carrots with mint*)

¾   pound carrots, preferably small
     baby carrots
     Salt to taste
3   tablespoons heavy cream

Freshly ground pepper to taste
1   or 2 teaspoons chopped fresh
    mint.

1. Trim and scrape the carrots. If small, leave them whole. Otherwise, quarter or slice them. Add them to a saucepan with water to cover and salt to taste. Bring to the boil and simmer until tender, 15 minutes or less.

2. Drain the carrots and add the cream. Add salt and pepper and simmer about 3 minutes. Serve sprinkled with fresh mint.

Yield: Four servings.

THE WORLD OF FOOD HAS SUCH BROAD HORIZONS that it is as amusing as it is astonishing how deeply exercised "food enthusiasts" can become over one recipe or another. That is not to say that I will abide transgressions against classic French cooking and will not make my protests about misnomers in the name of Escoffier as loud as possible.

What I have in mind are the supposed "purists" who are opposed to variances from what their palates are accustomed to. For example, the purist who is vehemently opposed to putting any kind of sauce on fresh bay scallops because they suffer from any but the simplest preparations, namely broiling or sautéeing. My defense is that while I admire the simple preparations of the delicacy, cooking is an adventure and a well-made wine or cream sauce can be an admirable change.

In the same vein, whenever I print a recipe for almost any food—poultry, fish, or meat—to be combined in a recipe with berries or fruit, there is the inevitable response of those who deplore such liaisons. No need to point out the time-honored links of duck with orange (à l'orange); sole with grapes (véronique); or game dishes with current jelly among the ingredients.

One day I "created" a dish of pork chops with orange that was to my taste— and to the taste of those who dined at my table—a worthwhile experiment. It came about because I had pork chops (about three-fourths of a pound each) and a large, seedless orange that had been placed, accidentally perhaps, in a monthly shipment of grapefruit.

This is not a complicated recipe by any means. It requires little of the tedium, for example, of duck à l'orange or duck with cassis. The pork chops are cooked thoroughly for about half an hour (they will remain juicy). The chops are removed and onions plus various liquids are added (broth, lemon juice, and tomatoes). Orange slices are added and the chops are served with the sauce. Rice with parsley is the obvious accompaniment for the dish.

Côtes de Porc à l'Orange
(Pork chops with orange)

4 large pork chops, about ¾ pound each
Salt and freshly ground pepper to taste
3 tablespoons butter
1 large seedless navel orange

½ cup finely chopped onion
Juice of half a lemon
1 cup fresh or canned chicken broth
1 tablespoon tomato paste
½ teaspoon sugar.

1. Sprinkle the chops with salt and pepper.
2. Heat 2 tablespoons of the butter in a very hot skillet and add the chops.
3. Cook over moderately high heat about 10 minutes until nicely browned. Turn the pieces and cook 10 minutes longer. Continue cooking, turning the

pieces often so that they cook evenly. Turn the pieces on their sides to brown and crisp the fat around the rim. Total cooking time should be about 30 minutes.

4. As the chops cook, trim off the ends of the orange. Cut the unpeeled orange into eight rounds.

5. Remove the chops to a serving platter and pour off fat from the skillet.

6. To the skillet add the onion. Cook, stirring until wilted. Add the juice of half a lemon and stir. Add the broth and tomato paste and stir to blend, cooking gently. Add sugar, salt and pepper to taste.

7. Add the orange slices. Add any juices that have accumulated around the chops. Cook, turning the slices, about 3 minutes.

8. Remove the orange slices from the skillet and arrange them around the chops. Swirl a tablespoon of butter into the sauce and pour the sauce over all.

Yield: Four servings.

Riz Persillé
(Parsleyed rice)

3	tablespoons butter		Salt and freshly ground pepper
2	tablespoons chopped onion		to taste
1	cup raw rice		Tabasco sauce to taste
1½	cups water	2	tablespoons finely chopped
1	bay leaf		parsley.

1. Melt 2 tablespoons of the butter in a saucepan and add the onion. Cook until wilted. Add the rice and stir briefly.

2. Add the water, bay leaf, salt, pepper, and Tabasco.

3. Bring to the boil. Cover and simmer 20 minutes.

4. Add the remaining tablespoon of butter and parsley. Stir to blend.

Yield: Four servings.

IF I WERE ASKED TO SPECIFY THE EASIEST DISH TO prepare for entertaining from one to fifty or more people, it most likely would be choucroute garnie, or sauerkraut with the appropriate garnishes. It is a dish that even a beginner in the kitchen can master with absolute guarantee of success, provided, of course, that the cook can follow the most basic instructions. A sauerkraut dinner may be as simple or as elaborate as you may want it. The garnie can range from frankfurters to the best assortment of sausages, ham, salamis, and so on that the charcuterie can supply.

The best-known sauerkraut preparation in French kitchens is choucroute à l'alsacienne, or sauerkraut Alsatian style, for Alsace is thought of as the sauerkraut capital of the nation. The dish is also known as choucroute à la strasbourgeoise, and the two are essentially the same—garnishes for them vary and include an assortment of sausages plus, at times, smoked pork, or smoked goose.

The basic preparation of the sauerkraut simply involves cooking the pickled cabbage on a bed of onion and garlic that have been cooked in rendered bacon fat. Various seasonings are added (juniper berries are a traditional seasoning for the dish but they are not always easily obtainable in America; thus they are optional), then the meats. The dish is covered and cooked until done. Depending on the cook or chef, the sauerkraut is cooked for from one to four hours and many people consider it better when reheated the following day. Some cooks, particularly those of Swiss persuasion, add grated potato blended with milk to the cooking.

Here is how to make an excellent and easily made choucroute garnie that cooks in exactly sixty minutes. The dish includes, incidentally, boulettes (o. k., meatballs) of pork. They are optional.

Choucroute Garnie
(*Sauerkraut with meats*)

2	pounds sauerkraut		Salt and freshly ground pepper to
2	slices bacon, chopped		taste
1	cup finely chopped onion	4	pork meatballs, optional (see
1	teaspoon chopped garlic		recipe)
1	bay leaf	1	1-pound ham steak in a single slice
6	crushed juniper berries, optional	1	1-pound Polish sausage (kielbasi)
½	teaspoon caraway seeds		pricked in several places with the
½	cup dry white wine		tines of a fork.
½	cup chicken broth		

1. If you like sauerkraut that is reatively sour, do not rinse it, but simply squeze it dry. If you like it less sour, however, run it under cold water and drain in a colander. Press to extract excess moisture.

2. Heat the bacon in a casserole or Dutch oven and cook until rendered of fat. Add the onion and garlic and cook until onion is wilted.

3. Add the sauerkraut. Tie the bay leaf, juniper berries, and caraway seeds in a small cheesecloth bag and add it. Add the wine, chicken broth, salt and pepper to taste and bring to the boil. Arrange the meatballs, ham steak, and sausage in or over the saukerkraut. Cover closely and cook 1 hour. Discard the cheesecloth bag. Serve with steamed potatoes and mustard on the side.

Yield: Four servings.

Boulettes de Porc
(*Pork meatballs*)

⅓ **pound ground pork**	1 **teaspoon finely chopped parsley**
2 **tablespoons bread crumbs**	**Salt and freshly ground pepper to**
2 **tablespoons grated onion**	**taste**
½ **teaspoon finely chopped garlic**	⅛ **teaspoon freshly grated nutmeg.**
1 **tablespoon sour cream**	

1. Blend all the ingredients in a mixing bowl.
2. Shape into four balls. Use in cooking sauerkraut.

Yield: Four meatballs.

Pommes Vapeur
(*Steamed potatoes*)

1¼ **pounds "new" red, waxy**	**Salt to taste**
potatoes or 2 large Idaho	1 **tablespoon butter.**
potatoes	

1. Peel the potatoes. If they are new potatoes, there should be at least eight. Leave them whole. If they are large Idaho potatoes, quarter them, which is to say, cut each potato into four equal pieces.
2. Place the potatoes in a saucepan and add water to cover and salt to taste. Bring to the boil and simmer until tender, 15 or 20 minutes, depending on size. Do not overcook.
3. Drain and add the butter, shaking the saucepan until the pieces are coated.

Yield: Four servings.

SINCE COMING TO THIS COUNTRY IN 1939 TO WORK as a chef at the French Pavillon restaurant of the New York World's Fair, I have detected a certain snobbery in the public's mind when it comes to what are called "peasant dishes," on which I thrived as a child and which I still enjoy in maturity.

One such dish is a potée, a "country" dish that is popular in many areas of France. A potée is any kind of dish made in an earthenware casserole, but it usually consists of pork products such as sausages or smoked meats cooked with an assortment of winter vegetables, principally cabbage and potatoes.

I grew up in a very small town in Burgundy, not far from Chablis. One kind of potée that came out of my family kitchen consisted of smoked pork butt, cabbage, turnips, celery, and carrots, all of them cooked in a kettle suspended in the fireplace. I consider it an ideal dish for cold weather dining, and, happily, it takes slightly more than half an hour to cook.

Almost any supermarket or grocery store carries smoked pork butts (sometimes labeled porkettes). These are like small, boneless hams and they are fully cooked.

A potée, with its various ingredients, is a main course unto itself.

I have named this dish, incidentally, after my home town of Tonnerre. Although no potatoes are included in the recipe, there is no reason why four medium-size potatoes, washed and peeled, could not be added to the stew along with the cabbage, turnips, and carrots. After the main course—a romaine lettuce salad, with cheese, and for dessert a mélange of fruits. The melange should be made as the potée cooks.

Potée Tonnerreoise
(Boiled dinner with smoked pork butt)

1¼ pounds head cabbage	4 peppercorns
1½ pounds smoked pork shoulder butt (porkette)	2 sprigs fresh thyme or half a teaspoon dried thyme
4 ribs celery, trimmed and tied into a bundle	4 sprigs fresh parsley
	Salt to taste
2 leeks, trimmed, partly split and well washed	2 turnips, about ¾ pound total weight, peeled
1 small onion, peeled and stuck with 2 whole cloves	4 small carrots, about ⅓ pound total weight, trimmed and scraped
8 cups water	Dijon or Düsseldorf mustard.
2 allspice	
1 bay leaf	

1. Pull off and discard any tough outer leaves from the cabbage. Cut out the core. Quarter the cabbage and set aside.

2. Combine in a kettle the pork butt, celery bunch, leeks, onion, water,

allspice, bay leaf, peppercorns, thyme, parsley, and salt. Cover and bring to the boil. Simmer 10 minutes.

3. Add the cabbage, turnips, and carrots. Cover and simmer about 25 minutes longer or until the pork is fork tender. Serve the vegetables with the sliced pork butt. Serve with mustard on the side.

Yield: Four servings.

Mélange des Fruits
(Fruits and berries with spirits)

2 cups fresh strawberries or an equal amount of cubed fruits such as pears and apples	3 tablespoons confectioners' sugar
	2 tablespoons Grand Marnier
1 seedless orange	1 tablespoon kirschwasser
2 tablespoons orange juice	1 tablespoon cognac
	1 tablespoon framboise.

1. Rinse the strawberries. Remove and discard the hulls. Rinse well and add them to a mixing bowl.

2. Peel the orange. Cut it into sections. Add this to the strawberries. Add the orange juice.

3. Sprinkle with confectioners' sugar and refrigerate for 1 hour or longer.

4. When ready to serve, add the remaining ingredients. Toss well and serve.

Yield: Eight servings.

ANY AMERICANS SEEM TO LOOK WITH DISDAIN ON dishes made with ground meats, relegating them to a low position in the hierarchy of foods that fit in the "gourmet" category. The foundation for this attitude probably lies in the fact that the dishes called hash are often made with meat of one sort or another that has been ground and served, so to speak, the second time around.

Ground meat dishes are by no means an American monopoly. Italy has its polpette and polpettini; Germany its Klöpse; Sweden its Kottbullar and France its boulettes. Porjarski cutlets, one of the fine adaptations of Russian cookery, are made with ground meat such as veal, or salmon.

There are ways, of course, to elevate any dish, and two of the methods for upgrading ground meats are the judicious use of certain herbs and spices, and the serving of the ground meats in sauces that add character and interest.

The meatballs here (don't be put off by the number of ingredients; the meatballs can be made and cooked in much less than an hour) are stuffed with olives and serve in a cream sauce delicately flavored with tomato and mustard.

As always, the best way to approach this recipe—in the interest of conserving time—is to assemble all the ingredients for the main dish. Chop, slice, or otherwise get them ready and then set about making and cooking the meatballs. The total preparation time should be less than half an hour; the total cooking and finishing time, less than that.

The noodles to go with the dish take the briefest amount of preparation, and this can be done easily during the last few minutes of cooking the meatballs.

Boulettes de Viande aux Olives
(Olive-stuffed meatballs)

1¼ pounds ground meat, preferably pork and veal	Salt and freshly ground pepper to taste
1 tablespoon butter	16 small stuffed green olives
1 cup finely chopped onion	¼ cup peanut, vegetable, or corn oil
2 small cloves garlic, finely minced	3 tablespoons flour
½ cup bread crumbs	½ cup dry white wine
½ cup finely chopped parsley	1½ cups chicken broth
1 large egg	1 tablespoon tomato paste
1 cup heavy cream	Noodles with dill (see recipe)
⅛ teaspoon freshly grated nutmeg	1 tablespoon imported mustard such as Dijon or Düsseldorf.

1. Put the meat in a mixing bowl.

2. Heat the butter in a small skillet and add half the onion and half the garlic. Cook until wilted. Let cool briefly.

3. Add the onion mixture to the meat. Add the bread crumbs, parsley, egg, half the cream, the nutmeg, and salt and pepper to taste.

4. Mix well, preferably using the hands. Divide the mixture into sixteen equal portions.

5. Flatten each portion into a small patty and place one small stuffed olive in the center. Bring the edges of the meat together and seal in the olive. Press into a ball.

6. Heat the oil in one or two skillets large enough to hold the meatballs in one layer. Do not crowd them. Cook, turning and stirring often so that they brown evenly. When nicely browned, about 5 to 10 minutes, remove and keep warm.

7. Pour most of the fat from the skillet. To the fat remaining in the skillet add the remaining onion and garlic and cook, stirring, until onion is wilted. Add the flour and stir. Add the wine and let it cook about 1 minute, stirring constantly.

8. Add the chicken broth and stir with a wire whisk to remove any lumps. Stir in the tomato paste. When the sauce is thickened and boiling, add the meatballs. Cover and cook 10 minutes, shaking the skillet occasionally.

9. Meanwhile, cook the noodles so that they will be ready when the meatballs are ready.

10. Blend the remaining cream and mustard into the sauce.

Yield: Four servings.

Nouilles à la Scandinave
(*Noodles with dill*)

½ **pound thin noodles**
   Salt to taste
2 **tablespoons butter**

2 **tablespoons finely chopped fresh dill**
   Freshly ground pepper to taste.

1. Bring enough water to the boil to cover the noodles when they are added. Add the noodles and salt to taste. Cook 9 to 10 minutes or to the desired degree of doneness.

2. Drain the noodles and return them to the kettle. Add the butter and dill, salt, and pepper. Toss well.

Yield: Four servings.

I N THE HIERARCHY OF FOOD THERE IS NO DOUBT
that sausages in general are what could be called food for the
masses or a peasant concept in food preparation. It is true that
sausages are a far cry from foie gras and caviar, and yet I have yet to meet a
connoisseur of cooking or eating who doesn't, on frequent occasions, feel a
well-defined hunger for what are called, in my place of birth, saucisses de porc
or pork sausages. There are country sausages and sausages Toulouse-style,
sausages from Lyons and the notable garlic sausages or saucissons à l'ail which,
when wrapped in pastry, have been, for several decades, in luxury restaurants
and bistros in France as well as in America, a choice first course, more often
than not served with a wine-flavored warm potato salad judiciously seasoned
with herbs.

Sausages are, compared to many meats, relatively inexpensive because they
can be made from the odds and ends, the scraps of pork (of course you can use
other things, including veal and even goose). In my Burgundy childhood, we
were often served sausages at the family meal. It never occurred to me then that
one of the reasons for the frequency of sausages on our family table was not
only the fact that the sausages tasted good; they were a budget item in that
country hamlet where I lived.

One of my favorite preparations—because it was a considerable change from
the usual grilled sausages with mashed potatoes or sausages cooked with sauerkraut and white wine (two dishes that remain to this day personal favorites),
was sausages cooked and served with a light tomato sauce (generally of fresh
tomatoes) and rice.

This is a dish that can be prepared without strain within the space of one
hour, although it does include three separate but easily made components. The
sausages are simply put in the oven to grill; then a hasty tomato sauce and the
rice are prepared. There is a plus in the fact that the dish is very much sufficient to serve as a complete meal. The logical way to prepare the dish is to put
the sausages on to cook in the oven, proceed to the rice, which requires slightly
in excess of fifteen minutes, and then make the quick tomato sauce. The three
can be assembled in five minutes or less.

Saucisses au Riz
(Baked sausages with rice)

3	sweet or hot Italian sausages, or a combination of both, about 2 pounds	1	bay leaf
		1	cup rice
		1½	cups chicken broth
4	tablespoons butter	½	cup dry white wine
2	tablespoons finely chopped onion	2	cups fresh tomato sauce (see
1	clove garlic, finely minced		recipe).

1. Preheat the oven to 400 degrees.

2. Prick the sausages with a two-pronged fork in several places. Place them in a skillet with about one-fourth inch of water and bring to the boil on top of the stove. Put the skillet in the oven and bake about 25 to 30 minutes, or until the sausages are browned and cooked through. Check the sausages after about 10 minutes. If liquid has accumulated, pour it off. Continue baking.

3. Meanwhile, melt 2 tablespoons of butter in a small casserole and add the onion. Stir until onion is translucent, and add the garlic and bay leaf. Cook about 1 minute, stirring, and add the rice. Cook about 3 minutes, stirring. Add the broth and bring to the boil on top of the stove. Cover and place in the oven along with the sausages. Bake exactly 20 minutes. No longer. Uncover and stir with a fork to make the rice fluffy.

4. When the sausages are done, remove them. Pour off the fat from the skillet.

5. When ready to serve, add ½ cup of tomato sauce to the rice and stir to blend. Spoon equal portions of the rice in the center of four plates. Place one serving of sausage in the middle of the rice and serve the tomato sauce on the side.

Yield: Four to six servings.

Sauce Tomate
(*Tomato sauce*)

2 or 3 tomatoes, about 1¼ pounds or use	½ cup finely minced onion
3 cups of canned tomatoes	1 clove garlic, finely minced
2 tablespoons butter	Salt and freshly ground pepper to taste.

1. Remove the core from the tomatoes. Cut the tomatoes into one-inch cubes. There should be about 3 to 4 cups.

2. Heat half the butter in a saucepan and add the onion and garlic. Cook, stirring about 1 minute, and add the tomatoes, salt and pepper to taste.

3. Cook about 5 minutes. Pour the mixture into the container of a food processor or use an electric blender.

4. Blend to a fine sauce. Spoon into a saucepan. Add the remaining butter and serve.

Yield: About two cups.

HERE ARE VERY FEW DISHES THAT INSPIRE AS much controversy as those that combine meat or poultry with fruits. For example, in one article in *The New York Times*, Marcia Davenport, the author, placed herself solidly in the league of naysayers, stoutly and eloquently defending her notion that there is a place for all things and the place for fruits and/or berries is at the end of a meal or at the beginning of breakfast.

I don't feel strongly about the marriage of meat with fruits, and there are numerous dishes in the classic French repertory that link them—duck à l'orange, dishes called Montmorency, which means with cherries, and dishes véronique, which is to say with white seedless grapes. I find them all quite palatable if properly made.

Which brings up the subject of a dish I propose for those who would prepare a meal for four in less than an hour. To the best of my knowledge, it is an original creation and for the want of another name it might be dubbed ham véronique, in that it is made with boiled ham served with a light tomato and white wine sauce containing briefly cooked white grapes. What's more (to further alienate those for whom meat with fruit is anathema), I propose a side dish of baked and broiled quartered apples.

The logical way to prepare this meal is to begin with the sauce. As it simmers, prepare the grapes. Peel and prepare the apples and then proceed to rolling the ham slices and arranging them on a platter for baking. The ham, of course, is purchased.

It is recommended that this menu include the usual salad, with cheese as a second course, and, if desired, a final course of a purchased or previously made dessert.

Roulades de Jambon Véronique
(*Ham rolls with grapes*)

1 pound thinly sliced boiled ham	Salt and freshly ground pepper to taste
2 tablespoons butter plus butter for greasing a baking dish	6 tablespoons dry white wine
1 tablespoon finely chopped shallots	1 cup heavy cream
1 cup cubed, cored, red, ripe tomatoes or use 1 cup canned imported tomatoes	1½ cups fresh whole, small white seedless grapes.

1. Preheat the oven to 400 degrees.
2. Melt 1 tablespoon of butter in a saucepan and add the shallots. Cook briefly and add the tomatoes, salt, and pepper. Cook about 10 minutes, stirring occasionally, and add 4 tablespoons of white wine. Cook about 3 minutes and

add the cream. Simmer about 15 minutes and put through a fine strainer. Cook about 5 minutes longer.

3. Meanwhile, prepare the grapes and add them to a small skillet with remaining 2 tablespoons of wine. Bring to the boil and cook, shaking the skillet and stirring, about 3 minutes. Do not overcook or the grapes will become mushy. They must retain a nice texture and shape. Add the sauce, stirring, and bring to the boil.

4. Butter an oval baking dish (a dish measuring about 19 x 12 x 2-inches is convenient). Roll the ham slices into cigarette shapes not quite an inch in diameter. Arrange the rolls close together, parallel and in a neat row. Brush with a tablespoon of melted butter and set aside.

5. As the sauce is finished, place the ham in the oven and bake about 5 minutes, just to heat through. Pour the sauce over the ham and serve. Serve, if desired, with the apples (see recipe) on the side.

Yield: Four servings.

Pommes au Four
(*Baked apples*)

1¼ **pounds (about 3) firm, unblemished apples**	2 **teaspoons melted butter** 1 **tablespoon confectioners' sugar.**

1. Preheat the oven to 400 degrees.
2. Peel the apples. Quarter them and cut away the core.
3. Arrange them cored side down in a buttered dish and brush with melted butter. Sprinkle with the confectioners' sugar.
4. Place in the oven and bake 10 minutes. Before serving, run briefly under the broiler.

Yield: Four servings.

THE TWO BASIC AND MOST DESIRABLE QUALITIES in food are flavor and texture. One vegetable that yields a fascinating, different, and admirable combination of both is endive, that white, pointed member of the chicory family that is a specialty of Belgium.

Endive is most commonly thought of as an ingredient for the salad bowl (and its eminence and elegance in that uncooked state is not to be disputed).

When cooked, Belgian endive takes on a flavor that is slightly bittersweet, full-bodied, but not overpoweringly so.

One of the best-known family-style dishes in France is Belgian endive (asparagus is also similarly utilized) wrapped in thin slices of ham, covered with a mornay sauce, preferably made with genuine Gruyère cheese, and baked.

Some meals, if they are to be prepared within the course of an hour, must be plotted with special care. This one is a case in point.

The endive requires approximately thirty minutes to cook. As it cooks there will be ample time to prepare the cheese or mornay sauce for the ham, and, if desired, to prepare a salad such as cucumber with dill. The baking time for the dish is approximately ten minutes.

Endives et Jambon au Gratin
(Endives and ham baked in cheese sauce)

8	thin slices cooked ham, about ½ pound		Salt and freshly ground pepper to taste
8	whole braised endives, drained (see recipe)	⅛	teaspoon freshly grated nutmeg Cayenne pepper or Tabasco to
3	tablespoons plus 1 teaspoon butter		taste
¼	cup flour	¼	pound grated Gruyère cheese, about 1½ cups
2½	cups milk	2	egg yolks.

1. Preheat the oven to 425 degrees.

2. Place the ham slices on a flat surface. Place on each slice a braised endive crosswise in the center. Roll the ham slices to enclose the endive.

3. Melt the 3 tablespoons butter in a saucepan and add the flour, stirring with a wire whisk. When blended, add the milk, stirring rapidly with a whisk. Add salt, pepper, nutmeg, and cayenne. Cook, stirring often, about 5 minutes.

4. Add about 1 cup of the cheese and stir until melted. Add the yolks, stirring rapidly with the whisk. Bring just to the boil, stirring, but do not boil or the sauce will curdle.

5. Rub the bottom of a baking dish (a dish that measures 13 x 8 x 2-inches is suitable) with the remaining 1 teaspoon butter.

6. Arrange the ham rolls over the baking dish. Spoon the sauce over all. Sprinkle with the remaining grated cheese.

7. Place in the oven and bake 10 minutes or until piping hot and bubbling and browned. If the top is not uniformly brown, run the dish briefly under the broiler to brown.

Yield: Four servings.

Endives Braisées
(*Braised endives*)

8 large, unblemished endives, about 1½ pounds	**Salt and freshly ground pepper to taste**
2 tablespoons butter	**Juice of half a lemon**
	½ cup cold water.

1. Wash the endives in cold water and drain.
2. Butter a heavy skillet in which the endives will fit in one layer. Sprinkle the pan with a little salt and arrange the endives over the pan. Sprinkle with salt and pepper.
3. Sprinkle with lemon juice and add the ½ cup of water. Cover closely and cook 30 minutes. Watch carefully that the cooking liquid does not boil away and the endive burn. If absolutely necessary, add a little more water to prevent sticking and burning.

Yield: Eight pieces.

Salade de Concombres à la Scandinave
(*Cucumber and dill salad*)

1 to 3 cucumbers, depending on size	**2 tablespoons chopped fresh dill**
1 tablespoon sugar	**Freshly ground pepper,**
Salt to taste	**preferably white pepper, to**
¼ cup white vinegar	**taste.**

1. Peel the cucumbers and split them in half. Scoop out the seeds with a melon-ball cutter. If so-called "gourmet" cucumbers are used, it is not necessary to cut in half or to remove the seeds.
2. Slice the cucumbers crosswise. There should be about 4 cups. Put the slices in a mixing bowl. Add the remaining ingredients and toss to blend. Add more seasonings such as vinegar, sugar, and so on to taste, if desired.

Yield: Four servings.

Pasta

THE COOKING OR CULINARY HABITS OF VARIOUS countries have intrigued me since I first became a chef a good many years ago. A friend of mine, an Italian, reminded me once again recently that tarragon is almost unknown and little used as a flavoring in Italy. In fact, there are very few Italians who know that the name of the herb is dragoncelle.

It isn't so curious, I thought, when I recalled that in my early youth the sweet herb known as basil (basilique in French), so much prized in Italian cooking, was practically unknown in the kitchens of Burgundy where I was raised.

Similarly, I had never heard of dining on freshly cooked and hot pasta tossed with a cold and well-seasoned fresh tomato sauce. For my taste, the combination is as irresistible as it is intriguing. I have dined on that combination on many occasions with numerous friends from Italy within recent years.

In preparing such dishes, my Italian friends remind me, they must be made at the heart of the tomato season, when the tomatoes themselves have been sun- and vine-ripened, for that is also the time when fresh basil flourishes best and is at its most potent.

The essentials for these dishes (and various kinds of pasta can be used, from the ubiquitously known spaghetti or spaghettini to tubular pasta like penne) are, in addition to the red ripe tomatoes and fresh basil, a good grade of olive oil, garlic, parsley, salt, and pepper. There are, I have discovered or surmised, numerous variables, including chopped chiles or dried pepper flakes.

I have heard lengthy discussions on whether cheeses are appropriate to include or serve with these cold-sauce dishes, and on this matter I take no sides. I have had it with and without cheese and am happily pleased with either version.

Two recipes for these dishes are outlined here. The first, and most basic, is hot spaghetti with cold tomato sauce. In this version a couple of tablespoons of Gorgonzola cheese may be added. The second recipe is made with penne (tube-shaped, they resemble straight broken macaroni), and it contains Fontina cheese plus grated Pecorino or Parmesan cheese.

The cold sauces, incidentally, are far more quickly made, for obvious reasons, than a cooked spaghetti sauce.

Ed Giobbi's Hot Spaghetti with Cold Tomato Sauce

2 pounds fresh, red, ripe tomatoes at room temperature (see note)	**⅓ cup olive oil, plus additional olive oil for the cooked spaghetti, optional**
2 cloves garlic, finely minced	**Salt and freshly ground pepper to taste**
⅓ cup fresh basil leaves, coarsely chopped and loosely packed	**1 pound spaghetti or spaghettini.**
¼ cup coarsely chopped parsley, loosely packed	

1. Combine the tomatoes, garlic, basil, parsley, ⅓ cup olive oil, salt and pepper to taste in the container of an electric blender or food processor.

2. Blend thoroughly.

3. Drop the spaghetti into boiling water and cook, stirring as necessary, to the desired degree of doneness. Drain. Return the spaghetti to the kettle and add, if desired, a touch of olive oil. Immediately add the tomato sauce. Toss quickly and serve immediately. This dish is generally not served with grated cheese.

Yield: Four to six servings.

Note: It is imperative that the tomatoes be at room temperature. Two tablespoons of Gorgonzola cheese may be added to the tomato mixture before blending.

Sirio Maccioni's Pasta de l'Estate
(Pasta with fresh, uncooked tomato sauce)

3	large, red, ripe tomatoes, about 2½ pounds		Salt and freshly ground pepper to taste
4	large whole cloves garlic, peeled but left whole	½	cup olive oil
1	small hot red or green chili, chopped, or use about ½ teaspoon or less red pepper flakes	1	pound penne or other tubular pasta
		¼	pound Fontina or Muenster cheese
½	cup coarsely chopped fresh basil	½	cup grated Pecorino or Parmesan cheese.

1. Wash and wipe the tomatoes. Remove the cores from the tomatoes. Chop the tomatoes. There should be about 6 cups. Put them in a large bowl.

2. Add the garlic, chopped chili, basil, salt, pepper, olive oil. Let stand at room temperature several hours. Or chill overnight. But let return to room temperature before serving.

3. Cook the penne according to package directions.

4. Meanwhile, grate or shred the Fontina, using the coarse blade.

5. When the pasta is cooked, drain it. Spoon off about ¼ cup of the surface oil from the tomatoes and add it. Add the Parmesan cheese and toss. Add half the tomato sauce and toss. Add half the remaining sauce and Fontina cheese and toss. Serve in soup bowls with remaining sauce spooned on top.

Yield: Four servings.

I HAD RARELY EVER DINED ON ITALIAN COOKING before I came to America in 1939. I had never eaten pizza (they tell me that the pizza craze in this country is relatively recent, at least since World War II) and the only time we served pasta in France was as a garnish for a "foreign" dish such as veal milanese.

In the intervening years I have become much taken with some Italian specialties, be they the full-bodied tomato sauces of the south or the more refined dishes of Tuscany and the North.

One dish which I admire and make fairly often (fairly often in my kitchen means about once a year) is spaghetti alla puttanesca, which means, in low humor, spaghetti street-walker's style (at least one lady I know once served this dish to me in her home and called it spaghetti angel-style). The hackneyed story goes that it was a dish made in one of the more raffish quarters of Naples to lure customers.

In any event, the sauce for the spaghetti is about as tasty and zesty and as easy to make as rolling dice. It consists of cooking tomatoes with seasonings including basil and oregano and parsley. An essential for piquancy is a dried, hot red pepper or hot red pepper flakes. Spiciness is characteristic of the dish.

In addition to this there are chopped anchovies, capers, and pitted black olives. It is important in making the dish properly that you use imported black olives such as those from Italy or Greece or the South of France. The California black olives are simply too bland to produce the necessary earthy character of the sauce.

Some years ago, I made this sauce in advance (it keeps well in the refrigerator and can be reheated to advantage) before going out clamming behind my house. Just before we sat down to dine, I tossed a few clams into the sauce to reheat it. I found it to be an agreeable and highly complementary addition. The sauce with spaghetti, plus a romaine lettuce salad with garlic croutons, would make a highly satisfactory and hastily made meal.

Spaghetti alla Puttanesca with Clams

2 tablespoons olive oil
1 tablespoon finely minced garlic
1 tablespoon finely chopped fresh basil or half the amount dried
1 teaspoon crumbled dried oregano
4 cups tomatoes, crushed
¼ cup freshly chopped parsley
1 dried hot red pepper
Salt and freshly ground pepper to taste

12 pitted black olives, preferably imported
2 tablespoons drained capers
1 2-ounce can anchovies, drained
½ cup bottled clam juice, optional
18 littleneck clams, the smaller the better
1 pound spaghetti or spaghettini cooked to the desired degree of doneness and drained.

1. Heat the oil in a saucepan or in a small, deep skillet, and add the garlic. Cook briefly without browning and add the basil, oregano, tomatoes, and parsley. Add the hot dried pepper.

2. Add salt and pepper to taste and bring to the boil. Cook about 30 minutes. Add the olives and drained capers.

3. Chop the anchovies and add to the sauce. Reheat, stirring. If the sauce seems too thick, add the clam juice. Add the clams, cover closely, and let the clams heat until they open, about 5 minutes. Discard the hot red pepper.

4. When the spaghetti is cooked and drained, spoon it into bowls and add sauce with clams onto each serving.

Yield: Four servings.

Salade avec Croûtons à l'Ail
(Romaine lettuce with garlic croutons)

1 small head romaine lettuce	**Salt and freshly ground pepper to**
3 very thin slices white bread	**taste**
3 tablespoons olive oil	2 teaspoons red wine vinegar
2 cloves garlic, peeled but left whole	¼ cup olive oil.
2 teaspoons imported mustard	

1. Trim off the ends of the lettuce. Pull the leaves apart and rinse well. Pat dry.

2. Trim the bread of crusts. Cut the bread into half-inch cubes or smaller. There should be about 1 cup.

3. Heat the oil in a skillet, and when hot add the bread and garlic cloves. Cook, shaking the skillet and stirring, until cubes of bread are golden brown. Drain in a sieve. Discard the garlic cloves or not, as you wish.

4. Cut or tear the lettuce leaves into bite-size pieces. There should be about 8 cups loosely packed. Put the leaves in a salad bowl and sprinkle the croutons over the leaves.

5. Put the mustard in a small mixing bowl with salt and pepper to taste. Add the vinegar and beat with a wire whisk. Add the oil, beating briskly with the whisk. Pour the dressing over the salad and toss.

Yield: Four servings.

TASTE IS ONE OF THE MOST SUBJECTIVE THINGS ON earth. I have no quarrel with the man who despises caviar. At today's prices, I might even envy him. I have one very close friend, a professional in the field of food, who can't abide the smell or taste of cheese. Even cream cheese. Since my childhood, I have had drilled into my skull the philosophy of Lucretius who lived more than two thousand years ago: "What is food to one, is to others bitter poison."

All this is by way of introduction to the following recipe, which will be to some palates the most mundane of all dishes, spaghetti with meatballs. It may not be gourmet fare to some, it is not authentically Italian (and it certainly isn't French), but it is a dish that delighted my children (now grown) throughout their childhoods.

As a matter of fact, there was a gathering of my offspring one evening recently and one of them asked for the dish specifically. I turned to the family kitchen, and about forty-five minutes later we sat down to dine on the dish, along with a loaf of homemade French bread and a salad.

In the course of the evening, one of them suggested that if it was good enough for their palates, it was good enough for this book, and, on reflection about the subjective nature of taste, I could not disagree.

In all honesty, I don't know when this "recipe" came about. It is simply a blending together of compatible flavors which seem logical. And perhaps, just a touch Neapolitan.

Over the years I have been told by Italian cooks that most of their tomato sauces are long simmered, and I knew one old lady who told me that three days were required to make her family's ancestral salsa di pomodoro alla napoletana.

As far as this recipe is concerned, the most time-consuming thing is the preparation of the meat balls, a simple blend of meat with onions cooked until translucent, plus bread crumbs, egg, and parsley. It does take a moment or two to shape them. But once the meat is browned and the tomatoes added, that's all there is to it. While the sauce simmers there's plenty of time to make ready a simple tossed salad.

Spaghetti with Meatballs

1¼	pounds ground chuck	1	cup finely chopped onion
1	teaspoon peanut, vegetable, or corn oil	1	teaspoon finely minced garlic
½	cup finely chopped onion	1	1-pound 12-ounce can imported tomatoes with tomato paste
½	cup finely chopped parsley	¼	to ½ teaspoon rosemary leaves
½	cup fresh bread crumbs	¼	teaspoon marjoram
1	egg, lightly beaten	¼	teaspoon oregano
	Salt and freshly ground pepper to taste	1	hot dried red pepper, optional
1	tablespoon olive oil	1	pound spaghetti or spaghettini
		2	tablespoons butter.

1. Put the meat in a mixing bowl and set aside.
2. Heat the oil and cook the onion until wilted. Let cool slightly.
3. Add the onions to the meat. Add the parsley, bread crumbs, egg, salt, and pepper. Blend well with the hands.
4. Shape the mixture with the hands into approximately sixteen balls.
5. Using a large skillet, heat the oil and add the meatballs. Cook, turning the balls as necessary, so that they brown evenly, about 5 minutes.
6. Holding the lid over the skillet, drain off the fat.
7. Scatter the onions and garlic around and between the meatballs.
8. Crush the tomatoes and add them. Add the rosemary, marjoram, oregano, dried red pepper, salt, and pepper. Bring to the boil. Cover and simmer 20 minutes.
9. Cook the spaghetti to desired doneness. Add butter, salt, and pepper and serve with meatballs and sauce.

Yield: Four servings.

Salade de Cresson et Endives
(*Watercress and endive salad*)

1	large or 2 small bunches watercress	2	teaspoons imported mustard
1	head Belgian endive		Salt and freshly ground pepper to taste
½	to ¾ cup thinly sliced, loosely packed cucumber slices	4	tablespoons oil, preferably walnut oil.
1	tablespoon lemon juice		

1. Cut off the tough stems of the watercress and discard.
2. Cut off the end of the endive and cut head into bite-size pieces.
3. Rinse watercress and endive in cold water and drain or spin dry. Add to a salad bowl. Add the cucumber slices.
4. Add the lemon juice, mustard, salt, and pepper to another small bowl. Using a wire whisk, beat in the oil. Pour the dressing over the salad and toss.

Yield: Four servings.

ONE OF THE GREAT POSITIVE ASPECTS OF LIVING IN New York is the ability to sample to one degree or another almost all the world's assorted cuisines—Chinese, Russian, Japanese, Greek, Italian, and many others.

One of the most appealing of the "foreign" dishes encountered during my stay here, which spans about thirty years, is the Italian (and I am told Neapolitan) creation, linguine with white clam sauce. Although I have eaten clams or palourdes of one sort or another (there are many different kinds of clams) all my life, I had never eaten a cooked clam dish until my arrival in America.

Years ago an old Italian chef taught me his "secret" of making linguine with clam sauce and his recipe is by far the best I've tasted. Most clam sauces are too liquid to coat the strands of pasta with which they are served. Thus when you finish the dish you are left with a puddle of clam liquid. I am opposed to "thickening" the sauce with cornstarch, as a few cooks do; it sort of vulgarizes the concept.

My Italian friend told me that he always uses the clam juice plus water to cook the linguine in. This gives the clam flavor to the pasta. At the end, he makes a quick clam sauce with the chopped clams, garlic, oil, and parsley. The end result is a fine, harmonious blending of clams and linguine.

A white clam sauce is one of the most quickly prepared of all sauces, assuming, of course, that the cook can open clams quickly. If you live in a clam area (and clams are sold in most fish shops in coastal areas), you can have the clams opened by the fish merchant, but make certain that he saves both the clams and their natural juice.

A fine accompaniment (or first course) for linguine with white clam sauce would be roasted peppers sautéed with garlic and oil and vinegar. You could use canned pimentos with anchovies (plus chopped garlic, oil, and vinegar). But home-roasted peppers, cooked under the broiler and peeled before sautéeing, are more special. The peppers can be made in advance and kept in the refrigerator. They are as good a few days later as they are when freshly cooked.

Linguine with Clam Sauce

---

36 littleneck clams	¼ cup finely chopped parsley
1 pound linguine	Freshly ground pepper to taste
⅓ cup olive oil	⅛ teaspoon hot red pepper flakes.
1 tablespoon finely chopped garlic	

1. Open the clams or have them opened. Save both the clams and the juice. There should be about 1½ cups of clam juice and 1 cup of clams. Chop the clams coarsely. Set aside.

2. Add six cups water and clam juice to a kettle for cooking the linguine. Bring to the boil and add the linguine. Cook until tender but al dente.

3. Heat the oil in a skillet and add the garlic. Cook briefly, stirring. Do not

brown. Add the chopped clams and cook, stirring, briefly. Add the parsley and pepper flakes and cook briefly.

4. Add the drained linguine and toss to blend. Spoon out into hot soup bowls. Serve equal portions of the sauce that concentrates on the bottom of the skillet onto each serving. A brief sprinkle of more olive oil on the dishes before serving is not amiss.

Yield: Four servings.

Poivrons Sautés à l'Italienne
(*Sweet peppers sautéed Italian-style*)

---

5 to 6 sweet red or green (bell) peppers	**½ teaspoon dried oregano**
¼ cup olive oil	**Salt and freshly ground pepper to taste**
4 peeled cloves garlic, each cut in half	**2 tablespoons red wine vinegar.**

1. Preheat the broiler to high.

2. Line a baking tray with aluminum foil and arrange the peppers on it. Place about four or five inches from the source of heat and cook, turning occasionally, until the skin of the peppers is slightly burnt and charred all over.

3. Hold under cold running water and pull away the skin of the peppers. Drain well. Cut away and discard the cores. Cut peppers in half and scrape away the seeds.

4. Heat the oil in a skillet and add the garlic. Cook briefly until the garlic starts to brown. Do not brown. Add the pepper halves and stir over high heat, turning the pepper pieces. Add the oregano, salt and pepper to taste. Cook about 2 minutes altogether.

5. Add the vinegar and cook just to heat through, about 10 seconds. Remove from heat.

6. Transfer the pepper halves to a serving dish and pour the sauce with garlic over them. Chill before serving. The peppers are better if left to stand overnight.

Yield: Four servings.

SHRIMP BELONG TO THAT CATEGORY OF FOODS that, by their nature, can be cooked to advantage in only a minute or so and are thus ideal for a hasty food preparation.

They are used here as a sort of "meal in one," cooked as they are with a tomato, anchovy, and caper sauce, and served with freshly cooked spaghetti.

To begin the meal, start cooking the tomatoes. The tomato sauce for this dish requires about thirty minutes.

As the sauce cooks, peel the shrimp—unless you want to go to the additional and generally useless expense of buying the shrimp already peeled.

One of the quickest and most effective methods of peeling shrimp is to use a pair of kitchen shears. Clip from the torn-off head and back toward the tail end. This will simultaneously open the housing of the dark vein down the back, and the shell can be quickly removed with the fingers, while holding the shrimp under cold running water. Drain in a colander and, preferably, pat dry with kitchen toweling.

When the shrimp are ready, assemble all the ingredients that must be added to the sauce at the last minute. About five minutes before the sauce is ready, add the spaghetti to the kettle of boiling water with salt to taste. Stir it often to keep the strands from sticking. Cook the shrimp quickly and add them to the sauce. When the spaghetti is ready (test it often and do not overcook), drain it. Serve.

It is recommended that this menu include the usual salad, with cheese as a second course, and, if desired, a final course of fresh fruit or a purchased or previously made dessert.

Shrimp with Anchovy Tomato Sauce and Spaghetti

1½ pounds raw shrimp in the shell
 4 tablespoons olive oil
 2 teaspoons finely minced garlic
 4 cups canned plum tomatoes
 1 teaspoon crushed dried oregano
 1 tablespoon crushed dried basil
    Salt and freshly ground pepper
    to taste

 2 tablespoons anchovy paste
 ¼ pound mushrooms, thinly sliced
 1 dry, small, hot red pepper,
    crushed
 ¼ cup drained capers
 1 pound spaghetti or linguine.

1. Peel and devein the shrimp. Rinse and pat dry. Set aside.

2. Heat half the olive oil in a small skillet and add half the garlic. Cook briefly and add the tomatoes, oregano, half of the basil, salt and pepper to taste. Cook, stirring often, about 30 minutes. Add the anchovy paste.

3. Heat the remaining oil and add the shrimp, the remaining garlic and basil and mushrooms. Cook, stirring, until shrimp turn bright red, about 1 minute. Add the mixture to the sauce. Add the hot pepper, capers, salt and pepper. Bring to the boil and serve on spaghetti or linguine cooked according to package directions.

Yield: Four servings.

ONE OF THE MOST COMMON QUESTIONS PUT TO anyone who gives serious thought to cooking—particularly if he works at it professionally—is what is a "gourmet" dish? It's a question I've given an appreciable amount of thought to and discussed at some length with my colleagues. And, to my mind, a "gourmet" dish is difficult if not impossible to pigeonhole or categorize, except to say that it is any food prepared with a mixture of conscience, care, and intelligence.

It might be a liverwurst sandwich on good bread with lettuce and mayonnaise. It might be a platter of long-simmered sauerkraut with well-chosen sausages—to name but two of the things that have given pleasure to my palate over the years.

Thus the recipe on this page. Who on earth, you might ask, would call the likes of spaghetti with meatballs a gourmet's delight? I would, provided the dish is made with "conscience, care, and intelligence."

The meat must be tender, succulent, and lean. But not too lean, otherwise it will taste dry. The tomato sauce must be simmered until well concentrated and tastefully seasoned. Incidentally, "gourmet" cooking does not imply blandness. A touch of piquance in certain foods is, at times, highly desirable. Think of diable sauces, sauce Robert, and sauce charintière.

Actually, spaghetti with meatballs (boulettes de viande sounds more rarefied) is not the quickest dish in the world to prepare. It can be made, however, in less than an hour, and with a tasty green salad, a loaf of crusty bread, and a good bottle of red wine, it would happily meet my qualifications for a gourmet dish.

Boulettes de Viande "Marinara"
(*Pork meatballs in marinara sauce*)

1½ pounds ground pork, beef, or veal or a combination of meats	1 egg
	1 tablespoon olive oil
¼ cup chopped parsley	2 cups marinara sauce (see recipe)
1 clove garlic, finely chopped	1 pound cooked spaghetti (see recipe)
¼ cup grated Parmesan cheese	
½ cup bread crumbs	Grated Parmesan cheese.
Salt and freshly ground pepper to taste	

1. In a mixing bowl, combine the pork, parsley, garlic, ¼ cup grated Parmesan cheese, bread crumbs, salt, pepper, and egg. Blend well and shape into sixteen balls of equal size.

2. Heat the oil in a skillet large enough to hold the meatballs without touching. Cook until nicely browned all over, at least 10 minutes.

3. Combine the meatballs with the marinara sauce and simmer 15 to 20 minutes. Serve on pasta; sprinkle with grated Parmesan cheese.

Yield: Four to six servings.

Sauce "Marinara"
(*Marinara sauce*)

4 cups canned Italian plum tomatoes	3 tablespoons chopped parsley
1 tablespoon olive oil	Salt and freshly ground pepper to
1 teaspoon finely chopped garlic	taste.
2 teaspoons dried oregano	

1. Place the tomatoes in a saucepan and cook until reduced by half. Stir often to prevent sticking.
2. Heat the oil in another saucepan and add the garlic. Cook briefly, and add the tomatoes, oregano, parsley, salt and pepper to taste, and blend.

Yield: About two cups.

Spaghetti Cooked by a New Technique

Bring 5 quarts of water to a vigorous boil and add salt to taste. Add 1 pound of spaghetti. Stir well until water returns to the boil. Cook 2 minutes.

Remove the pot from the heat and cover first with a clean cloth, then with a lid. Let stand 9 minutes without uncovering the pot. Drain and toss with 1 tablespoon butter or olive oil. Serve with a sauce.

Yield: Four to six servings.

Cold Dishes

WHEN I NOTED THAT CHICKEN, MORE THAN ANY other food, is the most ubiquitous "meat," employed by the rich and poor alike, I failed to add that this is not only true of Western cuisines; it is also true in Asian kitchens. Some of the greatest "foreign" dishes in the world are based on chicken cooked in one form or another. The Indonesian table is well known for its satays of chicken, the Japanese dine finely on mizutake, chicken cooked at table in a broth with noodles and vegetables (and in Japan there are also specialty restaurants serving nothing but chicken where the raw breasts are thinly sliced and eaten raw like sashimi). Java, Vienna, and the American South are noted for their fried chicken, although the techniques and flavors are disparate.

One of the most interesting and spiciest chicken dishes with which I am familiar, and for which I have a particular liking, is a cold chicken dish made with shredded cooked boneless breast and served on a bed of cold noodles with a sesame paste made biting hot with hot chili oil. Over the years I have spent many hours in the kitchen with Virginia Lee, and the recipe came to my attention while she was preparing recipes for her Chinese cookbook.

The dish, which looks fairly complicated, is as easy as the breeze to prepare. It is made with skinless boneless chicken breast which is simmered briefly until cooked through. The breast is shredded and set aside. The fine noodles are cooked for a very few minutes in the broth and the sauce is nothing more than a quick blending of assorted ingredients, which include vinegar, sugar, and finely minced garlic. Although it is normally served as an appetizer at a several-course Chinese feast, it can be served as an admirable main course for warm weather dining.

A bit less exotic for the warm season is another cold chicken dish that can be made similarly from breast cooked briefly, or it could be made with leftover boiled chicken from another meal. This is a salad known in France as a mayonnaise de volaille or "chicken mayonnaise." In the version printed here, which can also serve as a main course, the salad is garnished with anchovies, which offer a curiously compelling contrast in flavors.

Mayonnaise de Volaille aux Anchois
(Chicken salad with anchovy garnish)

---

4 cups cooked, skinless, boneless chicken cut into bite-size cubes	4 to 8 anchovy fillets
1 cup finely diced celery	2 giant-size or large stuffed olives
¼ cup drained capers	2 hard-cooked eggs, peeled and quartered
1½ cups mayonnaise	1 or 2 red ripe tomatoes, quartered
¼ cup finely chopped onion	
Boston lettuce leaves	

1. Put the chicken cubes in a mixing bowl and add celery, capers, 1 cup of the mayonnaise, and onion. Toss to blend well.

2. Arrange the Boston lettuce leaves with edges slightly overlapping to serve as a base for the salad.

3. Spoon the salad into the center and smooth it over like a mound. Spoon the remaining ½ cup of mayonnaise all over it.

4. Garnish the salad with the anchovy fillets, overlapping or in a pattern.

5. Cut the olives into thin crosswise slices and garnish between the anchovies. Arrange the eggs and tomatoes around the base and serve.

Yield: Four servings.

Poulet aux Nouilles Froides Façon de Virginia Lee
(Virginia Lee's chicken and cold noodles with spicy sauce)

1 large chicken breast	3 tablespoons light soy sauce
6 ounces fine egg noodles	2 tablespoons red wine vinegar
¼ cup sesame paste	1 teaspoon plus 1 tablespoon sesame
3 tablespoons water	oil
2 teaspoons hot chili oil, optional	¼ cup peanut or corn oil
	2 tablespoons finely chopped garlic.

1. Bring about 6 cups of water to the boil and add the breast. Do not add salt. When the water returns to the boil, simmer about 10 or 15 minutes. Remove the breast but save the broth.

2. Bring the broth to the boil and add the noodles. Cook, stirring occasionally, about 5 to 7 minutes. Drain and run under cold water until chilled. Drain thoroughly and add to a mixing bowl. Add the teaspoon of sesame oil and toss.

3. Cutting with a knife or using the fingers, cut or pull the chicken into fine shreds.

4. Add the sesame paste to a bowl and add the water, stirring. Add the chili oil, soy sauce, wine vinegar, the tablespoon of sesame oil, peanut oil, and garlic.

5. Arrange the noodles on a serving dish. Cover with the chicken and spoon the sauce over.

Yield: Four servings.

IN SOME WAYS, AMERICA'S DINING HABITS ARE curious. There is a vegetable that I have known since my cradle days that is widely used all over Europe in salads, in soups, in marinades, and so on, which is, for no accountable reason, treated as a rare oddity in this country. The vegetable is known in France as céleri-rave, and in America and England as celery root, knob celery, or celeriac.

By far the best known use for the vegetable in this country is as an appetizer known as céleri rémoulade, in which the raw vegetable is cut into the finest julienne strips and blended with a well-seasoned mayonnaise. The vegetable is splendid when whipped and creamed and served like mashed potatoes, but that is another matter.

It is certainly true that céleri-rave, or celery root, is grown and can be purchased in America. It is a more or less round root, generally quite large and "knobby" in appearance. When it is in season it is a delight to dine on. In French restaurants in this country, where it enjoys its greatest popularity, it is generally served alone as a first course, or in combination with slices of pâtés or terrines or other cold meats or salads.

A salad of céleri rémoulade—with a few embellishments—can make an excellent luncheon dish with a loaf of French bread, followed by a fine, imported cheese.

The embellishments I have in mind are either a fine julienne of salami or cold mussels. Mussels, incidentally, cook quickly and cool quickly. They could, of course, be cooked the previous night.

The rémoulade sauce is easy to prepare. Although it is preferably made with homemade mayonnaise, a good grade of the commercial variety is certainly acceptable. The only really time-consuming factor in preparing céleri rémoulade is actually the preparation of the celery root itself. It must be peeled and then cut into the thinnest possible slices. The slices are stacked and cut into the finest possible shreds.

Céleri Rémoulade avec Moules
(Celeriac in mayonnaise sauce with mussels)

---

1 knob celery (also called root celery and celeriac), about ¾ pound	1 tablespoon prepared mustard such as Dijon or Düsseldrof
1 quart mussels	Salt and freshly ground pepper to taste.
2 tablespoons wine vinegar	
1 cup mayonnaise, preferably homemade	

1. Place the mussels in a saucepan and add half the wine vinegar. Cover and bring to the boil. Cook about 5 minutes, or until the mussels open. Remove. Let cool.

2. Remove the mussels from the shells. Discard the shells but save at least 2 tablespoons of liquid.

3. Peel the celery and cut into thin slices an eighth of an inch thick or less. Stack the slices, a few at a time, and cut them into the finest possible strips. If a food processor is available, the celery may be quartered and shredded, using the fine shredding blade. Add the celery to a mixing bowl.

4. Add the mussels to the celery. Blend the mayonnaise, remaining vinegar, and the reserved mussel liquid. Add this to the celery mixture. Add salt and pepper to taste, and toss well to blend. Serve.

Yield: Eight or more servings.

Céleri Rémoulade avec Salami
(Celeriac in mayonnaise sauce with salami)

1	knob celery (also called root celery and celeriac), about ¾ pound	1	cup mayonnaise, preferably homemade
¼	pound thinly sliced salami	1	tablespoon white vinegar
1	tablespoon prepared mustard such as Dijon or Düsseldorf	1	tablespoon water if the mayonnaise is very thick
			Salt and freshly ground pepper to taste.

1. Slice the celery and cut it into thin slices about one-eighth inch thick or less. Stack the slices, a few at a time, and cut them into the finest possible shreds. If a food processor is used, the celery may be quartered and shredded, using the fine shredding blade. Add the shredded celery to a mixing bowl.

2. Stack the salami and cut it into very thin strips. Add it to the celery. Add all the remaining ingredients and toss well to blend thoroughly. Serve.

Yield: Eight or more servings.

THERE ARE SOME "HASTY" FOODS IN THIS WORLD that I consider culinary abominations. I would count among them instant rice and the frozen dinners that abound on the freezer shelves of supermarkets. There are some pre-cooked foods, however, that are an absolute boon to anyone who has menu planning and cooking by the kitchen clock in mind, and one of them is sliced boiled or baked ham. For the most part, the quality of store-bought hams is uniform and they have—generally speaking—been cooked in the simplest manner possible. Plain, sliced boiled ham can be transformed in a hundred different ways into main dishes—baked in cheese sauce, gratinéed with potatoes, and tossed in cold salads for summer.

One of the most interesting salads we've contrived combines a basic bowl of cubed boiled ham with cut-up endive, two foods which, cold or hot, complement each other. The crispness and slightly sweet-bitter taste of raw endive make a fine foil for the texture and flavor of the ham.

The tie that binds the two is a ravigote sauce in the classic French tradition. It consists basically of a vinaigrette sauce (vinegar and oil) plus capers, parsley, chopped onion, chives, and tarragon. In preparing the dish, fresh herbs are worth searching for, although dried herbs may be used, or the herbs may even be omitted. Ravigote, if you care about etymology, has to do with "re-invigorating" or making fresh.

A boiled ham and endive ravigote salad makes an excellent warm weather dish and could be served as a light repast—at lunch, for example—with hot French bread. Or it could be served with one or more salads, such as sliced tomato or cucumber.

One of my personal favorite salads for summer or winter is a salade pommes vin blanc, which is to say, a potato salad with a white wine dressing. This salad is traditionally served lukewarm and contains, in addition to the potatoes and a light sprinkling of white wine, the simple additions of oil, salt, and pepper.

Both the salads could easily be made within the space of an hour.

Salade de Jambon et Endives Ravigote
(Ham and endive salad)

The ham and endive:
1¼ pounds thinly sliced boiled ham
2 large heads of Belgian endive

The sauce ravigote:
2 teaspoons imported mustard
1 tablespoon red wine vinegar
Salt and freshly ground pepper to taste
½ cup peanut, vegetable, or corn oil

1 tablespoon drained capers
2 tablespoons finely chopped fresh parsley
2 tablespoons finely chopped onions
1 tablespoon finely chopped fresh chives
1 tablespoon finely chopped fresh tarragon.

1. Stack the ham slices on a flat surface and cut into half-inch cubes. There should be almost 4 cups. Put the ham in a bowl.

2. Trim off the base of each endive. Pull off and reserve about twelve of the best outside leaves of endives to be used as garnish. Coarsely chop the remaining endive. There should be about 2½ cups. Add this to the ham.

3. Put the mustard, vinegar, salt, and pepper in a small mixing bowl. Add the oil gradually, stirring vigorously with a wire whisk. Add the capers, parsley, onions, chives, and tarragon. Blend well.

4. Pour the sauce over the ham mixture and stir to blend.

Yield: Four to six servings.

Salade de Pommes Vin Blanc
(*Potato salad with white wine*)

2½ pounds potatoes (see note) Salt and freshly ground pepper to taste	⅓ cup dry white wine ½ cup peanut, vegetable, or corn oil (or use olive oil if you prefer)

1. Rinse the potatoes and put them in a large saucepan with cold water to cover. Bring to the boil and simmer until tender, 20 minutes or longer, depending on size. Do not cook until mushy.

2. Preheat the oven to 200 degrees.

3. Drain the potatoes and when they are cool enough to handle, peel them. Cut them into quarter-inch-thick slices and put into a heatproof mixing bowl. Sprinkle with salt, pepper, wine, and oil. Toss while warm. Cover the bowl with foil and put in the oven briefly to warm through. Turn into a serving dish and serve while warm.

Yield: About eight cups. To prepare half that amount, simply divide all ingredient amounts in half.

THERE ARE A LOT OF LUXURY OR GRAND LUXE RES-
taurants around the world that offer specialties that never appear on the menu. The dishes are available for very subtle
psychological reasons best known to the restaurant's proprietor and maître
d'hotel. Such unadvertised dishes offer the owner or maître d'hotel the opportu-
nity to whisper into a favored customer's ear, "I have something created
especially for you and I think you'd like it." Very comforting to the customer's
ego and an enticement for continued patronage.

When I was chef at Le Pavillon, when it enjoyed a considerable esteem in
America, the owner, Henri Soulé, had one particular specialty that he'd ask to
have prepared for his pet customers. The dish was a great favorite of the Duke
and Duchess of Windsor and of Cole Porter, and it was always available to
them.

It is a delicate and interesting creation and it is especially good for summer
dining. It consists of small, cold omelets, flavored with fines herbes and bits of
tomato, and served cold with a crabmeat filling.

This is not your usual rolled omelet but rather a "flat" omelet. That is to
say, it is cooked more like a pancake, turned once in the skillet, rather than like
a hot, oval-shaped omelet with pointed ends, which might be filled with any
number of fillings.

The omelets, quite small in size, are cooked in advance and removed from
the skillet to cool. They are then filled with a stuffing that consists of crabmeat
(it was always snow-white lump crabmeat at Le Pavillon) bound with a light,
tomato-flavored sauce containing parsley, finely chopped shallots, and the least
trace of cognac.

The omelets, generally two to a guest, are sufficient unto themselves for a
meal, but a cold tossed salad would not be out of place. And the omelets go
well with a nice, not too dry, chilled white wine such as a Rhine or Alsatian.

The omelets are easily made within the space of an hour and probably with
minutes to spare. The filling can be made in advance; the omelets shortly
before the guests arrive. They should be filled at the last moment with more of
the tomato mayonnaise on the side.

Omelettes Froides au Crabe
(Cold omelets with crabmeat)

8 large eggs	Salt and freshly ground pepper to
2 tablespoons finely chopped	taste
parsley	4 teaspoons butter
1 tablespoon finely chopped fresh	Crab dressing (see recipe)
tarragon or 1 teaspoon dried	Tomato mayonnaise left over
¼ cup heavy cream	from crab dressing (see recipe)
¾ cup peeled, red, ripe tomatoes cut	Parsley sprigs for garnish.
into ½-inch cubes	

1. Break the eggs into a mixing bowl. Beat lightly. Add the parsley, tarragon, cream, tomatoes, salt and pepper to taste. Beat well.

2. Use a small omelet pan or preferably a 7-inch Teflon pan. Heat about ½ teaspoon of butter in the pan. Add about ⅓ cup of egg mixture. Let cook until firm and lightly browned on the bottom, stirring quickly with a fork until the omelet starts to set. When set, slip a large pancake turner under the omelet and turn it quickly to the other side. Let cook about 5 seconds. Remember, you want to produce a flat omelet, not a typical folded omelet. Turn the omelet out flat onto a sheet of waxed paper. Continue making the omelets until all the egg mixture is used.

3. When ready to serve, add equal portions of the crab dressing to the center of each omelet. Fold over. Garnish with parsley sprigs. Serve with the leftover tomato mayonnaise.

Yield: Four to eight servings.

Garniture de Crabe
(Crab dressing with tomato mayonnaise)

---

1 whole egg	2 tablespoons finely chopped
1 teaspoon imported mustard	parsley
½ teaspoon Worcestershire sauce	1 tablespoon finely chopped shallots
Salt and freshly ground pepper to	1 teaspoon cognac
taste	1 pound crabmeat, preferably lump
1 cup peanut, vegetable, or corn oil	crab
2 tablespoons bottled chili sauce	Juice of half a lemon.

1. Break the egg into a mixing bowl and add the mustard, Worcestershire, salt, and pepper. Beat with a whisk.

2. Gradually add the oil, beating constantly until thickened. Add the chili sauce, parsley, shallots, and cognac to blend. Set aside.

3. Add the crabmeat to a mixing bowl. Add half the sauce. There should be just enough to bind.

Yield: Four to eight servings.

ARLIER IN THIS BOOK WE SUGGESTED THAT CERtain recipes may be cooked in "deliberate excess" in the interest of the hasty preparation of a meal. The point of that exercise is to insure that there will be leftovers, which can be put to excellent advantage in a subsequent meal. I have pointed out that, to my mind, there are many foods that taste best "second time around." The list of good, inspired uses for leftover foods is practically endless, and there is practically no food that can't be put to a second purpose. I feel quite certain that it was a cautious and thrifty chef who first conceived the idea of what is called consommé célestine, a chef who, on one occasion, found himself with an excess of crêpes and decided not to throw them out. Consomme célestine consists of a rich beef broth that is garnished with finely shredded crêpes plus a few chopped choice herbs. And there is more than one Scandinavian sandwich or canapé that calls for cold (leftover, perhaps) scrambled eggs as a topping. One of the choicest is made with cold scrambled eggs and smoked eel, with a dill topping.

Another suggestion for an excellent original dish, the leftovers of which could be put to prime use, are moules, or mussels, marinière. To my taste, moules marinière are one of the most gratifying of dishes when served with their own liquid hot off the fires. In retrospect, I can recall only one place in the world where I was served so many mussels that it took a bit of force to down the last one, and that was in one of the restaurants of Brussels, where mussels are something like a national dish.

The preparation of moules marinière is triflingly simple. It consists of combining the well-scrubbed mussels (the scrubbing is the only tedious part) with white wine, shallots, and other seasonings, and putting them on to steam. The moment the mussels open (four to five minutes, more or less) they are ready to serve with the kettle juices. When cold (or simply lukewarm) they can be transformed—quickly and simply—into excellent cold dishes, ideal for summer dining, by blending them, in or out of the shell, with a variation of a mayonnaise or a vinaigrette dressing. The recipe outlined here is for a vinaigrette with chopped hard-cooked eggs and herbs. With a loaf of French bread and a salad. This dish is sufficient for a meal.

Moules Marinière
(Mussels in white wine)

4 quarts freshly scrubbed mussels	2 sprigs fresh parsley
6 tablespoons finely chopped onion	Freshly ground pepper
3 tablespoons finely chopped shallots	3 tablespoons butter
1 bay leaf	1 cup dry white wine.
2 springs fresh thyme, or half a teaspoon dried thyme	

1. Combine all the ingredients in a kettle and cover. Bring to the boil.

2. Let steam 4 to 5 minutes, or just until mussels open. The mussels may be served in soup bowls with the liquid.

Yield: Six to eight servings.

Moules Vinaigrette en Coquilles
(Mussels vinaigrette on the half-shell)

---

2 quarts steamed mussels (see recipe)	**2** hard-cooked eggs, peeled
1 tablespoon imported mustard	**2** tablespoons red wine vinegar
3 tablespoons finely chopped onion	Salt and freshly ground pepper to taste
1 tablespoon finely chopped shallots	**1** cup peanut, vegetable, or corn oil.
1½ teaspoons chopped parsley	

1. The mussels may be steamed immediately, or they may be left over from an earlier cooking. Remove the top shell of each mussel and discard. Leave the mussels on the half-shell.

2. Put the mustard in a mixing bowl and add the onion, shallots, and ½ teaspoon parsley.

3. Add the eggs to a sieve and push them through with the fingers. Add half the eggs to the mustard mixture. Reserve the remainder for garnish.

4. Add the vinegar, salt, and pepper to the mustard mixture. Stir rapidly, gradually adding the oil.

5. Pour the sauce over the mussels. Place mussels on a serving platter and sprinkle with the remaining hard-cooked eggs and a teaspoon of chopped parsley.

Yield: Four servings.

I HAVE BEEN ASKED A FEW THOUSAND TIMES OVER the years if I ever eat and savor foods that come in cans, and the answer, of course, is yes. There are times when my appetite craves sardines; on occasion I will dine on canned tuna with a good deal of relish; and if there is absolutely no fresh salmon to be had, I can willingly feast on the canned variety.

Although I hope destiny will forbid the day when I have to exist on foods from the pantry shelf, my larder is well stocked with a variety of items which can and have come in handy in certain "emergency" situations: a return home after a long weekend; a lazy Saturday lunch between fishing forays in Gardiner's Bay; an impromptu lunch for unexpected guests (and no time for shopping in town).

The fact is that there are numerous dishes that can be made from pantry items that are highly palatable.

One year, on a trip through Italy, we were twice served tuna (I will vouch that in both cases the tuna had come from tins) that had been blended with the cooked white kidney beans that are known as cannellini. In an "emergency" situation I have reproduced this dish using canned cannellini, which are quite commonly found in supermarkets in this country. Mind you, I do not contend that canned beans are the equal of those cooked from a dried state. I do say that the tinned version makes a highly acceptable substitute, even if the beans en boîte, to use the French phrase, are a trifle overcooked and somewhat less than firm to the bite. Suffice it to say that this particular salad (it can serve as an appetizer or a main course) consists of simply opening two cans and blending the contents with various seasonings, plus oil and vinegar.

There is also another "pantry salad" listed here. It is similarly made with tinned chick-peas, drained and blended with canned salmon. If you have the time, cook the beans or peas from the dried state. And by all means, use cooked, fresh salmon if it is available. These recipes are for "emergency" occasions. But good.

Haricots Secs avec Thon
(Cannellini beans with tuna)

---

1 **20-ounce can cannellini (white kidney beans) drained, about 2 cups**	1 **tablespoon red wine vinegar**
	Juice of half a lemon
¼ **cup finely chopped scallions or onions**	¼ **cup olive oil**
	Salt and freshly ground pepper to taste
½ **teaspoon finely minced garlic**	2 **7-ounce cans tuna packed in oil**
½ **teaspoon crumbled dried oregano**	**Tomato slices for garnish.**
2 **tablespoons finely chopped parsley**	

1. Put the drained beans in a mixing bowl and add the scallions, garlic, oregano, parsley, vinegar, lemon juice, olive oil, and salt and pepper to taste.

2. Drain the tuna and flake it (not too finely). Add it to the bean mixture and toss gently. Serve garnished with sliced tomatoes.

Yield: Four servings.

Salade de Saumon et Pois Chiche
(Salmon and chick-pea salad)

3 cups freshly cooked or canned chick-peas, drained
½ cup finely chopped onion
½ cup finely chopped celery
1 teaspoon garlic
4 tablespoons finely chopped parsley
4 tablespoons finely chopped dill
3 tablespoons red wine vinegar

½ cup olive oil
Salt and freshly ground pepper to taste
2 cups freshly cooked or canned salmon, drained
1½ cups peeled, seeded, red ripe tomatoes cut into cubes, optional.

1. In a mixing bowl combine the drained chick-peas, onion, celery, garlic, parsley, dill.
2. Add the vinegar, oil, salt, and pepper, and toss to blend.
3. Drain the salmon and pick over to remove bones and soft skin. Add the salmon and, if desired, cubed tomato to the peas and toss to blend. Serve chilled, garnished with cucumber slices.

Yield: Four servings.

ONE OF THE GREAT, UNQUESTIONABLE CULINARY blessings of the summer season, particularly, perhaps, for those who are concerned about cooking times, are lobsters. A one and one-half to two-pound lobster, which is sufficient for one (and oftentimes two) servings, steams in about twelve minutes. One says "steams." Actually, the lobsters are cooked in a quantity of water with such seasonings as bay leaf, thyme, and, if desired, a hot dried pepper. It may be neither here nor there to the reader, but many home cooks tend to overcook lobsters, just as they do shrimp, by half an hour or longer.

Lobster is superb, of course, hot from the kettle. Or at room temperature. Or cold. This is another of those foods which might be cooked in quantities larger than what are needed for one feast. Leftover lobster meat is a gustatory delight in salads, recipes for which number in the thousands.

Three recipes for summer feasting are outlined here. One is for basic steamed lobsters. Another is for a sauce verte or green mayonnaise to be served with them (if you're not up to making the mayonnaise, go ahead and use your melted butter and lemon halves). And a third is for a memorable lobster salad.

There are many variations of sauce verte in this world (it is salsa verde in Italian). Some recipes for making the green mayonnaise call for an assortment of greens and herbs such as spinach, sorrel, tarragon and so on. The version here simply calls for mayonnaise with the addition of a quick purée of watercress, parsley, and dill. The flavor is as fresh as spring water.

The lobster salad is a quick version of a salad we dined on when exploring restaurants for that much publicized and costly meal we dined on at Chez Denis, in Paris, some years ago. The salad, lightly flavored with tarragon, is "bound," as we say in French, with fresh mayonnaise and tossed with finely shredded—a chiffonade—of romaine or other lettuce. It should be eaten the moment it is prepared; otherwise the lettuce will lose its crisp texture.

Homard à la Sauce Verte
(*Steamed lobster with green mayonnaise*)

4	1½-pound lobsters	2	bay leaves
16	cups water	2	sprigs fresh thyme or ½ teaspoon
	Salt to taste		dried thyme
16	peppercorns	1	hot dried red pepper.

1. Select a kettle large enough to hold the lobsters when they are added.

2. Add the water, salt, peppercorns, bay leaf, thyme, and hot red pepper. Bring the water to a full rolling boil. Add the lobsters and cover. When the water returns to the boil, let cook for 12 minutes.

3. Remove the lobster and hang them by the tail to drain.

4. Split two of the cooked lobsters lengthwise. Discard the tough sac near

the eyes. Arrange the halves on two or four platters and garnish with parsley. Serve with green mayonnaise (see recipe).

Yield: Two to four servings.

Sauce Verte
(*Green mayonnaise*)

1 **egg yolk**
1 **tablespoon vinegar**
1 **tablespoon prepared mustard**
Salt and freshly ground pepper to taste

1 **cup plus 1 tablespoon peanut, vegetable, or corn oil**
½ **bunch watercress, rinsed, patted, or spun dry**
1 **tablespoon chopped parsley**
1 **tablespoon finely chopped dill.**

1. Put the egg yolk in a mixing bowl and add the vinegar, mustard, salt and pepper to taste.
2. Start beating with a wire whisk and gradually add the oil, beating vigorously. When thickened and smooth, set aside.
3. Put the watercress, parsley, dill, and 1 tablespoon of oil in the container of a food processor or blender. Blend to a fine purée. Add this to the mayonnaise.

Yield: About one-and-one-quarter cups.

Chiffonade de Homard
(*Lobster in tarragon sauce with lettuce*)

4 **1½-pound lobsters, steamed (see recipe), or use 3 cups lobster meat**
1 **egg yolk**
2 **teaspoons tomato ketchup**
1 **teaspoon imported mustard**
1 **tablespoon tarragon vinegar**
½ **teaspoon Worcestershire sauce**

Salt and freshly ground pepper to taste
1 **cup peanut or olive oil**
2 **teaspoons finely chopped fresh tarragon or half the amount dried**
1 **teaspoon cognac**
10 **or 12 romaine lettuce leaves, rinsed and patted dry.**

1. Remove the meat from the lobster; cut into bite-size slices and set aside.
2. Add the egg yolk, ketchup, mustard, vinegar, Worcestershire, salt, and pepper to a bowl. Start beating with a wire whisk, gradually adding the oil. When thickened and smooth, add the tarragon and cognac.
3. Stack the lettuce leaves and shred them. Add the lobster and sauce to the lettuce and toss. Serve before the lettuce wilts.

Yield: Four servings.

T HAS BEEN NOTED BEFORE THAT THERE ARE NU-
merous admirable pre-cooked foods in supermarkets and grocery stores which, when brought home and properly enhanced
can be a blessing for the palate. And a time saver. I do not, naturally, mean
frozen dinners, most, if not all, of which would be beyond repair, even if you
smothered them with the likes of truffles and foie gras.

The list would include ham and salamis and a whole packed cooked beef
tongue. I know. Tongue is not caviar to the general public, but for many an ep-
icure in this world, it ranks high on the list of delectables. That is not to
propose that you can bring the food home and transform it into its grandest
classic usage, tongue with sauce maderè, or Madeira sauce with freshly cooked
spinach en branche or en purée. The Madeira sauce alone requires a few days
of cooking time.

But one of the great taste liaisons is cold, sliced tongue (or tongue at room
temperature) served with a slightly mordant mustard and dill sauce. There is
one sauce given to us some years ago by a Swedish friend that is absolutely
sublime when served with tongue (or other foods, for that matter). It is made
with imported mustard plus dry mustard (which gives it an additional bite),
sugar, vinegar, oil, and chopped fresh dill. If there is no fresh dill in your
market, don't worry; the mustard sauce is excellent without it.

I have, in my years as a chef, found "cooked" tongues in groceries that
seemed to my taste slightly underdone when sliced directly from the package.
Thus, I generally cook the tongue for about ten minutes (in its tightly sealed
package if the instructions tell you so) to insure that it is not underdone.

When I serve that tongue with mustard sauce (it is generally on summer
menus) I consider a lentil salad to be just about ideal as an accompaniment.
This, too, is a hastily cooked and prepared dish. The lentils require about thirty
minutes cooking time, after which they are drained and dressed with a vinaigrette sauce made with finely chopped onion, garlic, and tomato cut into small
cubes, plus oil and vinegar, of course. The lentils are delicious when served
lukewarm or at room temperature.

Langue de Boeuf à la Moutarde
(*Tongue with mustard and dill sauce*)

---

1 cooked beef tongue, available in plastic wrap in supermarkets	⅓ cup peanut, vegetable, or corn oil
¼ cup prepared imported mustard	Salt to taste
1½ teaspoons dry mustard	2 tablespoons finely chopped fresh dill.
3 tablespoons sugar	
2 tablespoons white vinegar	

1. The size of cooked beef tongues varies greatly. If you have too much to
serve your guests, simply save leftovers for another use, such as in sandwiches.

You may wish to reheat the tongue briefly as indicated on the package, in the plastic bag, about 10 minutes without boiling.

2. Cut away and discard the gristly, throaty, and unsightly lower part of the tongue. Peel and slice as much of the tongue as desired and arrange it on a platter.

3. Put the prepared mustard into a mixing bowl and add the dry mustard and sugar. Stir with a whisk to blend. Gradually add the oil, stirring. Add sugar, vinegar, and salt. Stir in the dill.

Yield: Tongue with about three-quarters of a cup of mustard sauce.

Salade de Lentilles
(Lentil salad)

½	pound dried lentils	2	sprigs fresh thyme or use ½ teaspoon dried thyme
3	cups water		
½	bay leaf	2	tablespoons finely chopped onion
1	clove garlic, peeled	1	tablespoon finely chopped parsley
1	small onion stuck with one clove	½	teaspoon finely minced garlic
	Salt and freshly ground pepper to taste	½	cup diced, peeled, seeded tomatoes
3	sprigs fresh parsley	1	tablespoon red wine vinegar
		3	tablespoons olive oil.

1. Wash the lentils and pick over them. Drain and put in a saucepan.

2. Add the water, bay leaf, garlic, onion stuck with a clove, salt, and pepper. Tie the parsley sprigs together with the thyme into a bundle. Add this. Bring lentils to the boil and cook, partially covered, until tender, about 30 minutes. Do not overcook. The lentils must be tender but not mushy. Remove from the heat. Remove the onion, garlic, bay leaf, and parsley bundle. Discard.

3. Drain the lentils well. Add the lentils to a large mixing bowl. Add the chopped onion, chopped parsley, garlic, tomatoes, vinegar, olive oil, salt, and pepper. Toss to blend well.

Yield: Four to eight servings.

ALTHOUGH AVOCADOS ARE NO NOVELTY TODAY IN the metropolitan areas of France, they were a total rarity in the days of my youth there. The first time I recall ever seeing an avocado—they are known in French as avocats—was after my arrival in America during the New York World's Fair in 1939, and to me they seemed wholly exotic.

I greatly enjoy avocados today, but to my taste they are, in one sense, a bit like snails or spaghetti. It is what you put on them that gives them their deserved stature in the world of food. It may be a simple dressing with lemon and a fine olive oil. Or avocado halves may be stuffed with a seafood or other salad, to describe but a few of their multitude of uses.

It is a commonplace that the specialties of any region are made with the ingredients that are native to that region. Thus the crayfish of Louisiana, the Dungeness crabs of the West Coast, the snails of Burgundy, and the corn-based specialties of the American South.

I am convinced that had avocados been native to Provence they would have been an inevitable ingredient in the celebrated salad of that region, the salade niçoise. Cubed avocado in a traditional niçoise is a "natural," as you will discover if you try the quickly made avocado and tuna salad listed below.

One of the most natural "teamings" in the world of food is the West Coast specialty, crab Louis in avocado halves.

There are many versions of the Louis dressing, and no one apparently knows the origin of the name. The dressing itself is sometimes attributed to an early chef of the St. Francis Hotel, in San Francisco. There is a recipe for the sauce in an early edition of the *Hotel St. Francis Cook Book* which I have in my library. That version calls for mayonnaise blended with French dressing, chili sauce, and Worcestershire sauce.

The recipe below for crab Louis with avocado halves is my own version of several Louis dressings that I have sampled. Either of these dishes would serve as a complete lunch for a summer menu.

Salade Niçoise aux Poires d'Avocat
(Tuna and avocado salad)

½ pound fresh mushrooms
2 tablespoons lemon juice
  Salt and freshly ground pepper to taste
1 large or two small avocados
2 7-ounce cans tuna fish packed in oil
1 2-ounce can flat anchovy fillets
1 red, ripe tomato, about ½ pound
1 small red onion, peeled

Rind of one lemon, cut into very fine strips
8 black olives
8 stuffed green olives
6 tablespoons olive oil
2 tablespoons red wine vinegar
1 teaspoon finely chopped garlic
2 tablespoons finely chopped parsley
2 hard-cooked eggs, peeled and quartered.

1. Thinly slice the mushrooms. There should be about 3 cups. Put the mushrooms in a mixing bowl and add the lemon juice, salt, and pepper. Toss to blend.

2. Peel the avocados and cut them in half. Discard the pits. Cut each half into four lengthwise slices. Cut the slices into large cubes. Add this to the mushrooms and toss to coat.

3. Drain the tuna and break it into bite-size lumps. Add this to the bowl.

4. Drain the anchovy fillets and cut them into small pieces. Add them to the bowl.

5. Core the tomato and cut it into one-inch cubes. Add this to the bowl.

6. Cut the onion into thin slices. Break the slices into rings and add them to the bowl.

7. Add the lemon rind and olives.

8. Blend the oil, vinegar, garlic, salt and pepper to taste. Beat well to blend and pour this over the salad. Sprinkle with parsley. Toss well before serving. Garnish with hard-cooked egg quarters.

Yield: Six or more servings.

Poires d'Avocat avec Mayonnaise de Crabe
(*Avocados with crab Louis*)

---

1   egg yolk
2   teaspoons prepared imported mustard
½   teaspoon Worcestershire sauce
2   teaspoons red wine vinegar
    Salt and freshly ground pepper to taste
½   cup peanut, vegetable, or corn oil
1   tablespoon chili sauce
¼   cup finely chopped scallions, green part and all

4   large stuffed green olives, chopped, about ¼ cup
1   pound lump crab, picked over to remove all trace of shell and cartilage
4   ripe avocados
    Lettuce leaves
2   hard-cooked eggs, sliced, optional.

1. Put the yolk in a mixing bowl and add the mustard, Worcestershire sauce, and vinegar. Beat with a wire whisk. Add the oil gradually, beating rapidly with the whisk.

2. When thickened and smooth, add the chili sauce, scallions, and olives. Blend.

3. Put the crab in a mixing bowl and add half the sauce. Blend gently so as not to break up the crab lumps more than necessary.

4. Split the avocados in half and discard the pits. Pile equal portions of the crab into the avocado halves. Spoon the remaining sauce over. Serve on a bed of lettuce leaves. Garnish the crab filling, if desired, with egg slices.

Yield: Four servings.

Metric Conversion Tables

TEMPERATURES

Fahrenheit°/Celsius°	(Actual Celsius°)	Fahrenheit°/Celsius°	(Actual Celsius°)
− 5°F/ − 20°C	(− 20.6°C)	180°F/82°C	(82.2°C)
32°F/0°C	(0°C)	190°F/88°C	(87.8°C)
37°F/3°C	(2.8°C)	200°F/95°C	(93.3°C)
50°F/10°C	(10°C)	205°F/96°C	(96.1°C)
60°F/16°C	(15.6°C)	212°F/100°C	(100°C)
70°F/21°C	(21.1°C)	225°F/107°C	(107.2°C)
75°F/24°C	(23.9°C)	228°F/109°C	(108.9°C)
80°F/27°C	(26.7°C)	238°F/115°C	(114.4°C)
85°F/29°C	(29.4°C)	250°F/120°C	(121.1°C)
100°F/38°C	(37.8°C)	275°F/135°C	(135°C)
105°F/41°C	(40.6°C)	285°F/140°C	(140.6°C)
110°F/43°C	(43.3°C)	300°F/150°C	(148.9°C)
115°F/46°C	(46.1°C)	325°F/165°C	(162.8°C)
120°F/49°C	(48.9°C)	350°F/180°C	(176.7°C)
125°F/52°C	(51.7°C)	375°F/190°C	(190.6°C)
130°F/54°C	(54.4°C)	400°F/205°C	(204.4°C)
135°F/57°C	(57.2°C)	425°F/220°C	(218.3°C)
140°F/60°C	(60°C)	450°F/230°C	(232.2°C)
150°F/66°C	(65.6°C)	475°F/245°C	(246.1°C)
160°F/71°C	(71.1°C)	500°F/260°C	(260°C)
165°F/74°C	(73.9°C)	525°F/275°C	(273.9°C)
170°F/77°C	(76.7°C)	550°F/290°C	(287.8°C)

POUNDS TO GRAMS AND KILOGRAMS

Pounds	Convenient Equivalent	Actual Weight
¼ lb	115 g	(113.4 g)
½ lb	225 g	(226.8 g)
¾ lb	340 g	(340.2 g)
1 lb	450 g	(453.6 g)
1¼ lb	565 g	(566.99 g)
1½ lb	675 g	(680.4 g)
1¾ lb	800 g	(794 g)
2 lb	900 g	(908 g)
2½ lb	1125 g; 1¼ kg	(1134 g)
3 lb	1350 g	(1360 g)
3½ lb	1500 g; 1½ kg	(1588 g)
4 lb	1800 g	(1814 g)
4½ lb	2 kg	(2041 g)
5 lb	2¼ kg	(2268 g)
5½ lb	2½ kg	(2495 g)
6 lb	2¾ kg	(2727 g)
7 lb	3¼ kg	(3175 g)
8 lb	3½ kg	(3629 g)
9 lb	4 kg	(4028 g)
10 lb	4½ kg	(4536 g)
12 lb	5½ kg	(5443 g)
14 lb	6¼ kg	(6350 g)
15 lb	6¾ kg	(6804 g)
16 lb	7¼ kg	(7258 g)
18 lb	8 kg	(8165 g)
20 lb	9 kg	(9072 g)
25 lb	11¼ kg	(11,340 g)

OUNCES TO GRAMS

Ounces	Convenient Equivalent	Actual Weight
1 oz	30 g	(28.35 g)
2 oz	60 g	(56.7 g)
3 oz	85 g	(85.05 g)
4 oz	115 g	(113.4 g)
5 oz	140 g	(141.8 g)
6 oz	180 g	(170.1 g)

Ounces	Convenient Equivalent	Actual Weight
8 oz	225 g	(226.8 g)
9 oz	250 g	(255.2 g)
10 oz	285 g	(283.5 g)
12 oz	340 g	(340.2 g)
14 oz	400 g	(396.9 g)
16 oz	450 g	(453.6 g)
20 oz	560 g	(566.99 g)
24 oz	675 g	(680.4 g)

LIQUID MEASURE CONVERSIONS

Cups and Spoons	Liquid Ounces	Approximate Metric Term	Approximate Centiliters	Actual Milliliters
1 tsp.	¹/₆ oz	1 tsp	½ cL	5 mL
1 Tb	½ oz	1 Tb	1½ cL	15 mL
¼ c; 4 Tb	2 oz	½ dL; 4 Tb	6 cL	59 mL
⅓ c; 5 Tb	2⅔ oz	¾ dL; 5 Tb	8 cL	79 mL
½ c	4 oz	1 dL	12 cL	119 mL
⅔ c	5⅓ oz	1½ dL	15 cL	157 mL
¾ c	6 oz	1¾ dL	18 cL	178 mL
1 c	8 oz	¼ L	24 cL	237 mL
1¼ c	10 oz	3 dL	30 cL	296 mL
1⅓ c	10⅔ oz	3¼ dL	33 cL	325 mL
1½ c	12 oz	3½ dL	35 cL	355 mL
1⅔ c	13⅓ oz	3¾ dL	39 cL	385 mL
1¾ c	14 oz	4 dL	41 cL	414 mL
2 c; 1 pt	16 oz	½ L	47 cL	473 mL
2½ c	20 oz	6 dL	60 cL	592 mL
3 c	24 oz	¾ L	70 cL	710 mL
3½ c	28 oz	⁴/₅ L; 8 dL	83 cL	829 mL
4 c; 1 qt	32 oz	1 L	95 cL	946 mL
5 c	40 oz	1¼ L	113 cL	1134 mL
6 c; 1½ qt	48 oz	1½ L	142 cL	1420 mL
8 c; 2 qt	64 oz	2 L	190 cL	1893 mL
10 c; 2½ qt	80 oz	2½ L	235 cL	2366 mL
12 c; 3 qt	96 oz	2¾ L	284 cL	2839 mL
4 qt	128 oz	3¾ L	375 cL	3785 mL
5 qt		4¾ L		
6 qt		5½ L (or 6 L)		
8 qt		7½ L (or 8 L)		

INCHES TO CENTIMETERS

Inches ("in")	Centimeters ("cm") (Nearest equivalent)
$^1/_{16}$ in	¼ cm
⅛ in	½ cm
$^3/_{16}$ in	"less than ¼ in/¾ cm"
¼ in	¾ cm
⅜ in	1 cm
½ in	1½ cm
⅝ in	1½ cm
¾ in	2 cm
1 in	2½ cm
1½ in	4 cm
2 in	5 cm
2½ in	6½ cm
3 in	8 cm
3½ in	9 cm
4 in	10 cm
5 in	13 cm
6 in	15 cm
7 in	18 cm
8 in	20 cm
9 in	23 cm
10 in	25 cm
12 in	30 cm
14 in	35 cm
15 in	38½ cm
16 in	40 cm
18 in	45 cm
20 in	50 cm
24 in	60 cm
30 in	75 cm

Index

Acorn squash, baked, 267
Agneau, 172-190
  bitoks d', 180-181
    aux câpres, 182-183
  brochettes d', à l'Indienne, 190
  carré d'
    persille, 178-179
    au romarin, 176-177
  côtes d'
    grillées, 174
    poêlées, 175
    à la Provençale, 184-185
    Rouennaise, 186-187
  noisettes d', à l'anglaise, 188-189
Almonds, rice with raisins and, 51
Alose à la crème, 104
Anchovy
  garnish, chicken salad with, 302-303
  hamburger with egg and, 246-247
  tomato sauce and spaghetti, shrimp in,
    297
Applejack sauce, chicken with, 44-45
Apples
  baked, 283
  loin pork chops with, 262-263
Asparagus
  buttered, 243
  chicken breasts with carrots and, 26-27
  with nutmeg butter, 81
  sautéed with sesame seeds, 37
  vinaigrette, 85
Asperges
  au beurre, 243

  de muscade, 81
  sautées aux graines de sésame, 37
  vinaigrette, 85
Auberbines au four "parmigiana," 269
Aubergines à la créole, 111
Avocado(s)
  and broccoli salad, 73
  chicken and, in cream, 30-31
  with crab Louis, 319
  and tuna salad, 318-319

Bar rayé poché, 114-115
Beans. *See* Cannellini beans with tuna;
    Green beans; Lentil salad
Beef, 224-255
  hamburgers
    with egg and anchovy, 246-247
    with peppercorn sauce, 244-245
    with sour cream, 242-243
  meatballs with spaghetti, 292-293
  quick sauté of, 252-253
  rolls with egg filling, 254
  steak(s)
    in chive sauce, 230-231
    with crushed peppercorns, 232-233
    filet mignon in a Bordeaux wine
      sauce, 228-229
    filet mignon in Madiera wine sauce,
      226-227
    London broil with sauce chasseur,
      240-241
    with mustard cream sauce, 234-235

with mint, 271
  and zucchini, 29
noodles with dill and, 155
and poppy seeds, noodles with,
  133
and potatoes, puréed, 259
steamed, 121, 233
and zucchini with fresh mint, 29
Casserole, chicken and rice, 47
Cauliflower
  with sieved egg and parsley, 195
  veal chops with, 194
Cayenne, deviled chicken legs with,
  36-37
Celeriac in mayonnaise
  with mussels, 304-305
  with salami, 305
Chaudrée aux fruits de mer, 130-131
Champignons
  Bordelaise, 237
  foies de volaille et, 76-77
    au riz, 67
Cheese
  mashed potatoes baked with, 255
  mozzarella
    baked mélange of vegetables with,
    223
    veal scallopine with Parmesan and,
    204-205
  noodles with, 35
  omelet with chicken, tomato, and,
    82-83
  Parmesan
    baked eggplant with, 269
    rice with, 71
    veal chops with, in white wine,
    196-197
    veal scallopine with mozzarella and,
    204-205
  pork chops glazed with, 270-271
  sauce, endives and ham baked in,
    284-285
  soufflé, 86-87
Chicken
  with applejack sauce, 44-45
  and avocado in cream, 30-31
  breasts
    with asparagus and carrots, 26-27
    breaded, 28-29

and cold noodles with spicy sauce,
  303
  with grapes, 22-23
  with spinach, 24-25
broiled, 16-17
curried, 49-50
  and shrimp, 154-155
fricasse of, with tarragon, 60-61
grilled
  American-style, 54-55
  with mustard, 56-57
legs, deviled, 36-37
livers
  in creole sauce, 68-69
  lamp chops on liver toast, 186-187
  with mushrooms in Madiera wine
    sauce, 76-77
  pilaf with tomato and mushroom
    sauce, 72-73
  rice with, 21
  with sage, 75
  on skewers, 70-71
with mixed grill, 54-55
omelet with
  poached, 80-81
  tomato, and cheese, 82-83
paella, 170-171
parsleyed, with vegetables, 32-33
with parsley sauce, 18-19
poached
  with bourbon sauce, 42-43
  in cream sauce, 41
  omelet, 80-81
in the pot, 48-49
Provençale, 20-21
in red wine sauce, 34-35
and rice casserole, 47
salad with anchovy garnish, 302-303
sautéed, 14-15
  with rosemary, 15
  with tomatoes, 20-21
  with wine and herbs, 52-53
with tarragon, 58-59
  fricasse of, 60-61
in white wine, 38-39
  and herbs, sautéed, 52-53
Chick-pea and salmon salad, 313
Chive sauce, steak in, 230-231
Chopping boards, 4

Foods of France, The (Root), 130
Freezing foods, 9
French bread, herbed, 131
Fricassée de poulet à l'estragon, 60-61
Fruit(s)
　and berries with spirits, 277
　mixed, 10
Fruits de mer
　au riz, 127
　chaudrée aux, 130-131

Gadgets. *See* Utensils
Game hens. *See* Hens, game
Garlic
　croutons, romaine lettuce with, 291
　toast, 141
　tomatoes with
　　and marjoram, broiled, 181
　　and parsley, cherry, 117, 139
　　and rosemary, grilled, 179
　　and zucchini, cherry, 215
Garnish(es)
　Bordelaise, mushrooms with a, 237
　of hard-cooked egg, 115
　lemon and caper, breaded veal with,
　　202-203
　Provençale, 185
Garniture
　de crabe, 309
　d'oeufs durs, 115
　Provençale, 185
Giobbi('s), Ed, 38
　hot spaghetti with cold tomato sauce,
　　288-289
Grapes
　chicken breast with, 22-23
　ham rolls with, 282-283
Green beans
　with lemon, 241
　with parsley butter, 65
　and onions vinaigrette, 161
　with vinaigrette sauce, 189

Halibut baked with bread crumbs,
　120-121
Ham. *See* Pork

Hamburger. *See* Beef
Haricots
　secs
　　avec thon, 312-313
　verts
　　avec beurre persillé, 65
　　au citron, 241
　　et oignons vinaigrette, 161
　　vinaigrette, 189
Hens, game
　with potatoes and mushrooms, 62-63
　with prosciutto, 66-67
　with vinegar sauce, 64
Herbs, 6-8
　calves' liver sautéed with, 210-211
　French bread with, 131
　sauce vinaigrette with, 159
　sautéed chicken with wine and, 52-53
　veal scallopine with fine, 222-223
　whiting with, breaded baked, 108-109
　zucchini with summer, 97, 147
　See also specific herbs
Homard(s)
　chiffonade de, 315
　farcis à l'estragon, 142-143
　à la sauce verte, 314-315
Hotel St. Francis Cook Book, 318
Huîtres
　à la florentine avec pernod, 132-133
　de saumon fumé a la crème avec nouil-
　　les, 128-129

Jambon. *See* Porc
Julienne de poivrons au kari, 165

Knives, 4, 32
Kropotkin, Princess Alexandra, 248

Lamb, 172-190
　chops
　　broiled, 174
　　on liver toast, 186-187
　　pan-broiled, 175
　　with Provençale garnish, 184-185
　kebabs, 190
　medallions, breaded, 188-189

patties
  broiled, 180-181
  with sour cream and capers, 182-183
rack of
  parsleyed, 178-179
  with rosemary, 176-177
Lee('s), Virginia, 302
  chicken and cold noodles with spicy
    sauce, 303
Leeks, scallops and, with pernod,
    134-135
Left-overs, 6, 8
Legumes. *See* Vegetables; *names of
    specific vegetables*
Lemon
  butter, 151
    broccoli with, 19
  and caper garnish, breaded veal with,
    202-203
  sole with capers and, sautéed, 116-117
  string beans with, 241
  whiting with, deep-fried, 110
  zucchini with oil and, 59
Lentil salad, 317
Le Pavillon restaurant, 142, 144, 276, 308
Lettuce
  lobster in tarragon sauce with, 315
  romaine, with garlic croutons, 291
Linguine with clam sauce, 294-295
Liver(s)
  calves'
    and onions, 212-213
    sautéed with herbs, 210-211
    with vinegar, 214
  chicken
    in creole sauce, 68-69
    lamb chops on liver toast, 186-187
    and mushrooms in Madiera wine
      sauce, 76-77
    pilaf with tomato and mushroom
      sauce, 72-73
    rice with, 21
    with sage, 75
    on skewers, 70-71
Cornish game hens, rice with mush-
    rooms and, 66
Lobsters
  steamed, with green mayonnaise,
    314-315

in tarragon sauce with lettuce, 315
  tarragon stuffed, 142-143

Maccioni's, Sirio, pasta de l'estate, 289
Mackerel with tomato and pepper sauce,
    106-107
Madiera wine sauce
  chicken livers and mushrooms in,
    76-77
  filet mignon in, 226-227
Maís en épi au beurre de poivre vert, 143
Maquereaux Portugaise, 106-107
Marinara sauce, 299
  pork meatballs in, 298-299
Marjoram, broiled tomatoes with garlic
    and, 181
Marmite de légumes, 33
Mayonnaise
  de crabe, poires d'avocat avec, 319
  green, 315
    steamed lobster with, 314-315
  sauce
    with mussels, celeriac in, 304-305
    with salami, celeriac in, 305
    shrimp in, 151
  scallion, 123
  tomato, crab dressing with, 309
  de volaille aux anchois, 302-303
Merlan
  au citron, friture de, 110
  au plat avec herbs, 108-109
Mint, carrots with, 271
  and zucchini, 29
Moules
  céleri rémoulade avec, 304-305
  marinière, 310-311
  poulette, 140-141
  vinaigrette au coquilles, 311
Mozzarella cheese
  baked mélange of vegetables with, 223
  veal scallopine with Parmesan and,
    205
Mushroom(s)
  with a Bordelaise garnish, 237
  chicken livers and, in Madiera wine
    sauce, 76-77
  game hens with potatoes and, 62-63
  rice with liver and, 67
  sauce, deviled, 70

Rice
    with almonds and raisins, 51
    baked, 69, 135, 157, 165
        with pine nuts, 137
    baked sausages with, 281-282
    boiled, 163
    and chicken casserole, 46-47
    with chicken livers, 21
    curried, 23, 31
    with liver and mushrooms, 67
    mixed shellfish with, 127
    with Parmesan, 71
    with parsley, 273
        and peas, 153
    with peas, 177
        and parsley, 153
    with peppers, 149
    saffron, 167
    tumeric, 61
Rigatoni, shrimp Greek-style with,
    160-161
Riz
    créole, 63
    Egyptienne, 21
    foies de volaille et champignons au,
        67
    au four, 69, 135, 157, 165
        pignolats, 137
    fruits de mer au, 127
    à l'Indienne, 23, 31
    au Parmesan, 71
    Orientale, 51
    persillé, 273
    aux piments, 149
    aux pois, 177
    avec pois et persil, 153
    au safron, 167
    saucisses au, 280-281
    au tumeric, 61
Rock Cornish game hens. See Hens,
    game
Root, Waverly, 130
Rosemary
    chicken sauté with, 15
    grilled tomatoes with garlic and, 179

Saffron rice, 167
Sage, chicken livers with, 74

Salad
    avocado
        broccoli and, 73
        tuna and, 318-319
    chicken, with anchovy garnish,
        302-303
    cucumber and dill, 285
    ham and endive, 306-307
    lentil, 317
    mixed green, 199
    orange and black olive, 171
    potato, with white wine, 307
    romaine lettuce with garlic croutons,
        291
    salmon and chick-pea, 313
    watercress and endive, 293
Salade
    de brocoli et poires d'avocat, 73
    de concombres à la Scandinave, 285
    de cresson et endives, 293
    avec croûton à l'ail, 291
    de jambon et endives ravigote, 306-307
    de lentils, 317
    Niçoise aux poires d'avocat, 318-319
    d'oranges et olives noires, 171
    panachée, 199
    de pommes vin blanc, 307
    de saumon et pois chiche, 313
Salad oils, preserving, 8
Salami, celeriac in mayonnaise sauce
    with, 305
Salmon
    and chick-pea salad, 313
    fillets
        in bread crumbs, 122-123
        grilled dilled, 112-113
    smoked, with creamed oysters and
        noodles, 128-129
Salt, 9
Sauce(s)
    applejack, chicken with, 44-45
    bourbon, poached chicken in, 42-43
    butter, with shallots and white wine, 17
    chasseur, 241
        London broil with, 240-241
    cheese, endives and ham baked in,
        284-285
    chive, steak in, 230-231
    clam, linguine with, 294-295

Whiting
  with herbs, breaded baked, 108-109
  with lemon, deep-fried, 110
Wine
  Madiera, sauce
    chicken livers and mushrooms in,
      76-77
    filet mignon in, 226-227
  red, sauce
    chicken in, 34-35
    filet mignon in a Bordeaux, 228-229
    porterhouse in, 238-239
  white
    butter sauce with shallots and, 17
    chicken in, 38-39
    mussels in, 310-311
    oysters with spinach and pernod,
      132-133

  potato salad with, 307
  sautéed chicken with herbs and,
    52-53
  scallops and leeks with pernod,
    134-135
  veal chops with Parmesan cheese in,
    196-197

Yogurt sauce, cucumbers with, 191

Zucchini
  and carrots with fresh mint, 29
  and cherry tomatoes with garlic, 215
  with oil and lemon, 59
  and summer herbs, 97, 147
  with tomatoes, baked, 109

ABOUT THE AUTHOR

PIERRE FRANEY appears regularly in *The New York Times* with his own byline and with Craig Claiborne. He is the former chef of New York's Le Pavillon and one of the world's most respected food experts.